piano girl

*Lessons in Life, Music, and
the Perfect Blue Hawaiian*

by Robin Meloy Goldsby

Backbeat
Books
San Francisco

Published by Backbeat Books
600 Harrison Street, San Francisco, CA 94107
www.backbeatbooks.com
email: books@musicplayer.com

CMP
United Business Media

An imprint of CMP Information
Publishers of *Guitar Player*, *Bass Player*, *Keyboard*, and *EQ* magazines

Distributed to the book trade in the US and Canada by
Publishers Group West, 1700 Fourth Street, Berkeley, CA 94710

Distributed to the music trade in the US and Canada by
Hal Leonard Publishing, P.O. Box 13819, Milwaukee, WI 53213

Composition : Maureen Forys, Happenstance Type-O-Rama
Cover Design: Richard Leeds—bigwigdesign.com
Front Cover Photo: John Popplewell

Library of Congress Cataloging-in-Publication Data

Goldsby, Robin Meloy.
  Piano girl : lessons in life, music, and the perfect blue Hawaiian / by Robin Meloy Goldsby.
     p. cm.
  ISBN 0-87930-824-9 (alk. paper)
  1. Goldsby, Robin Meloy. 2. Pianists—United States—Biography. I. Title.

  ML417.G63A3 2005
  786.2'092—dc22   2005005525

Printed in the United States of America

05 06 07 08 09   5 4 3 2 1

Contents

Dedication

For John,
because kissing the bass player
is the smartest thing I've ever done.

Author's Note

The events described in the *Piano Girl* stories are true.
Some of the characters were given
fictitious names and identifying features.

Introduction

Life from the Other
Side of the Steinway

*I*t's not always a Steinway. Sometimes it's an ugly-looking, beautiful-sounding white Bösendorfer concert grand or a Yamaha conservatory grand with a high-gloss mirrored surface, so polished that I can see the mood of the evening staring back at me. Sometimes the instrument I play barely qualifies as a piano. Sometimes it's an Army-surplus spinet made by a firm that is a subsidiary of a toy company. Sometimes it's a beat-up upright piano with four broken strings—and when I press a key I can hear several distinct tones fluttering together and laughing at me with their out-of-tuneness. Sometimes it really *is* the perfect Steinway Model B, a seven-foot grand with a sound warm enough to make me stay at the piano forever, just listening. I play. I make music. I am the tall blond woman in the strapless cocktail dress, and I sit in the corner and play the piano.

I didn't set out to be a cocktail pianist. But here I am, wearing something black, a little eyeliner, a little lipstick, high heels. I'm not Shirley Horn, or Diana Krall, or Marian McPartland, or Bobby Short in a blond wig. Not even close. But I work all the time and I'm pretty good at what I do.

There are many terms for my profession. I am called a cocktail pianist, a bar pianist, a hotel pianist, and a lounge pianist.

I perform background music that enhances a dinner, a lunch, a chilled prosecco; or atmosphere music meant to embellish a business meeting, a wedding, an illicit affair—without getting in the way. I play music that is comforting, gentle enough to pacify, melodic enough to nudge my audience into the folds of their own memories.

I've spent many years underestimating the validity of my job. I'm not really a bar pianist, I tell myself, because I want to be more than that. I'm a student. I'm an actor. I'm a writer. I'm a composer. I'm a single woman living in New York City standing on the edge of a nervous breakdown. I'm a citizen of the world. I'm happy. I'm a mother. I'm a wife. I'm all of these things, true, true, true. But I'm able to be all of these things because playing the piano in a hotel continues to pay the bills. Now, with the wisdom of a maturity that was bound to catch up with me, I realize that being a cocktail pianist is a lovely way to make a living. It started out as a way to earn money for college. It ended up being my profession for thirty years and counting.

I play medleys of great songs and obnoxious songs and make them all sound, well, nice. Plus I've been questionably blessed with the ability to be polite, to smile, and to remember the first names of the customers who stray into the joints where I'm playing. These days, some of the joints are castles in Europe. I've traveled a long way from the Nantucket Club Car and the Redwood Motor Inn on Banksville Road in Pittsburgh where I had my first steady gigs as a teenager, but basically the scene is the same. Fancier clothes, slightly better piano, same ratio of lunatics to normal people. I play.

Sometimes I'm treated like visiting royalty from a mysterious land, flown to the job in a private jet, showered with roses, fine wine, and compliments from people whose pashmina socks cost more than my entire wardrobe. Sometimes I feel like a frazzled waitress with eighty-eight keys strapped around my neck, taking orders from drunken shoe salesmen who would prefer to see me go-go dance in a green fringed bikini on top of the piano rather than make any sense out of the instrument in front of me.

Every job presents the chance to be a musical fly on the wall—providing a piano score for life as it's served, straight-up with a side of olives, to the droves of people who pass through the world's bars and restaurants. Over the years I've been appalled, attacked, blown away by kindness, cajoled into fits of giggles, and moved to tears by the tiny dramas that unfold before my eyes and ears. I cry. I laugh. Laughter is a kind of music—the best kind. I've always wanted to write the score for a film. But maybe this is better. I'm writing and playing music for life, as it happens. It's like recording live on tape, without the tape.

One day I'm eighteen years old, sitting down to play my first job. Startled, I wake up on a bright spring morning and realize that I'm forty-six, and that my entire adult life can be documented by a series of forty-minute sets and twenty-minute breaks. I fret about missed opportunities—how I've spent the peak years of my life behind an instrument that fights back more often than it complies with my wishes—and the way real time slips away from me like runaway triplets at a children's piano recital.

I have moments of artistic satisfaction. Many of them. On a typical night—in between requests and idle chit-chat with guests from, say, Helsinki, or Bogata, or Hackensack—I play the music that I want to play, the way I want to play it. I feel peaceful, exhilarated, and sure that I've chosen the right profession. It's almost a magical feeling, and I allow it to sweep me away. Then some drunk-on-his-ass sales rep from a surgical supply company sends me a cocktail napkin with a request for "Memory" from *Cats*, a twenty-dollar bill, and—as an afterthought—his room number. I check out the man who has sent the note. He is sprawled on the burgundy velvet banquette, smoking a cigar and drinking a brandy. He looks like a cross between a sloth and a walrus. I play the song, keep the money, and make sure a taxi is waiting for me at quitting time.

I go home, slightly amused, a little disgusted. But I come back the next day to play again. In fact, I look forward to it. The smells of cigarette smoke, grilled steak, and too much Chanel No. 5 waft in my direction like a big cloud of fairy dust blown in from a distant yet familiar planet. I sit at the piano. The customers briefly acknowledge my presence, then resume talking. It's time for my first set. I place my hands on the instrument, not quite sure what to play. I never know what the first song will be until exactly this moment. In front of me is a maze of ebony and ivory, but I don't see the keys anymore. I see the faces of 30 years of guests, friends, bartenders, and waiters morphing into an impressionistic canvas of something remarkable.

So I play a song to remember.

> *The sweetest sounds I'll ever hear*
> *Are still inside my head.*
> *The kindest words I'll ever know*
> *Are waiting to be said.*
> *The most entrancing sight of all*
> *Is yet for me to see.*
> *And the dearest love in all the world*
> *Is waiting somewhere for me.*
>
> —Richard Rodgers

Part I

1976–1979

Play Something You Know

"**D**id you leave anything at home?" Dad says as he heaves the first of my five suitcases into the big green taxi. "Or did you bring it all with you?"

The distance from Pittsburgh to Nantucket is 633 miles. It is the summer of 1976—the bicentennial summer. I've just arrived on Nantucket Island with an ancient Schwinn bicycle, two frazzled parents, a lot of music banging around in my head, and a vast amount of self confidence. Having just completed my freshman year of college, I'm looking forward to the beach, an army of Ivy League boys, and a waitressing job at a little Italian place called "Vincent's Italian Family Restaurant." I'm going to be a real woman and a superb waitress—sexy and sophisticated—conquering the world, one meatball at a time. On my days off I'll frolic on the beaches of Nantucket wearing a white bikini and no sunscreen. I'll gain my independence, make some money, have a string of boyfriends, and get a tan. This is my plan.

I own fourteen bathing suits, some blue jeans, a couple of black turtlenecks, and a dozen pairs of shoes. Not much else. But when you're eighteen and going away from home for the first time what else do you need? Most of the suitcases contain books. I've never been able to go anywhere without them. When I ran away from home at the age of eight, I packed eleven Nancy Drew books in my pink-and-orange paisley vinyl suitcase and stomped out the front door, making sure to let it slam behind me. I didn't have any food or clothing. Just the books. I didn't get very far. My valise was too full.

This time around the suitcases are much heavier.

It has taken us thirteen hours to drive from Pittsburgh to Cape Cod, then another few hours on the ferry over to Nantucket. It's the fifteenth of May. The sky is gray and the wind blows little circles of fallen magnolia blossoms around my feet. The taxi driver watches as my father loads each suitcase into the back of the wood-paneled station wagon. My dad moves in slow motion. The bike won't fit.

"Bob," says my mother. "You just go ahead with the bike and meet us there. Robin and I will accompany the bags to the rooming house. I'm sure the nice driver will give you the directions."

"Yep, up the road a piece, then make a left at the rotary, first fork, second right, till you hit the cobblestones," says the driver. "That'll be Main. Yep. You want Union, third turn on the right after you make that second left."

My father, who through the years has earned the nickname "Mr. Maps" for his inability to give simple directions, whips out his brand-new carefully folded street map of downtown Nantucket and squints at it, hard.

"Got it, Dad?," I say. I am so full of impatience I feel like I am going to just blow up, right there on Straight Wharf.

"Got it," he says. "Wait a minute. Wait a minute. Just wait a minute. Look here. What if I go left here at the corner and then cut over to Main, taking the left fork before I get to the right on Union?"

"Well," says the driver. "You could do that. Yep. You could do that. Cobblestones might be a little rough on that bike though. Yep."

"Maybe I'll do that," says Dad. "Or what about taking this route, here? Over Orange, down Main, hit the rotary go right." He jabs at the map. "That's it, that's the ticket. Or…"

"Could we *please please please* go?" I say. I am anxious to see where I will be living. But my Dad is holding on to the last few moments of my childhood. He is stalling.

"Bob, step on it," says my mother, coming to the rescue. "Let's get this show on the road." My mother has been saying "let's get this show on the road" to my Dad at least twice a day for as long as I've been alive.

What show? What road?

The rooming house is a fine establishment run by the ever-vigilant Mrs. Dunham, who likes to think she is New England's number-one deterrent to teenage sex. There are six girls living in several bedrooms on the second floor. Most of the girls, myself included, will spend the summer inventing clever ways to sneak boyfriends upstairs so we can screw our brains out while Mrs. Dunham is off chasing after her own teenage sons who are sneaking into other boardinghouses elsewhere on the island. Posted in bold letters by the front door is a sign that reads NO BOYS PERMITTED ABOVE THE THIRD STEP. My father thinks this is an excellent thing. He arrives thirty minutes after us, a bit rattled after riding my old Schwinn over two hundred yards of Nantucket cobblestone. Years later, if I close my eyes, I'll still be able to see him bouncing along, all six feet of him on a skipper-blue bike built for a twelve-year-old girl, with those ridiculous fringy things attached to the handlebars flying out behind him, delivering his little girl's bike to the place where she won't be needing it anymore.

"Those cobblestones are brutal," he says. "My head is still vibrating."

My parents depart on the early boat the next morning. They get the show on the road, and sneak out of town before I've crawled out of bed. This is a good thing, because my mom and I can avoid the Crying Ritual. Here's how the Crying Ritual goes. She cries, then I cry, then we cry together. Then we talk about how silly we are for crying, and cry some more. Big babies, that's what we are. It's exhausting.

~

I've got enough money to pay my rent for a week, plus enough extra to buy my waitress uniform. The uniform, which I purchase at a store on Main Street, appropriately called Butt-ner's, is a white polyester shift with a zipper up the front, possibly the only garment ever designed with the specific intent of making an attractive teenage girl look like Eleanor Roosevelt.

I start working at Vincent's Italian Family Restaurant that week. They give me a red-and-white-checked apron to wear over my frumpy frock. Someone tells me I have to wear a hair net, which is humiliating since I have about a yard of hair. The hair net is horrid—it's like having my head caught in a giant spider web. And it slips down over my eyes at the most inopportune times, causing me to swat at my head like a crazy person. But here I am: uniformed, accessorized, hair net in place, and ready to go. I even have a HI MY NAME IS ROBIN! badge.

I am a disaster. We aren't just talking about spilled red wine and dropped plates of lasagna. There are, I'm ashamed to say, several incidents involving blood. I'm a far cry from the sexy and sophisticated waitress I want to be. I'm a gawky and uncoordinated teenager wearing a hair net and sensible shoes, fumbling plates and making a mess. And the worse part is, I know it. I finally understand why my mother has refused to allow me in her kitchen all these years.

This is my first excursion away from home. I've got enough money, a place to live, and a job. But I'm all twisted up inside. I'm the opposite of lonely, meeting too many people and making too many new friends. There are too many choices, too many options, too many boys. My life is chaotic. I'm tasting the murky waters of independence without a filter system in place.

I miss my piano. I don't expect to miss it, but I do. I miss the routine of practicing. I need something to hold onto. Structure. I hate my job. I hate my uniform. And I really hate the friggin' hair net. It might give structure to my hair, but not my life. I need a hair net for the soul. So I decide to try to find a piano to practice during the day, when I'm not maiming innocent diners and children in highchairs with flying carafes of Chianti.

Right on Main Street in downtown Nantucket is a famous old restaurant and bar called the Club Car. Jens, a hulking blond Swedish waiter I've met in the alley behind Vincent's Italian Family Restaurant, a man who is obsessed with putting his hand up my frumpy frock and breaking Mrs. Dunham's third-step rule, suggests the Club Car would be a good place to practice. I show up there one morning at nine and ask to speak to the manager, and I'm introduced to a very kind but lecherous older gentleman named Lino Tambellino. He agrees to let me practice at the Club Car every morning from nine to eleven.

"So, let me get this straight. You wanna play here in the mornin' for nobody?"

"Well, yes, Mr. Tambellino."

"Call me Lino, sweetheart."

What a name, Lino Tambellino. He could join the My Name Is a Poem Club. I'm always on the lookout for new members.

"Okay, Lino. I just need someplace to practice. I'm studying music in college, well music and theater both, actually, and I need to practice the piano over the summer."

"You wanna eat here, too?"

"No, Mr., uh, Lino, I just want to practice in the morning."

"You gotta eat sweetheart."

"Thank you, but that's not necessary."

"What are you crazy? RICARDO! Get the babe somethin' to eat! What do you want, a steak?" Lino obviously has a warped sense of time. I guess when you live in a cocktail lounge it's easy to become a nocturnal creature, confusing breakfast with supper, and dawn with dusk.

"Lino, it's pretty early for me. Maybe a bagel or something, if you insist. But then I'd like to practice, if that's okay."

"Ricardo, we need bagels! And coffee. And juice. You want bacon? We got bacon. Go practice. Ricardo! We need some fuckin' bacon over here! Sweetheart, Ricardo will let you know when the food is ready."

Ricardo, I can tell, is going to be duking it out with the Swede on the third step of Mrs. Dunham's Home for New England

Virgins. He is short and swarthy with a full head of dark brown curls and big brown eyes. I'll bet he's at least thirty. *A professional waiter.* Wow! I haven't been on the island for a week and I'm becoming an American clearinghouse for serious waiters from European countries. Where are all those Ivy League boys I've heard about? I want Harvard, Yale, and Brown, but I'm getting Stockholm, Fuerteventura, and Sarajevo. It's early in the summer. Maybe the Ivy League guys are still in school. Ricardo winks at me.

I go to the piano. It's an old upright grand, ornately carved ebony with lots of water stains and cigarette burns. But it's almost in tune and it has character. Oh, it feels so good to play. So, so good. I make up a song and play for about five minutes when Ricardo comes to announce the arrival of the breakfast. Drat. Reluctantly, I follow him to Lino's table. Ricardo winks again.

Stop that. Don't wink. Just don't. Wiggle your eyebrows if you must, but don't wink at me—it gives me the heebie-jeebies.

"Tell you what, sweetheart," Lino says in a low voice. I feel like I'm in a scene from *The Godfather* and Lino is about to whisper his plan to put a horse head in Ricardo's bed or something. I lean closer. "How's about you play here five nights a week?"

I am shocked. "For people, you mean?"

"Yeah, sweetheart, for people. I never heard of no piano player playin' for nobody. You sound nice. The people, my people, they'll like it. Eat your bacon. You want some shrimp salad? How about a lobster?"

"Oh, no thank you. I mean, no thank you to the food, I'm fine really." I'm flustered. "But thank you for the job offer. Wow. I'm very flattered. But there's a problem. I've got my waitressing job at Vincent's Italian Family Restaurant. And I work at night."

"So quit, sweetheart. I'll give you fifty bucks a night to play here. That's 250 clams a week. You ain't gonna make that schleppin' no minestrone at Vincent's. Can you start next week?"

∾

I manage to get around the corner from the restaurant before I start jumping up and down and making whooping noises. This is like winning the lottery! I have a job, a real job, in show business!

No more hair net.

I run to Vincent's, resign, give my uniform to another trainee, toss the hair net in the dumpster in the alley, and race to the pay phone to call my parents with the news that their eighteen-year-old daughter is now a professional bar pianist.

My dad, Bob Rawsthorne, is a professional drummer and vibes player in the greater Pittsburgh area. He knows the score, and I think he'll be excited for me.

"Robin, get hold of yourself," my Dad shouts into the phone. "You only know twelve songs and eleven of them are Bach. *What are you going to play!?*"

Dad ships a crate of fake books—volumes of popular songs in easy-to-read arrangements—to me. My mother scrounges around and finds some passable evening gowns for me to wear and throws them in with the music. The crate is like the cocktail-piano version of the Popeil Pocket Fisherman. Dad has tucked in a note:

Bob's Excellent Rules for Success on a GIG:
1. *Don't drink on the job.*
2. Don't let the management push you around.
3. Always carry a roll of duct tape and an extension cord with you because with those two items you can solve virtually any problem.

Sure enough, there's a roll of duct tape and an extension cord in the crate. Dad has also shipped a small sound system, since, heaven help us, I'll be singing. In spite of my father's doubts and warnings, I'm completely confident that I'll be successful. I've got a couple of old prom gowns and lots of undiscovered music in me, just waiting to be played. Nothing can go wrong.

‹›

After calling my parents, I race back to the Club Car to start practicing.

"Thank you again, Lino. I promise you I'll try my best."

"You're welcome sweetheart. I got a nice stuffed pork chop on the lunch menu. You like pork chops?"

Nantucket Sound

The summer of 1976 will be long and warm and full of surprises. My work is cut out for me. I stash my big crate of music next to the piano and start playing songs that I like and songs that I hate, thumbing my way through fake books, trying to find tunes that are a good match for my musical limitations.

This is good. This will work. This sounds hideous. This one, that one. I'll try anything. Sit up straight, curve my fingers, keep the thirds out of my left hand, don't rush.

On my very first night on the job, about eight minutes into the first set, a customer offers to buy me a drink. My knowledge of alcohol is limited to the time I drank half a fifth of vodka at a high school party and allowed my football-player boyfriend to take off my bra, after which I spent the next three days throwing up. But the first night at the Club Car, wanting to be hip and sophisticated and above all polite, I accept a drink from the first sunburnt man in a yachting cap to offer one. He's drinking a dreadful concoction called a Godfather—scotch and amaretto on the rocks. I place the full glass, brimming over with ice cubes, on the top of the piano, and watch it overflow as the ice melts. An hour later there are six drinks there, lined up like ducks swimming in a little lake. Men keep sending drinks and I keep not drinking them.

In my second week of work, I discover the tip jar. I stick a big brandy snifter on top of the piano, with a decoy dollar in it. When someone offers a drink, I smile, say I'm too young to drink legally, and glance longingly at the tip jar, which I call my College Tuition Fund. Works like a charm. Some nights I collect more money in tips than I do in salary.

It's easier to sing and play at the same time. I'm not a great singer, but I'm not a great player either, so one thing cancels out the other. Each day I walk through the foggy Nantucket morning to the bar, practice for two hours, eat lunch, go to the beach, go for a boat ride, or play tennis. Then I slink back to Mrs. Dunham's house, scrounge around for food in the community refrigerator, take a bath, and coordinate my wardrobe for the evening. My female roommates are very helpful in this area. Most nights I arrive at the Club Car looking like beach-blanket Barbie.

Maybe it's my wardrobe, maybe it's the amount of alcohol being consumed by the Club Car customers, or maybe it's my enthusiasm for my job—but for whatever reason, they like me. The restaurant itself is spacious and quaint in a "yo-ho-ho and a bottle of rum" nautical style, but the bar area where I play is an actual railroad car. It's long and narrow, as railroad cars tend to be. When the bar fills up with customers, I must squeeze between the tables to get to the piano, which is stuffed in the back of the railroad car, next to the restroom. The Club Car bar is no place for chubby people. But this is good. Lino will never be able to get back here to fire me.

My audience consists of two distinct groups of men. Drunken sailors and artistic gay guys. I'm accepted by both groups, although I prefer the gay men, who show up on Thursday nights. The gay guys come to hear my Bette Midler tunes and give me fashion tips; the drunken sailors come to look at my cleavage and see if my tube-top falls off.

I call my Dad for advice. "Should I go around and listen to other piano players to get ideas about what to play?" I ask. There are more than a dozen piano players working in various restaurants and bars on the island.

"No," he says. "Play what you want to play, then you won't sound like everyone else." This is great advice for several reasons: First, I can't sound like anyone else even if I want to. I'm not good enough and I know it. Second, it's more fun to play the music I want to hear.

"If you like what you're playing, the audience will like it, too," says Dad.

People jabber and laugh and drink and smoke like chimneys. They scream insults at each other across the bar, trade dirty jokes, eat heaping plates of calamari, seem to pay no attention to the music whatsoever, and still manage to absorb just a little of what I play. They clap, they don't clap. They give me tips, they send me drinks. They make requests, they don't.

I feel powerful. I watch every evening unfold, knowing that the songs I sing and play might guide the night in any possible direction.

I take little American flags with me to the gig. It is, after all, the *bicentennial year*. I pass the flags around, and we have tremendous fun singing the "Marine's Hymn" and "Anchors Aweigh." On Thursdays the Kate Smith impersonators show up, so we always finish the evening with "God Bless America." There's nothing better than a large group of gay men marching in place, waving flags, and singing "God Bless America" at the top of their lungs. Pure heaven.

Then there's my serious side. When you're eighteen, you've got to have a serious side. I learn as many Carole King songs as possible. Carole is my idea of a serious artist. About a month into the gig, I have most of the *Tapestry* album memorized. I fool around with some standards I like—"Skylark," "Laura," "Old Cape Cod"—and begin writing my own material. I go in a dozen different directions and have fun with all of them. I hit lots of wrong notes and forget lyrics halfway through songs, but no one notices. Or if they do, they're drunk and polite enough to let me slide.

ॐ

I narrow the field of eligible young waiters down to one guy. His name is Joe and he's a business major from the University of Pennsylvania. He's from a Philadelphia Main Line old-money family. I've got the honor of being the first girl he dates who is not in the social register. Joe has been going out with debutantes. I lure him to me by singing a Keith Carradine song called "I'm Easy" while he's picking up his order of Singapore Slings at the bar. I look him right in the eye, sing the song, and it's a done deal. I don't have a Blue Book listing or a pedigree name, but I've got the blond hair, the pretty dress, and my secret weapon: the piano. Aha! My ability to play the piano, once a source of embarrassment in my early teenage years, can help me get the things I want, even if I'm not a debutante. Joe's parents are aghast as they watch the heir to the family fortune fall for a scantily-clad bar pianist with a following of flag-waving homosexuals, but they try to be nice to me, really they do. I put up with their condescending smiles because I'm nuts about their son. It only bugs me a little when they insist on introducing me to their upscale, lockjawed friends as Robin Meloy Rawsthorne, of the *Pittsburgh* Rawsthornes, a trained concert pianist.

Yeah. My ancestors were the lounge act on the Mayflower.

ॐ

Mrs. Dunham, who really wants to believe she's running a chastity training center, goes into Code Red Alert when she realizes I have a steady boyfriend. I sneak Joe in and out of Mrs. Dunham's windows several times, but then I start to feel guilty about tarnishing her sterling reputation. So Joe and I spend most of our days and nights at his parents' home, a lovely shingled house up on the cliff overlooking Nantucket Sound. There are eighty-three wooden steps that take me down the cliff to the water. On the roof of the house is a widow's walk with a view of Nantucket Sound that goes on forever. From here you can see everything, and nothing. In the evenings the sky turns shades of purple and orange, and I think about music even when my fantasies are full of teenage love and dreams and desires.

I play and play and play. I've grabbed hold of the opportunity presented to me by Lino Tambellino, and I'm not letting go. I started the summer—three short months ago—as a girl, but I'm more grown-up these days. The piano has smoothed the rough edges of this transition, and continues to guide me through the labyrinth of adult choices I need to make. My music, influenced by the rhythmic slapping of the waves and the sensation of the coarse Nantucket sand as it passes through my fingers, seems a flawed—but somehow perfect—soundtrack for my journey, which is just beginning.

Roses and Daffodils

I arrive home from Nantucket Island with a heap of luggage, a sound system, a microphone boom stand, a box of sheet music, and a collection of new bikinis. I also have the foundation of a musical repertoire and one of those trendy baby-oil and iodine suntans. I'm back in the Golden Triangle, my hometown of Pittsburgh, Pennsylvania, for my sophomore year at Chatham, a private college for women located on the old Mellon estate in an area of Pittsburgh called Shadyside. My cocktail piano earnings will pay for room and board, books, and my incidental expenses, most of which happen to be shoes.

My classmates at Chatham are academic overachievers. I don't fit into this category of student, but I figure if I hang out with the smart girls long enough, some of their organizational skills might wear off on me. Many of the girls, or *women* as we like to call ourselves, come from wealthy families. Some of my classmates are minority scholarship students. I'm one of the in-between kids; too middle-class and mainstream to qualify for financial aid, too poor to get through school without working.

I land a piano job at the Pittsburgh Grand Hyatt, a beautiful new hotel right smack in the middle of the city, directly across from the Civic Arena. It's a popular locale, with lots of chrome fixtures and big rubber trees lining the bustling lobby. I play the happy-hour shift in the lounge, from five to eight on weekday evenings. I love the term: *happy hour.* We should have designated drinking hours for all of our emotions: *sad hour, bored hour, hopeful hour, if-only-I'd-listened-to-my-mother hour.* Or how about the *indecisive hour?* I'd be the first one there, walking around trying to decide where to sit. Two drinks for the price of one, if you can make up your mind what you want to order.

To the credit of my classmates, not one of them, as far as I know, makes a snide comment about the girl in the four o'clock French class wearing a beaded, backless cocktail dress and high heels. Everyone thinks I have a cool job, which I do. Monday through Friday, directly after school, I dash downtown in my grandmother's 1969 fawn-colored Plymouth Valiant, pass off the car to the valet-parking guy, and run into the Hyatt cocktail lounge with just enough time to do my sound check—*on-off-high-low-finished*—and start the five o'clock set. At eight I hightail it back to the campus to make an evening rehearsal of whatever obscure and wonderful play is being produced in the college theater. It's a crazy schedule but I'm doing everything I love, making money, and having a ball.

The *Pittsburgh Press* runs a feature article on me:

CO-ED BY DAY, LOUNGE PIANIST AT NIGHT!

The article includes a revealing photo of me sitting at a desk holding a Shakespeare anthology and wearing an obscenely cut satin evening gown. The Associated Press picks up the article and it's published in newspapers around the world. Then I get a few letters, delivered to the college, from prisoners wanting to *date* me when they get out of jail. One guy compares himself to Angela Davis and Jesus.

They say that there's no such thing as bad publicity, but I beg to differ.

ॐ

At the Hyatt, I'm tucked into a safe corner playing a generic-brand studio-upright piano. It's not the greatest instrument, but the Hyatt keeps it tuned, better than the Club Car piano, anyway. One evening, a vaguely familiar-looking man with friendly eyes comes over to my piano, just as I'm playing the song "Charade" in five-four time. "Charade" is written in three-four waltz time, but I think I'm clever playing it in five.

"My dear," he says. "Playing the piano in a bar is one of the most difficult jobs in music, and you are doing it very well. I just wanted you to know that."

"Thank you, Sir," I say, shaking his hand, my standard cautious greeting for strange men carrying martini glasses. "I'm Robin Meloy."

"Nice to meet you, Robin. I'm Hank Mancini. Nice work on 'Charade.'" He gives me a jaunty little wave and walks off to wherever it is that famous composers go.

"Wait a minute!" I want to yell. "You wanna hear a little 'Moon River'? I can play that one just the way you wrote it!"

But he's gone.

Hank?

Well, knock me over with a feather. This is my first real personal contact with a famous person—unless you consider the time Smokey Robinson came to the side of the stage and kissed me at the Allegheny County Fair, which doesn't count, because my dad was in the band. I heard Mr. Mancini was in town, but never in a million years did I expect him to show up at my gig and talk to me. Now I'll spend the entire evening trying to figure out how many mistakes I'd made while playing his piece. Unless you are Dave Brubeck, you probably shouldn't play a three-four piece in five. Especially when the composer is sitting there listening to you.

∽

My roommate at Chatham College is Debra McCloskey. Debra comes from Ellwood City, Pennsylvania, where she's a local hero for having won the Lawrence County Junior Miss Pageant. The day she won, the Ellwood City newspaper ran a two inch bold headline that said:

DEBBIE MCCLOSKEY WINS JUNIOR MISS!!!

The entire front page was dedicated to descriptions of the pageant, the talent presentation, Debbie's wardrobe, and interviews with her proud parents, Blanche and Harry. At the bottom of the page, in fine print, was the single sentence:

Richard Nixon Resigns—story page 6

At Chatham, Deb is a political science and theater major. She grew up in a blue-collar working-class home. Even though my father is a jazz drummer, Deb thinks my family is rich because we've got matching towels in the bathroom. I think she's rich because she has an entire town worshiping at her feet. My other roommate, Peggy Melozzi, is a Heinz Scholar with an English and theater double major. She spent a semester at Oxford and is a brilliant actor and writer. Most of the time I feel like the campus idiot around Peg and Deb, but their determination and ingenuity give me a much needed academic nudge.

Deb and Peg are frequent guests at the Hyatt. Sometimes we have famous people staying at the hotel, and Deb and Peg like to tag along, hoping to see someone they recognize. We spot celebrities in various stages of fame, including Art Garfunkel, Flip Wilson, Jonathan Winters, and members of every professional hockey team in the USA. As Deb and Peg sip their diet sodas, their shining eighteen-year-old faces, sincere and beautiful, beam out at me from the dark and smoky recesses of the Hyatt lounge. They think I'm glamorous. I think they're intellectuals.

♪

Make the bed and light the light, I'll be home, late tonight, Blackbird, bye-bye!

It's one o'clock in the morning and Deb, Peg, and I are high on orange juice and chocolate cake, the kind with four layers and dark, gooey icing. Peggy has strung her rather large collection of Lily of France ice cream–colored bras like a banner across our sitting room, and we're singing "Bye Bye Blackbird" in goofy three-part harmony. The more we sing, the more convinced we become that we are God's gift to the world of entertainment. We add a few dance steps: a shuffle to the side, a cute little turn, a waving of the arms.

We're sure we are on to something *big*.

"This is good. Really. This is good stuff."

"Well, it's as good as any of these other nightclub acts you see."

"There are no other nightclub acts in Pittsburgh. I mean, not like this."

"I'll say."

"Exactly. We're great. We really are. That's the point. Pittsburgh needs a great nightclub act. Especially an all-girl nightclub act."

"All-women."

"Whatever. I'll call my agent."

"What agent? There are no agents in Pittsburgh. Who do you think you are, Marlo Thomas?"

～

Diamonds, daisies, snowflakes, that girl! The TV series *That Girl* was our favorite piece of show-biz propaganda. I might not have a swanky Manhattan apartment and a cute boyfriend named Donald, but I do actually know an agent, one I've worked with on piano jobs. His name is Pete Frank and he has an agency in Pittsburgh called Ultimate Entertainment, a name that sort of sets you up for disaster, if you ask me.

Pete once sent me on a job and neglected to mention that there was no piano at the restaurant. I got to the place, a fancy locale on the outskirts of Pittsburgh, and there was a massive Hammond organ, with foot pedals and everything. The restaurant manager—who had been told by my lying agent that I was a fabulous concert organist fresh from a tour of European cathedrals—had to turn the organ on for me. I had no clue how to get a sound out of it. Then I stepped on one of the bass pedals, scared myself silly, and screamed. I spent the rest of the evening worrying about where to put my feet and adjusting to playing with my hands on two different levels. No matter what I played, it sounded like ice-skating music. "Ladies choice," I announced to the dazed couples seated in the dining room. "Couples skate only, and then we'll take a little break and bring out the Zamboni machine." No one laughed. But they paid me a hundred bucks at the end of the night and Pete got his fifteen percent.

Soupy Sales once said, "I don't have an agent, I have an Egyptian curse."

Here's Pete's philosophy: Book anything, send a resourceful musician, or at least someone who looks like a musician, and hope and pray that it works out all right. This is the guy I call to book Deb and Peg and me. Just askin' for trouble, we decide to call our act Ladies.

&

"We need a picture. Pete can't book us without a picture."

"How about an act? We don't have an act. Don't we need an act first?"

"No. He told us to worry about the act later. First we need the picture."

"What will we wear?"

"But we've got no act."

"First things first. What will we wear?"

"The Danskin leotard-skirt things. We all have them."

"That makes me look too fat."

"That makes me look too skinny."

"That makes my boobs look too big."

"Perfect."

&

A nerdy photography major from the senior class volunteers to take a photo of us hanging over the carved-oak banister of one of the campus mansions. Pete lands our first booking in about ten minutes. Unfortunately, we still only know one song.

With a meager two weeks to go, we *zip zip zip* into action. Of the three of us, Deb is the only one who can actually sing. Singing a couple of choruses of "Bye Bye Blackbird" is quite different from singing—full voice—a ninety-minute cabaret show.

Peg and I panic and persuade Deb to sing really loud, convinced that she will pull us through. Peggy and I will function as the comic relief and the dramatic force, intentionally or not.

We hire a piano player named Ricky Ritzel, a name we love because it reminds us of a cracker. I could play myself, but we need the three bodies down front, plus I'm anxious to get out from behind the keyboard. Very anxious. Ricky isn't the perfect accompanist for us, but he is sweet and funny and when we pay him he says things like, "Oh, thanks, now I can buy my Uncle Ed a new raincoat." He even puts on a hard hat and lets us play his head with drumsticks on one number. Ricky is about five feet tall, and I swear he gets shorter every time we practice.

Like the beat beat beat of the tom-tom, when the jungle shadows roar...

We rehearse day and night, night and day. We think we're really good. Twenty-four hours before the first booking we schedule a dress rehearsal. Our only invited guest is a rather large and messy girl named Rita, a good friend of Peg's. Rita is the most intelligent girl in the school, and we're sure she'll be able to give us some constructive criticism. About halfway through our dress rehearsal, after we've wailed and brayed our way through a song from the musical *Shenandoah* called "Freedom," Rita stands up and says—very calmly—"This is horrible." Then she walks out.

I get extremely huffy.

"That's not nice."

"We can't be that bad. She's just not on our level."

"What does she know about show biz anyway. I mean, isn't she studying philosophy or opera or something?"

"Never trust a woman with rigatoni stains on her shirt."

৵

Pete Frank books us at the Oakdale Army Support Base, not too far from Pittsburgh International Airport.

"Good," says Deb's boyfriend George, who functions as our driver for the evening. "You'll be able to make a quick escape to

Toronto if they start throwing tomatoes." George doesn't have much faith in us, but that doesn't bother us, not one bit.

With our make-up bags and big hair, we march into the club like *real professionals* and ask where our dressing room is located. We're pointed to the women's restroom.

"At least with the name 'Ladies' we'll always have our name on the dressing room door," says Peg.

"Hey, check this out," says Ricky Ritzel. He's eating a banana and pointing to a big poster with our press photo on it.

APPEARING TONIGHT AT

THE OAKDALE ARMY SUPPORT BASE NIGHTCLUB

"LADIES" SNAKEDANCERS EXTRAORDINAIRE.

ONE NIGHT ONLY!

There is a long silent pause.

"Well. I don't know what snakedancers do, but I'll bet they don't open the act with 'Everything's Coming Up Roses,'" says Peg.

Pete Frank is in excellent form. On our very first job, he has booked us as snakedancers.

We'll be swell, we'll be great, gonna have the whole world on a plate!

We're so bad we're sort of good. After a few numbers, the audience stops looking for the snakes. Deb sings several selections from *Chorus Line*, I do a Carole King tune. We do "Boogie Woogie Bugle Boy" with me playing the piano and Ricky Ritzel, cracker boy, playing an old bugle. Deb, the skinny one, sings a parody of "The Way We Were," substituting the word *mammaries* for memories while Peg and I walk back and forth behind her with our chests puffed out. It's awful. Really awful. I realize this as I'm performing. But it works, and I can't help myself, I'm having fun.

⌇

For several months we're on the animal circuit: the Elks Club, the Moose Club, the Lions Club. We stomp our way through half a dozen shows before one of our drunken audiences turns on us and begins booing and throwing things. No tomatoes, but still.

It's not pleasant getting hit with peanut shells when you're trying to sing a romantic ballad. Peg and I—in the middle of a meaningful duet called "We Make a Beautiful Pair"—hear a man in the audience whisper very loudly, "They stink! Those two can't sing worth shit." The novelty wears off. The three "Ladies" retire and retreat to the safety of studying T.S. Eliot, Debussy, and Abnormal Psych. I return to my solo piano job, where, once again, I stay in the background, smile at famous and not-so-famous people, and make music without getting hurt or insulted.

ॐ

It will take me almost three decades to appreciate the beauty of our college-girl bravery; our naive willingness to sing and dance and act like fools and just assume that the whole world would be fascinated enough to watch and listen. Where does that courage go when we grow up? Maybe it floats out the door one day when we're not paying attention, and is gone forever. Or maybe it lurks outside, just around the corner, searching for a way to sneak back into our lives, through a window we've forgotten to close. I hope so. I will check my windows every day, and leave them open, just a crack.

Deb will become a Superior Court Justice for the state of Pennsylvania. Peg will move to Providence, Rhode Island, and have a successful career as a writer. I'll bet every dollar I have that both of them, no matter what, will always remember the words to "Bye Bye Blackbird."

We were great. We really were.

Sand Dunes and Salty Air

A musician will rarely survive a change in hotel or restaurant management. When the new manager comes in, the first thing he'll do is change the bar snacks. Then he'll fire the musicians, order thousands of dollars' worth of new uniforms for the waiters, and reprint the menu in so many different typefaces that it looks like a kidnapper's ransom note. The turn-over rate for management in the restaurant and hotel business is ridiculously high, which means that most musicians can count on being fired more times in a year than many people will be in a lifetime.

"Remember, Robin," my Dad reminds me. "You'll get fired from every job you have. Don't take it personally."

I expect to spend my second summer on Nantucket back at the Club Car, older and wiser, with a bigger repertoire and a more sophisticated wardrobe. But while I'm off playing tunes in the Pittsburgh Grand Hyatt, Lino Tambellino retires from the Nantucket Club Car. He's replaced by a woman who has her own ideas about bar snacks and piano players. She switches from pretzel twists to Pepperidge Farm Goldfish and replaces me with a blind sixty-year-old male stride pianist who bangs out Scott Joplin tunes. I'm out of there. With the help of a local Nantucket artist named Marshall DuBock, I land a nice job at a family-owned and -operated place called The Gordon Folger Hotel. The hotel restaurant, known as the Whale, seats about sixty people and is spacious and comfortable, with big wooden ceiling fans that stir the cool Nantucket evening air over the heads of guests devouring big bowls of chowder and enormous buckets of steamed mussels. It's a family place, with lots of old people and kids, quite a contrast to the Club Car with its bevies of drunken yachtsmen and gay Kate Smith impersonators. I miss those guys, but I adjust quickly to my new clientele.

I have trouble getting paid the first summer I play at the Whale. The proprietors are a friendly couple in their fifties, and even have teenage children of their own, but for whatever reason they "forget" to pay me. I'm living from my tips, but I'm not sending money home for the college tuition fund. My parents aren't pleased.

When I was about five years old, my father taught me how to take money from a nightclub manager. "Here," he would say. "Pretend that you're a musician and I'm a nightclub manager and I'm about to pay you. What do you do?"

The answer, of course, was to say, "Gimme the bread," snatch the money out of his hand and run. Although I've never actually performed the snatch and run with a real nightclub manager, after six long weeks of not being paid at the Whale, I finally take my father's advice. I throw a fit and threaten legal action. The owner immediately forks over the cash, and I snatch the money and run. Okay, I don't exactly run, but I do walk directly to the First National Bank with a satisfied bounce in my step. Later in the week the *Inquirer and Mirror*—the local Nantucket newspaper—publishes a glowing review with the title:

ROBIN MELOY DELIGHTS THE WHALE!

I am, at the age of nineteen, developing a sordid file of press clippings, most of which have titles that made me sound like a supporting player in a porn film.

☙

In addition to the tourists, there are many regular customers at the Whale; even some Nantucket natives, like Marshall DuBock. He shows up once a week—usually with a lovely blond coed on his arm—to have a couple of drinks, hear his favorite song, and check the progress of my suntan. But my favorite guest is Mrs. Graham, a meticulously dressed, salt-preserved ancient woman who arrives precisely at six every evening, orders a Manhattan, and holds her ears when I start to play. The staff offers to move Mrs. Graham to a different table, farther away from the grand piano, but she insists on her regular seating arrangement.

"I've been sitting at table nineteen for the last thirty-two years," she says with a booming voice. "I'm not going to move now because of *her*." And then she picks up her cane and points it toward me while tossing a haughty look in my direction. "I'd like my Manhattan please."

Every night at 6:15, Walter, the handsome host of the restaurant, escorts Mrs. Graham and her cane to the salad bar at the back of the restaurant, a procedure Walter calls the Salad Bar Safari. Mrs. Graham insists on performing the salad bar activities herself, and because of her flailing cane and failing eyesight, she has a tendency to fling lettuce leaves and macaroni salad all over herself and anyone standing within arms reach of her. Walter sometimes returns to his podium with mayonnaise splattered on his glasses.

The piano at the Whale—a thirty-five-year-old Mason Hamlin that probably hasn't been tuned since the day it was purchased—is situated right next to the front door, close to the cash register and bar. It's a drafty but profitable location. Walter finds the world's largest brandy snifter for me—I think it's actually a fishbowl—and we're surprised by the way it fills with dollar bills. The guests pay for their dinners, get their change, and throw a couple of bucks in the fishbowl. Even Mrs. Graham makes a contribution now and then.

"Get that girl some piano lessons!" she shouts at Walter as she exits the restaurant.

Once, when Mrs. Graham is on her way into the restaurant, my sister Randy—who is on the island conducting a study of boys and Brandy Alexanders—jumps up to hold the screen door open for her. Randy's hand slips, and the persnickety screen door slams shut in Mrs. Graham's face, making an explosive noise and knocking Mrs. Graham and her cane halfway across the porch, flat on her rinky. Walter races to her rescue. Uninjured, Mrs. Graham orders a double Manhattan, straight up. My sister apologizes to the shaken Mrs. Graham and returns to the bar. Randy stays another five minutes, but I make her leave when she has a big laughing fit right in the middle of my hip bossa-nova rendition of "It's Too Late."

I will play at the Whale on and off for the next eight summers. Mrs. Graham will live to be 100 years old. She wins.

Playback 1977

It's ten minutes past six on a Saturday night on Nantucket Island. I've spent the day sailing on Nantucket Sound, and because of the wind, or lack of it, I'm very late getting back to town to start my piano gig. There's no time to go to my apartment to change clothes, and I'm desperate. I scurry from the dock of the Nantucket Yacht Club to the employees' dorm, a dark and dismal cave underneath the restaurant that is home to the many Ivy League waiters and waitresses working at the Whale. Amy, a short brunette majoring in art history at Princeton, greets me at the door.

"Here. Wear this."

"I can't wear that. It's a nightgown."

"So what? That thing you had on last night looked like a nightgown."

"Well it wasn't a nightgown. It was an evening gown. It was an emerald-green satin evening gown from my Aunt Jean, thank you very much. A Halston knock-off, but still."

"Aunt Jean must be a swinger. I'm telling you, it looked like a nightgown. Anyway, what difference does it make? This will look great on you."

"But it's polyester."

"Jesus, Robin, you're already ten minutes late, you're standing there in cutoffs and a bikini top when you should be upstairs playing the piano, and you're arguing about polyester? Wear the damn nightgown. No one will notice. Who's gonna care? Mrs. Graham? She can't see past the tip of her cane."

I strip off the shorts and the bikini top and kick them into the corner of the musty dorm room. Amy pulls the nightgown over my head. It's pink with little purple flowers and dancing bears. She gives me some gold sandals and lipstick. I run up the steps to the restaurant. The sandals are two sizes too small and I trip just as I make my entrance.

Screech, bang. That damn screen door. Oops, shit!

Walter, the host of the restaurant, catches me just before I spin out of control and careen into a party of five being seated near the piano.

"What in the world are you wearing?" he says. "That thing looks like a nightgown."

I don't have time to reply. Walter seats the family and returns to the piano.

"Where have you been?" he asks. "You're always on time. Mrs. Graham is complaining that there's no music. She's having a fit that you're late."

"Mrs. Graham hates my guts, Walter," I say as I do my sound check—*on off high low finished*—and get my tip jar out from behind the bar. "It would make her evening to hear that I drowned in a waterskiing accident. She'd like it even better if I were caught in a trawling net and pulled in with the catch of the day."

"Yeah, but she has her routine," Walter says. I play an arpeggio. I'm completely frazzled. Mrs. Graham stands up, shoots poison darts at me with her eyes, and hobbles back to the salad bar.

"See what I mean? I think she secretly admires you," says Walter. "She won't go to the salad bar until she knows you're here."

"Walter!" shouts Mrs. Graham from the salad bar. "Where is the three-bean salad? And what's this concoction next to the Jello? It looks like dog doo!"

"Uh-oh," says Walter. "She's got hold of the giant salad tongs. I'd better go help her."

I play "Hello Young Lovers." One of the people seated near the piano sings along. These shoes are killing my feet. My hair is stiff from the salt water and I can feel the sunburn on my nose.

Walter returns from the salad bar.

"Another tie bites the dust." He has pieces of cabbage and cucumber clinging to his suit. "I should *never* let her get hold of the giant tongs."

"Robin! Hi!" Fulton the bartender has returned from the kitchen and is stocking the bar.

"Nice, uh, dress."

"Thanks." Okay, so maybe it's not so bad. I just wish it didn't have bears on it. I play a Chopin Nocturne because I know he likes Chopin. This guy is really sexy, I think.

Screech, bang. I wish someone would oil that door.

It's my friend Marshall DuBock with his date of the week. He looks nervous and I can see why. His date has the biggest breasts I've ever seen. Walter greets Marshall and his date, sees the breasts, and turns bright red.

"Good evening," Walter says. "Welcome to the Whale. I'm Walter. Tonight your Peter will be a waiter."

Oh my God. I play "All of Me" and hide my face with my hair.
Screech, bang.

Two men in Navy blazers and Nantucket-red pants enter and sit at the bar.

"Martini, straight up, shaken not stirred, three olives and a side of flavored rocks. What are you havin' Jim?"

"Scotch and Squirt."

Scotch and Squirt?

Fulton smiles at me. I want to play more Chopin for him, but I only know the one piece. Actually what I want to do is jump over the bar and tackle him. Man, do I have a crush on this guy. I get out my flute. I can play the flute and the piano at the same time. How about that, boys?

"Look at that, Jim," says Martini Man. "That girl can play the flute and the piano at the same time." I'm ridiculous. I'm playing a song I wrote with only five notes in the melody, which is all I can play with my left hand holding the flute. I play some goofy chords with my right hand. Everyone stares at me.

"Now that's talent," says Scotch and Squirt.

I could probably win the talent portion of the Miss America contest with this act. But first I would have to learn how to twirl the flute. I'll work on that.

Everyone claps.

I play and sing "The Girl from Ipanema."

Tall and tan and young and lovely, the girl from Ipanema goes a-walkin'...

"How the hell do I eat this thing?" The coed with the huge breasts has ordered lobster, a really bad choice for a first date. Walter almost has a heart attack as he ties the bib around the girl's neck. Marshall, her date, tries to extract a piece of claw meat from the pile of shells on his plate and sends the entire claw across the table directly into the girl's lap.

"Allow me," says Walter.

But each day when she walks by the sea, she looks straight ahead, not at me...

"Another round here, bartender," says Martini Man. "And one for the piano girl."

I give them my best underage coed smile.

"She's too young to drink," says Fulton. "But you can put money in the fishbowl on the piano. It's her College Tuition Fund."

I love this guy Fulton. Even if he is in dental school.

Uh-oh. Man your battle stations. Here comes Mrs. Graham.

I play "I Wish You Love."

I wish you bluebirds in the spring...

"IT'S TOO LOUD, WALTER," Mrs. Graham shouts as she hits the leg of the piano with her cane. "I CAN'T TOLERATE IT. AND THAT FIFE THING SHE PLAYS IS HORRIBLE. I CAN'T ABIDE FIFING!"

"It's a flute, Mrs. Graham," says Walter. She puts a dollar in my tip jar.

"DREADFUL."

I sing, "And in July, a lemonade, to cool you in the leafy shade…"

"What?" says Scotch and Squirt. "I like the fife. The fife is good."

"It's a flute," I say.

"Piano fingers, flute mouth. What more could you ask for in a girl?" They order another round.

Some family restaurant this is.

Screech, bang.

Mrs. Graham exits, but I can hear her yelling from the front porch.

"AND FURTHERMORE, WALTER, SHE NEEDS SOME PROPER CLOTHES. THAT THING SHE HAS ON LOOKS LIKE A NIGHTGOWN."

Screech, bang.

Walter returns.

"Another satisfied customer," he says.

I think my nose is starting to peel.

Someone to Watch Over Me

There's a piano. There's a bar. Now go play.

To me, making a living as a musician seems like the natural thing to do.

My childhood was a symphony of musical adventure, a fantasy land of song, dance, and laughter; a cacophony of scales, jazz records, and practice sessions. I learned jazz slang before I was six years old, calling money "bread" and referring to my playmates as "the cats."

"Hey Mommy, lay some bread on me, please. The cats and I need a five-spot to buy a Mister Softee, you dig?" This drove my mother crazy, but my dad thought it was a riot.

My sister and I memorized the words to Peggy Lee and Sammy Davis hits and did after-dinner shows for my parents and our little brother, selling them tickets and forcing them to sit, pinned to the sofa, as we chirped through endless choruses of "Fever" and performed our choreographed version of "I've Got You Under My Skin."

Mom took us, on a regular basis, to see my dad perform and record in nightclubs, concert halls, and television studios. Pittsburgh in the sixties was a swinging place, and Dad was a busy guy.

Grandma Rawsthorne, my father's mom, was the choir director of our church. She had a genuine contralto voice, perfect for singing "O Holy Night," "Up from the Grave He Arose," and other Methodist classics. Grandma also played the violin and the piano and made the best Christmas cookies in Pittsburgh while singing in the kitchen. Aunt Pinky played the french horn and a little bit of everything else, even though she was really an R&B fanatic. Aunt Jean and Uncle Bill had an organ in their home, and I'm positive the two of them were the best jitterbug dancers in Western Pennsylvania. I played the flute, my sister played the cello, my brother played the drums. Dad had timpani, a marimba, a xylophone, a vibraphone in the basement, every percussion instrument ever invented, and three or four sets of drums that he had stored all over the place. He even had a gong. My mother, also a first-class dancer, could play "Deep Purple" on the piano, and her mother, my Grandma Curtis, played an excellent "Star Spangled Banner" once a month at American Legion Auxiliary meetings. We had visitors and friends who sang the blues, played the bass, played the trombone, or banjo, or the guitar. No one ever had to turn the volume up at my house. Most kids play hide and seek. My sister and I played Sound Check.

Even our vacations were full of music, paid for by my father's out-of-town gigs in exotic locations. I remember one summer holiday in Miami when he played in a Dixieland band for a Teamsters' convention at the Americana Hotel. We ate frogs' legs and wore hibiscus in our hair and marveled at the eight-story picture of Jimmy Hoffa projected on the hotel wall.

༄

When I turned nine years old, my mother started driving me every week, through rush hour traffic on Banksville Road, to the home of Mr. Bill Chrystal, a piano teacher with a formidable reputation and an army of capable students. Mom would pull the station wagon up to the side of his house on McCully Street, wish me luck, and wait for me to climb the long stone staircase that led to Mr. Chrystal's studio. I'd stand in front of his door with my fingers hovering over the bell, palms sweating, and try to think up ways to get out of my lesson. On the other side of the door, I would hear the cautious tempo of the student before me. I imagined the silent disapproval that met each mistake, and heard the *scratch, scratch, scratch* of Mr. Chrystal's blue and red pencils as they circled mistakes the student had made while plodding through the music. Red indicated a bad mistake. Blue signified a musical mortal sin—punished by Mr. Chrystal's withering stare and a week of practicing one passage until you got it right.

Eventually, I would muster up enough courage to ring his bell. He would answer the door, all smiles, and have me take a seat on the couch in his studio, where I sat and witnessed the praise, the humiliation, the confusion, the triumph of the student ahead of me.

Mr. Chrystal had two grand pianos in his studio. One of them, the one I got to play, was a Steinway with perfect action and a glorious sound. I adored playing it, even when Mr. Chrystal berated me for mistakes, bad posture, or poor preparation. He was a taskmaster, a drill sergeant, and a wizard pianist. He scared me with his stern voice and strict regimen, but I loved how he put ideas in my head and pulled music out of my fingers. It seemed a kind of magic. Later in life he became my friend. I even got to call him Bill.

But back then, he was still Mr. Chrystal. He bullied me into learning things. I would show up for my lesson with a new piece of music. "You'll never be able to play that," he would say. "You're not good enough. It's way too hard for you. Forget it." And then he'd slam the book shut and move on to the next thing. I would go home and start practicing like crazy just to prove him wrong. This isn't a technique I'd recommend to aspiring teachers, but it worked with me. If you wanted me to do something difficult, all you had to do was tell me I wasn't capable. I was the princess of reverse psychology.

∽

At my first piano recital, I played a Mozart Minuet. There was an "A" section that repeated and a "B" section that repeated. At the top of the first "B" section, I hit a clam—a bad one. Everyone in the audience winced. When I went back to repeat this section, I decided that if I played it correctly the second time around the audience would know that I had played it wrong the first time. So I played it wrong again. On purpose.

"You," my dad said in response to my nine-year-old logic, "are destined for a career in show business."

Mr. Chrsytal just smiled.

～

My mother spent the better part of fifteen years being a taxi driver for her children. In 1968 other people were burning their bras and their draft cards. Mom threatened to burn her driver's license. She took an extra two hours out of her hectic schedule every week to drive me to my piano lessons. My parents refused to select a teacher based on convenience. They wanted the best guy in town, even if that meant driving thirty minutes in each direction and spending money they didn't have.

During my lesson, Mom would zip to the shopping mall and browse around. She always bought me a hot soft pretzel and a frozen Coke for the ride home. Sometimes I'd be in tears from a particularly frustrating lesson with Mr. Chrystal. Occasionally I would feel proud of myself for accomplishing something I had thought was impossible. Whatever my mood, she talked me through it. The time it takes to support a child's artistic desires and dreams isn't mentioned in most parenting how-to manuals, but it should be. My mom could write the book.

～

Two years later, my sister Randy began taking piano lessons, too. But she hated them. She detested Mr. Chrystal and she despised practicing. In three years she learned to play one song— "Eleanor Rigby." We would go to our lessons together. I would play first, and Randy would volunteer to do office work for Mr. Chrystal just so my lesson would run longer and her lesson would be shorter.

"Okay, Randy, Robin's lesson is over. You're on."

"Oh, Mr. Chrystal," my sister would plead. "Please let me finish alphabetizing your wonderful collection of sheet music. I just need a little more time to complete this second shelf. Boy, this Bach guy sure wrote a lot of stuff. And how about this Beethoven fella? Tons of music! I'll need a few more minutes to get all of this sorted."

"Okay. Aren't you a nice girl? So efficient. Robin's lesson can go a little longer. She can certainly stand a little more work on those melodic minor scales. Robin, *how many times do I have to tell you this?* CURVE YOUR FINGERS, ROBIN, for God's sake!"

My sister's secretary act went on for months and months. My parents were paying thirty bucks a half-hour for my sister to do office work. She eventually got caught at her game and switched to ballet. She loved that. She can still play "Eleanor Rigby," though. She's a big hit at parties.

I almost quit playing a couple of times. Like most kids, I had a change of heart when I hit puberty. Until that point I had been improving at a steady pace, playing in competitions and developing a small classical repertoire. But then I started junior high school and a terrible thing happened. The other kids made fun of me because I played the piano. "Classical music," they said. "How queer." After a conference with my parents, Mr. Chrystal began encouraging me to play pop, rock, and folk music, teaching me how to read lead sheets and chord symbols. He taught me how to do my own arrangements. And he encouraged me to compose. I earned the respect of my classmates by playing Three Dog Night hits and I learned to quiet the adolescent noise in my head by writing innocent songs about growing up. I went from being an angst-ridden nerd to being cool. At thirteen, that's far more important than a Bach Invention. Mr. Chrystal had found a way to keep me playing the piano.

By coincidence, Bill Chrystal ended up at Chatham College and became an associate professor of music there. I had to stop calling him Mr. Chrystal and start calling him Bill when he began dating Peggy, my irresistible roommate with the large collection of bras. Bill was 53, Peg was 20. Bill wasn't the type to hang out in our dorm room and eat popcorn, but that was fine with me. I worried about those red and blue pencils. I didn't want him following me around and drawing blue circles around the mistakes I made in real life. At Bill's suggestion I began studying with the head of the Chatham music department, a classical teacher named Henry Spinelli.

Mr. Spinelli was a tiny man with an adorable pointy face. If you were casting elves for a Christmas play, he would be the man to call. Cheryl Hardwick, a good friend of my family and one of the musical directors for the television show *Saturday Night Live*, had attended Chatham years before and studied with Mr. Spinelli. He often asked about Cheryl, and I got the feeling that she was his all-time favorite student. She was certainly his most successful.

"Mr. Spinelli," I said one afternoon as I sat down at the 1899 Steinway grand positioned in his office. "I talked to Cheryl last night and she sends her best."

"Oh? How nice. She was always such a wonderful musician. Such excellent technique. You know, I saw her on that show the other night. That *Saturday Night Live* show." There was a long pause and then Mr. Spinelli's nose started to twitch. "She was dressed as a bee." He cleared his throat. "Such a waste."

I thought that getting paid to play music on television while dressed as a bee was a marvelous thing. Cheryl was one of my role models and musical heroes—a woman instrumentalist in a man's musical world, focused and driven and having fun. The bee suit was icing on the cake.

৴৹

For thirty years my dad was the drummer and vibes player for the *Mister Rogers' Neighborhood* television program, playing jazz for a children's show hosted by a man who taught kids about music, love, and self-respect. Fred Rogers was a family friend, an inspiration, and the kindest man I'd ever met. He had words of encouragement for me whenever our paths crossed; often on

Nantucket, and sometimes in Pittsburgh, where his show was taped.

"You make people feel good with your music," he said to me once. "What a wonderful feeling that must be for you, Robin. Isn't the piano a marvelous thing?" Fred understood, perhaps better than anyone, that playing the piano made me happy. He was a very musical person. He played the piano enough to express himself and had the wisdom to hire talented musicians to make his gentle lyrical themes come to life for the millions of children who tuned in to his show.

Once in a while, Dad took me to the studio with him to watch the recording of an episode. He worked with bassist Carl McVicker and pianist Johnny Costa, an extraordinary jazz musician and arranger. Costa's technical magic and artistic vision thrilled me—but it scared me, too.

Johnny kissed his own hands and credited God after he performed. But hard work played a more important role. "Bobby," he once said to my dad, "I decided when I was a kid that I would never have any dark areas on the keyboard." There weren't any shadows or sharp corners or hidden agendas on the Costa piano, only improvised music that spoke clearly of the fullness of the life swirling around him.

Costa was a tornado of talent. He was also eccentric, volatile, and insecure. He had a habit of lying on the floor in the middle of airports, simply because he was tired. He argued with waitresses over the quality of coleslaw. He made sexist comments about any woman who walked past him. He used the f–word every chance he got. And he was highly critical of other musicians—those of us who still had "dark places" on our instruments. Johnny, Carl, and Dad called themselves the Kamikaze Trio. Dad never knew what would be required of him, musically or emotionally, when he worked with Costa. But he said that performing with Costa was the biggest privilege of his professional life.

Knowing Costa, and listening to him, was a complex part of my musical education. Every time I heard him play I encountered a curious mix of motivation and defeat. His talent was so extreme that he made me want to quit playing the piano, but so beautiful that I couldn't.

⤳

I don't have to travel far to hear the musical voices of my childhood. All I have to do is sit down and play. Every time I touch the piano, Bill Chrystal is there, reprimanding me for a careless mistake or sloppy fingering. His imposing physical presence at the side of the Steinway has been replaced by a tiny voice in the back of my head. Sometimes, not often enough, I catch myself playing a passage the way he would have played it, clear and perfect and full of life, and it takes my breath away.

I turn on the PBS series *Mister Rogers' Neighborhood* and hear Johnny Costa playing, Fred Rogers singing, and my Dad backing them up with his tasteful percussive nuances and perfect time. Watching that show is a melodic time tunnel, a chance to revisit the playing and composing heroes of my youth. Fred and Johnny left behind a billion notes, a dizzying number of beautiful thoughts transposed into song, and a musical tapestry woven with the golden threads of optimism and inspiration. *Yes!* they seem to say over and over and over again. *There is music in life, but there should be life in music, too.* The show reminds me that each creative musician and each supportive person in a young person's life—teacher, parent, or friend—carries a torch that can spark the artistic flame that lives in every child's heart.

Music has always been a part of my life. I couldn't help but listen and fall in love with the sounds around me. Play the piano in a bar? It's a privilege.

Circus, Circus

I'm scheduled to play Maurice Ravel's *Piano Sonatine* for the spring music department recital at the Chatham College chapel. I know the material. I love the material. I've practiced it until the piece is playing me, instead of the other way around. I'm confident and secure with my interpretation of the composer's intention, and I'm looking forward to the night's performance.

I walk onstage, sit down at the Steinway concert grand, and adjust the height of the bench. There are about seventy-five people in attendance, a small crowd for such a big space.

Something is wrong with me. I feel, I don't know, hollow. My hands are tingling. I take a deep breath, and begin playing the first movement of the *Sonatine*.

That's when it hits me. About sixteen bars into Mr. Ravel's elegantly written composition, my heart starts pounding. *Boom. Boom. Boom.* My hands sweat and shake, and I'm moving in slow motion, except for my right knee, which has developed a high-speed twitch.

"You can do this, you can do this," I say to myself five or six times.

Another voice, a strange one coming from inside my head, starts poking at my self confidence.

"Who are you?" I think.

The Voice of Doom, he replies in a loud, whiny voice. I look around. No one else can hear the Voice of Doom. Just me.

Get...Out...Of...Here, I think, trying hard to concentrate on the notes.

Nope, he says. *I'm not goin'. You're a fake, and it's about time you realized it. Fake, fake, fake! You're gonna massacre this piece big time and all these people will hear you do it. You're nothing but a big faking faker. Fake, fake, fake, fake, fake.*

He's yelling at me from inside my brain, somewhere between my ears and the top of my skull, and he keeps getting louder and louder.

I try to argue back but I can't get a word in edgewise.

This is awful.

I can't locate the notes. Or if I find them I play them so slowly that I have no idea where I am in the piece. Everything I've learned is gone—out the window like bubbles blown through a ring on a windy day.

I steal a glance at the audience. Grandma Curtis and Grandma Rawsthorne are in the second row with Aunt Jean and Uncle Bill. They're all smiles and don't seem to notice anything wrong. That's good. My parents are in the row behind them, but I look away before I can catch their reaction to my train wreck. Oh no. There's Bill Chrystal, with a pained expression on his normally placid face, hovering on the side of the chapel, looking like he's ready to dash out the fire exit if things get any worse.

I'm freezing and my hands shake. I'm having an anxiety attack.

Oh. Wait. Now I get it. I'm onstage alone and the audience is paying attention. I've gotten used to the chatter and the laughter of the cocktail lounge. Where are the clinking glasses and the waiters barking orders at the bartender? Where is the whir of the blender, where are the cheerful hellos and goodbyes and how are yous? Where is all the *noise*? And how come these people are listening? What do they expect to hear?

No, no, no, no, no! Don't just sit there! Talk! Smoke a cigarette! Have an argument with your neighbor. Dispute the check with your overworked waitress, because you did, after all, only have two gin and tonics and you're being charged for three. Order another round of Strawberry Margaritas or some of those tasty chicken fingers. Do something, anything, but please please please don't listen to me. It is enough for me to listen to myself. Really, it's enough.

Well, there you have it, says Voice of Doom. *Another concert career comes to a screeching halt.*

$\backsim$

The next day I decide to audition to be a showgirl in the Ringling Brothers Barnum and Bailey Circus.

Maybe I'll be good enough for the circus.

No you won't, says the Voice of Doom. VOD is pushy and he's off to an excellent start.

Debbie McCloskey is going to audition, too. We get ourselves made up like a couple of teenage tarts, pack our dance bags with circus-appropriate items—blue eye shadow, little pots of glitter, hair clips with sequined fruit appliqués—and climb aboard the Fifth Avenue bus that takes us to the circus site, the Civic Arena in downtown Pittsburgh.

"Back door, please!" Deb yells at the bus driver. "I don't know about this bus stop," she says to me. "Isn't this a rough part of town?" Deb is from Ellwood City. Every part of Pittsburgh is a rough part of town for her.

"Naw, don't worry," I say. I'd taken the bus down there every Saturday for years for flute lessons. By the age of nine I'd been using public transportation to get everywhere in the city. I'm not scared, not at all.

Of course I've never hiked through this particular corner of the city dressed like a hooker. Showgirl makeup, big hair, and high heels at 8:30 A.M. have a tendency to make a girl look like last night's leftover, no matter how young she is. We endure and ignore the taunts and the leers, and run as fast as we can in our tight skirts and colorful heels. Out of breath, windblown, and short on composure, we drag our dance bags up to the guard at Gate B of the Civic Arena.

"Through the tunnel to the Center Ring, please, Ladies." We tiptoe past cages of tigers and lions. They're being fed huge chunks of raw meat on a hook. My feet feel like huge chunks of raw meat on a hook.

"You know," Deb says to me. "We really should wear sensible shoes to these things and change once we get where we're going."

"But I don't own a pair of sensible shoes."

A camel spits at Deb.

"Don't get too close to the cages, girls!" yells a very short (some might even say dwarf-like) man with huge arms. "These cats will have you for breakfast."

Maybe being a concert pianist isn't such a bad idea.

But you're not good enough. Remember? says VOD.

We reach the center ring. This is amazing. In the first ring The Flying Zucchinis—or whatever they're called—are practicing their trapeze act. I stand there, looking up, with my mouth hanging open, as a young female Zucchini releases the trapeze, hurls herself through the air, somersaults three or maybe even four times, completely misses the other trapeze, drops into the net, and laughs. In ring three is a leather-clad woman shouting commands in an Eastern European language at six stampeding horses. She has a whip and the horses are bolting around her in a circle. When she whacks her whip on the ground, the horses leap in the air, spin around, and gallop in the other direction. Wow! Heigh-ho Silver! Ride like the wind! I'm getting dizzy just watching. They make a lot of dust. I cough. The trainer looks over her shoulder at the large group of girls gathering for the audition, and her eyes narrow. She cracks the whip, three times, loudly, and turns her attention back to her animals.

"I love this," I say to Debbie. "It's like going to the circus for free!"

"Sign the sheet and go stand in the line, please. We're eliminating girls based on appearance."

Oh great! I have a lot of confidence in my ability to look like a circus showgirl. I've been practicing ever since my parents took me to Las Vegas when I was sixteen. We saw Sammy Davis, Jr., Gladys Knight and the Pips, Steve and Edie, and several hundred showgirls wearing nothing but feathers and sequins held together by dental floss.

Debbie and I shed our coats, brush our hair, re-apply our weather-worn fuchsia lipstick and do our best showgirl walks as we strut to the middle of the center ring.

I am wearing a white french-cut leotard and silver shoes.

"Robin," whispers Deb, as we take our places in the line. "That leotard is completely see-through!" We stand there posing, grinning at the choreographer as he looks us up and down. After his gaze moves on to the girl on my right, I glance down at myself. Double drat. My nipples are standing at attention like twin lieutenants at a West Point parade. *Merde.* Who knew it would be so cold in the Big Top.

"You in the white! And you next to her in the blue," shouts the choreographer. Debbie always wears blue because it makes her eyes stand out. My white outfit is having a similar effect, but not with my eyes, exactly. "Can you two dance?" he asks.

"Oh yes," we say in unison. This is a big fat lie. Deb can dance a little; she'd been the star majorette at Ellwood City High School. But I am certainly not a dancer. My sister is the dancer. I am the piano player.

No you're not, says VOD. *You just think you're a piano player.*

"Yes," I say again to the choreographer, "I'm a very good dancer."

"Can you do a time step?" he asks.

"Yes! I can do a time step!" I say. I turn to Deb and whisper, "What's a time step?"

"I can't teach you that in 30 seconds, " she says. "I barely know how to do one myself. Just move your arms around a lot and smile like crazy. In that outfit, they'll never notice your feet." She exits the ring to put on her tap shoes. I claim to have forgotten mine.

I notice a Channel Four camera crew setting up on one side of the ring.

Oh good—we'll be on the news tonight!

"That'll be a great story," says Deb. "Nipple Day at Ringling Brothers."

"Ah, come on, look, it's not so bad now. I'm getting warmer. Maybe the lights are helping."

I survive the time-step cut. I wave my arms around and smile and bounce and before I know it, I make it to the second round. So does Deb.

"And now for the ballet combination," says the choreographer.

Oh come on.

You know, I honestly thought that all I would have to do for this job was ride an elephant or hang from a ring. I mean, no one goes to the circus to see a ballet. This choreographer fellow is going way overboard.

I stumble my way through the ballet combination without harming myself or anyone else. The final part of the audition is coming up. We'll be required to do thirty chené turns across the ring, starting at one side and stopping when we get to the other. What is this, the Bolshoi? Sorry, but turning or spinning of any kind has never been one of my strong suits—I suffer from motion sickness, big time.

The assistant calls out the names of the girls who have made the third cut. I'm sure that I've failed the ballet combination and I'm already packing up my gear when I hear my name.

"Robin Meloy, you're up second for the chené turns," says the assistant. I look at Debbie for help, but she's busy practicing, twirling and revolving and pirouetting like a crazed dancing doll in a jewelry box. I don't want to rehearse—I'm afraid I'll get too dizzy before I have to do the real thing. All around me girls in bright leotards and metallic shoes are spinning, whipping their heads from side to side; whirling dervishes in high heels and lip gloss. I feel a little queasy. I stand perfectly still and try to focus on the horizon.

The camera crew positions itself on the far side of the ring, in the spot where we're supposed to stop. The first girl jumps gracefully off the edge of the ring and spins her way, in a perfect line, to the far side. She stops suddenly, strikes a perfect "live at Caesar's Palace" showgirl kind of pose, and ambles out of the center ring. I hope she'll be trampled by one of the stampeding horses, but alas, she is spared.

"Miss Meloy, you're on!" There is weird mazurka music playing—*hoopa, shoopa, shoy, yoy, yoy!* I have no idea if I'll make it to the other side—I've never tried this many turns—but I figure I've got nothing to lose. I leap from the border of the ring and start spinning. I try to "spot" my turns, snapping my head back and forth to prevent dizziness, but I can tell, after seven or eight revolutions, that it isn't helping.

You wouldn't want to throw up, now would you? says VOD.

As I approach the other side of the ring, I remember the camera crew. Oh no! I am hopelessly out of control by now, reeling toward the Channel Four news people like an albino bat with nipples who has lost its sense of direction.

I trip on the camera tripod and lunge into a rotund cable man.

"Whoa, lassie!" he yells. Together, we tumble onto the dusty floor. Down, down, all the way down.

Everything is spinning around me, there's a 250-pound union technician on top of me, electrical cable around my ankles and sawdust in my hair.

See? says VOD. *I told you. You're not even good enough for the goddamn circus.*

The cable guy takes his time getting back on his feet, helps me up, and brushes the straw off my leotard, an activity he seems to enjoy.

Deb, though not perfect, manages to execute her turns without knocking over the news crew. The audition is over.

"Thank you, Ladies!" says the choreographer. "Those of you who have been chosen will be notified in four weeks! We will only be selecting eight showgirls this year, and we've been holding auditions in every major city in the United States of America. So don't be sad if you don't get in. You've got some very stiff competition!"

The cable guy laughs, a little too loudly.

"Thank you for coming to audition for the greatest show on earth!"

"Well, that's that," says Deb. "I really think we need to finish college anyway, don't you? You know, interim semester in England and all of that. It would be a shame to toss it all aside to join the circus."

"Yeah. And I don't think I could deal with living on a train with all those animal smells."

"And the costumes. They look pretty from far away, but I'll bet up close they're really cheesy."

"And Lord only knows what they give you to eat. Slop or something."

"Right. And they probably make you clean up the elephant crap when the show is over. And you know that horse lady with the whip is some kind of S&M freak who is really nasty to everybody."

The choreographer walks past us.

"Excuse me, Sir!" I say. "I just want to tell you that we've had a fabulous time and that it would be a dream come true for us to work in the circus!"

"Oh yes," says Deb, batting her big blue eyes. "A dream come true! If a genie popped out of a magic lantern and gave us three wishes, being in the circus would be the first one!"

"Why, thank you, girls! You'll be hearing from us."

⌒

Later that same afternoon, I go to play a piano job at LeMont, a half-tacky-half-fancy restaurant with a great view of Pittsburgh's Golden Triangle. The event, a public-relations spectacle for a fashion company, will be attended by a large crowd of glittering guests. I hustle into the restroom, wipe off my excess circus-showgirl-hooker makeup and brush the lacquer out of my hair. Whew. That feels nice. I change into the little black Audrey Hepburn dress I'd thrown into my circus bag earlier this morning. As I make my way to the piano, I hear the welcome sounds of conversation and laughter. I play my first notes, relieved that no one is paying much attention. Voice of Doom won't find me here, I'm sure. I feel a tap on my shoulder.

"Hey there, lassie! You certainly do get around town, don't you girl?"

It's the cable guy I'd toppled at the circus audition. He's at the restaurant to videotape the fashion event.

"You won't be doin' any dancin' here, will ya? Let me know if you get the urge and I'll see if I can track down a helmet."

"Oh. I'm so sorry about that accident at the arena," I say. "Don't worry. I'm not at all dangerous while seated at the piano."

The Channel Four news runs footage of me twice on the evening broadcast. In the first story, I'm spinning like a mad-woman trying to get a job in the circus. In the second segment I'm sitting at the piano, perfectly content, playing "My Funny Valentine."

I hardly recognize myself.

॰ॢ॰

Four weeks later Debbie and I get letters welcoming us to the Ringling Brothers Barnum and Bailey Circus, Red Company. On the top of the stationery is a chain of elephants, linked together trunk to tail. We are to report to circus camp in Florida for training two months later.

The job pays $175 a week, thirty-five of which I'll have to pay back to them for weekly rent on the circus train. Circus food, or slop, is included in the rent. The contract covers a six-week probationary and training period, and then eighteen months on the road wearing scanty costumes—probably posing in a feather headpiece and a magenta sequined bikini while surrounded by lions, horses, and tiny people flying through the air with the greatest of ease. Predictably, my parents aren't thrilled about me ditching my college education to join a highfalutin version of the carnival. Debbie says no to the circus without a second thought. It takes me a little longer to make up my mind. I turn down the offer. But at least I know I'm good enough.

॰ॢ॰

The evening of the Ravel recital visits me as a recurring nightmare: I'm onstage, alone, and I can't find the notes that I need to play, I can't find the words to explain why I can't play them, and I can't find the strength to get up and leave the stage. I sit there, frozen, staring at the keyboard while the audience stares at me. It's a silent dream, and a lonely one. It's as if the music has been choked out of me and is hiding somewhere outside of the concert hall, waiting for me to find it.

When I play in a room full of noisy people, it's like playing alone. I own what I play, because no one is judging me. Why am I able to put myself in competitive and judgmental situations in other areas of my life? That's a big mystery to me. I can stand onstage and tell a story, I can act in front of a movie camera. I can sing and dance in front of thousands of people even though I'm not particularly good at either thing. But when it comes to playing a formal piano concert, a large dusty veil of fear falls over me and I can't work my way out. I punch and tear at the veil to try to grab hold of a phrase, a note, anything that feels like the familiar song I've spent months practicing. But what I play comes from far, far away and feels foreign to my hands and distasteful to my ears. It's never, ever good enough. Then, magically, when everyone stops listening, the music returns to my fingers and I like the way I sound.

I really don't want to play formal concerts anymore—it's too upsetting. But playing in a bar is fun. It might not be the concert career I once imagined for myself, but at least it's not the circus.

Handful of Keys

I'm often accused of assigning human qualities to inanimate objects. I admit I'm guilty, especially when it comes to the musical instruments I love.

The piano I played as a child was a gentle giant. It was an upright grand, six feet tall, at least 100 years old, and painted an antique Wedgewood green to match my mother's living room. Manufactured by Boardman and Gray, a company established in 1837, the piano had been a gift to my great-grandmother when she was a little girl. My father says that in the history of the world, it's the heaviest thing—ever. He might be right. Each time he moved it he swore he would never attempt it again. In spite of the unfortunate color, Big Green was a fine instrument. I'll never forget the feel of the worn ivory on my fingers and the sound of those elongated bass strings that stretched almost up to the ceiling. The real ivory keys on Big Green, although criminally murderous to the elephants that provided it, had an elegant touch not matched by modern synthetics.

The house we lived in was small and perfectly decorated. Big Green looked like a disgruntled hippopotamus tucked into a corner of the living-room, directly across from the front porch. In the summertime I practiced while I watched—through the screen door—the neighborhood kids zoom by on their bikes and roller skates. I'd see Wanda Wohlfarth in her tennis whites stroll past our home with her racket, off for an afternoon on the courts. I'd identify the *clip clop clip clop* of Barbara Forbes's cleated high heels as she returned from work in the late afternoons, and hear the pleasant voices of Mr. and Mrs. Oakes as they sat chatting on their front porch. While sitting at Big Green, I'd watch my brother go flying by the front door with his baseball glove or butterfly net, my sister chasing after him with her wild auburn hair trailing out behind her like ribbons in a windstorm. The screen door opened and closed, drinks were served, steaks were grilled, children were disciplined. I played on and on, feeling forever safe, unaware of how grateful I would one day be for the tranquility of those summers.

The Wilson family lived two houses down from us, and Mary Beth Wilson was my best friend. She would come and fetch me away from the piano, and the two of us would do cartwheels across the courtyard, leaving ourselves grass-stained and dizzy with laughter. Then I would go back to Big Green and practice some more.

In the winter it was more complicated. My brother and sister were less likely to play outside, and the little black-and-white Philips television in the living room became their main source of entertainment. This was a big conflict. I couldn't practice Schumann while my siblings were watching, or trying to watch, *The Flintstones*. I was playing "Scenes from Childhood" and they were yelling *yaba-daba-doo*. The bickering went on for several years until my parents broke down and bought earphones for the television. It wasn't ideal, but it was a good compromise.

At my weekly piano lesson with Mr. Chrystal I played a lovely Steinway grand piano. I looked forward to playing this piano every week, but I had grown used to Big Green and felt more comfortable with its touch. That's an expression you hear in music circles—*that piano has a nice touch*. It sounds as if the piano is touching the player, instead of the other way around. Well, it's true. Big Green touched me, whether because it was an excellent instrument or because it was my first love, I'm still not sure. Big Green reminds me of carefree seasons, of moments lost and memories found, of my parents in their youth, my siblings in their innocent glory, and a girlhood that was charmed by the gift of music. Maybe I'll get Big Green back someday and put it in front of a screen door of my own. But it's too heavy to move.

♪

My grandfather, Vernon Kingsley Curtis, died when I was nine years old, the year I started piano lessons. He was a coin collector. After his death his collection was sold and the profits were split among his seven grandchildren. I ended up with $900, not a penny of which was to be spent before my twentieth birthday.

From the minute I got that money, I started plotting about what I would do with it. I've had almost ten years to think, to daydream, to fantasize about what kind of treasure my little nest egg would buy—a car? Three months in Paris? Jewelry? A Chanel suit? No. I want something that will last, to remind me of my grandfather. On my twentieth birthday I make my decision: I will buy myself a piano. A grand piano.

The music building at Chatham College has two nine-foot grands in the main hall. One is a Steinway, one is a Baldwin. The action on the Steinway responds a little better, but I'm crazy about the sound of the Baldwin—the tone is golden and warm. With this in mind, I set out to find one. My $900 has grown to 2,000 bucks. Everyone tells me I'm crazy—that I'll never find a quality instrument in that price range.

I pore over the newspapers for months. When I spot the ad I've been waiting for—a small Baldwin grand piano for $1,800—I drive to the listed address and get there early enough to be first in line. By the time Frank Lavelle opens the door there are ten people behind me. I hesitate, then I walk into the ground floor studio. I'm nervous.

There it is. My piano. A five-foot, eight-inch Baldwin grand, manufactured in 1964, three years before I started piano lessons. It's shoved to the side of the room and is covered by jazz rubble— stacks of music, overflowing ashtrays, and old coffee cups—the debris of a working musician. The case is mahogany, scarred in several places by cigarette burns and brandy-snifter rings. Yet the piano has a graciousness to it, like a woman of a certain age who has led a hard life but maintained her dignity. I fall in love with the idea of the piano before I even touch a key.

I sit down to play. The piano is in tune, the action is good, and the sound! Oh, the sound! It's a smaller sound than the concert grand at my school, but it's no less mature. It's round and warm and everything I want. I write a check for Mr. Lavelle and we exchange phone numbers to arrange the delivery.

My father just about kills me. Being a guy who has never in his entire life made a purchase without Thinking It Over for a minimum of two months, he can't understand how I, without the help of an expert, could agree to spend all the money I have to my name on a beat-up old piano after playing it for twelve minutes. And there's another small problem. It will be a year before I move into my own apartment in New York, and I need to find temporary lodging for the instrument. The only logical option is my parents' home. Mom has an impeccable house with everything in its designated place—no exceptions. She never had a problem with one of us bringing home a stray animal. But bringing a kitten into the house isn't quite the same as having a grand piano shoved into the middle of her immaculate Ethan Allen living room. She can't even see her Williamsburg-blue floral print sofa. She is miffed.

I should have thought this through. But I'm happy I didn't. If I had hesitated for a minute, one of those people behind me on line would have snatched up the Baldwin and I would have been haunted for the rest of my life. Anyway, it all works out. My dad calls a piano technician he knows and has him examine the piano, thinking that we can cancel the check if the Baldwin turns out to be a lemon. It isn't. The technician says I've found a great instrument. Dad forgives me. Mom almost wigs out trying to find a spot for the piano between the dark green overstuffed chairs and the matching maple end tables, but her interior decorating instincts kick in before she takes a hatchet to both me and the piano. Eventually she gets used to having the Baldwin in the living room. I think she even likes it. Just a little.

The Baldwin will stay with me for over twenty-five years. It will see me through a failed first marriage, a divorce, a decade of elation and despair, another marriage, two children, a move to a different continent, and a career full of mixed blessings. It will be with me long enough to see me settle down. I've dug the Baldwin out from under the rubble. It will return the favor.

꜠

"Come on, Robin," a friend of mine says when we discuss the prospect of trading in the Baldwin for a better piano. "It's not real. It's just a piano. A hunk of wood with strings."

"Stop right there!" I say, feeling prickly and defensive. But I won't be able to explain myself. All I know is this: When I sit down to play, I swear I can hear the Baldwin smiling. The piano gives back what I put into it. I have it tuned, I dust it, I play it every day, and it makes me happy. That's real.

Wonderful Night

"Won't forget, won't regret, what I did for love!" Debbie McCloskey belts out the last few bars of her audition for Don Brockett. It is 1978, and everyone has a big crush on the music from *A Chorus Line*. Deb is a great singer, a trained soprano who can also manage a bit of Ethel Merman if her classical voice teacher isn't around to tell her she is ruining her voice. Deb is my best friend. I'm accompanying her on the upright piano in the corner of Brockett's downtown Pittsburgh studio. Don's assistant, Pam Golden, is seated to one side of him with a chaotic pile of notes.

There are only four of us in the studio, but because of the mirrors lining every wall. I feel like I'm in a crowd. Don, who wears hand-embroidered needlepoint pants and matching tennis shoes, lurches to a standing position and waves his arms. Don is a large, barrel-chested man. He lumbers across the room to the piano. With all the mirrors, it looks like an invasion of a needlepoint army.

His voice sounds like gravel being dropped onto more gravel. "Girls, girls, stop right there!" he growls. Actually, we've already stopped, but we pretend to stop again. "I can use you both in my new show!" Deb and I don't dare look at each other. Deb is beside herself with joy. Her glee bubbles around me and gives me a fizzy feeling in my stomach. I hadn't intended to audition myself, certainly not as a pianist—I already have my job playing cocktail piano at the Hyatt—but now I'm caught up in the audition frenzy, too. It sucks all the common sense right out of me.

"I need a pianist with some stage presence for this show," Don says to me. "You can sing! You can play! You can talk! And you'll look fabulous in a Donny Difonso glitter gown!"

I sign up without a second thought.

ىگ

My first Don Brockett production is a cabaret show called *TV or not TV*. It's a satire, a comment on the television culture of the seventies. We sing parodies of classic TV theme songs of the period, including *Green Acres*, *Beverly Hillbillies*, and *Gilligan's Island*. *TV or not TV* starts with me playing a tremolo with my left hand, standing on my piano bench, and screaming, "*Debbie McCloskey, come on down!*" in the style of *The Price Is Right*. Don is smart enough to figure out that people going to the theater to escape the doldrums of television will enjoy a show about, uh, television.

Brockett is a remarkable person. Using his skills as an actor, comedian, writer, director, and producer, he employs and educates young performers anxious to break into the "biz." He has become well-known locally for his high-quality dinner theater productions. He also writes and produces industrial shows, scripting corporate entertainment events for clients like Westinghouse, Milton Bradley, and Lean Cuisine. Low-fat chicken, elevator parts, children's board games—there's not a subject in the world that Don can't write about.

Don is everywhere. Three times a day he pops up on television wearing a chef's hat—baking cupcakes and whispering secrets in Purple Panda's ear on *Mister Rogers' Neighborhood*. He's frequently quoted and photographed for the society and entertainment sections of Pittsburgh newspapers. He plays supporting roles in Hollywood films and leading roles in charity events like the Special Olympics. A regular on the Pittsburgh cabaret circuit, Don can be seen every weekend onstage as he spits out jokes about Pittsburgh politicians and cheers on his partner, comedienne Barbara Russell, as she gargles the melody to "How Much Is That Doggie in the Window?" Don Brockett is a Pittsburgh icon. Everybody loves him. Except those of us who work for him. We love him and hate him in equal measure. But one day we'll look back and see only the love.

～

The Baldwin spinet piano is center stage, facing the audience. I sit there surrounded by singers and dancers, bottles of water, discarded leg-warmers, sheet music, and the samples of silver sequined cloth the set designer has brought in for the back side of the piano. We've just finished rehearsing the first half of a new Don Brockett cabaret production, scheduled to premiere later in the week. The dinner theater is in a tiny building perched on the side of Mount Washington.

Our backdrop is a wall of glass. The entire city of Pittsburgh, which sparkles next to the three rivers below us, is a canvas of tiny glittering jewels in the luminescent sky. The city fathers and founders of industry have gone overboard in their artificial illumination of the Golden Triangle, and the view leaves me breathless. I look over my shoulder at the city below me. I notice the clouds are moving west, giving me the feeling that the theater is slowly floating out of the mountainside into the dusk. Cool.

Don Brockett ambles back and forth, giving note after note after note to his assistant, who scribbles furiously on her yellow legal pad. We aren't sure what to expect.

Are we good?

Are we awful?

I know that my tempos aren't exactly in the pocket. Oh God, I hope he won't yell at me. I see the sweating foreheads of the performers around me, and I realize that they're thinking the same thing. Please, not me. Let him yell at someone else.

The air is pulsing with tension.

"Mr. Brockett, thir, may I make a thuggestion?" says the efficient-looking manager of the nightclub. His name is either Price or Brice—I can never get it right because he speaks with a lisp. He has slicked-back hair, a white John Travolta suit, and very erect posture. He smells like limes. He says, "I just thought that the intermithon could come a little thooner in the thow, then we could thell more…"

"I'M NOT GONNA LET SOME FIVE-DOLLAR-AN-HOUR PISSANT RESTAURANT MANAGER TELL ME HOW TO DO MY SHOW," shouts Don Brockett to Price-Brice. "I don't tell you how to make the salad dressing, you don't tell me how to do my show. Got it? Now get out of my rehearsal space and let my kids finish their work. You go back to the kitchen and make an omelet or something."

"Yeth thir, Mr. Brockett, thir," says Price-Brice. He pauses. "Would you like that omelet with cheethe, thir?"

"Jesus Christ," says Don. "I don't want a fucking omelet. I just want YOU to get out of here. NOW!!!" His booming voice bounces off the walls of the restaurant, whips around the bar, and plops at the feet of Price-Brice. Even with the gel, the poor guy's hair stands on end. He scrambles off to omelet-land, kowtowing and running backwards, banging through the double kitchen doors butt first. *Whack!* Silence. The singers and dancers on the stage are afraid to breathe. I hunker down on my piano bench and pretend to be studying my music. The wrath of Brockett hangs in the air like a cold fog. I can still smell the limes.

"Now where were we?" Don asks as he balances the bulk of his authority on a nearby cocktail table. "Take it from the bridge of 'Wonderful Night,' Robin. But just a minute!" He stops talking. We wait. Don throws his hands in the air and smiles a big wide grin that looks like sunshine. "You kids are going to look fabulous up there, the lighting is perfect. I've never had such a talented cast!"

Abruptly, he frowns and his thick eyebrows knit themselves into a dark horizontal line. Uh-oh.

"Richard!" he bellows. "You need to really learn the words to the damn song—you're doing that woo-woo thing that singers do when they don't know the words. I hate the woo-woos. We have three days until opening night. No more woo-woos. You look like a big baby in a playpen up there. NO MORE WOO-WOOS! Got it? Where's that little pissant manager? I need a coffee. Okay, Robin. Ready? One, two, one, two, three!"

On an evening like this I could kiss everybody, I'm so full of love and good will...

⚘

Don is physically disabled. His problem started at adolescence when his hips didn't develop correctly. "He was always 'different,'" says Don's wife, Leslie. "And much of the time he was in pain. His father was a salesman who was constantly on the road; his mother spent most of her time with Catholic ladies' organizations to escape being at home with her mother-in-law who lived with them and raised Don. Grandma was everything to Don. He adored her. It was her support and love that pulled him through those terrible teen years. After being taken to every doctor his grandmother could think of, Don finally ended up in the D.T. Watson Home for Crippled Children, where he was isolated in a room, unable to leave his bed because he was in some kind of medieval traction device. He was sixteen. The only contact he had with the outside world was his radio. He listened to variety shows like Arthur Godfrey and heard some smart, funny people doing satire for the first time in his life. That was the beginning of his career. At that time, the Watson Home allowed visitors only once a week, so Don's radio was very important to him. He didn't attend high school classes for the last two years but still managed to graduate from St. Mary of the Mount High School on Mount Washington. He attended Duquesne University with crutches and braces. He had been told that he would never walk again."

A determined man should not be underestimated.

Many things in my life change when I begin working for Don. I quit my piano gig at the Hyatt, and I'm not able to take part in my college theater production of *A Doll's House* because of a jam-packed Brockett rehearsal schedule. Perhaps I would learn a lot doing Ibsen, but my perverse logic convinces me I'll get a better education doing Don's show. Plus, the *Doll's House* costumes are a drag—all those Scandinavian earth tones. Blah. I opt for the Don Brockett Cabaret.

Don Brockett University
Entertainment 101

1. A costume can be changed in eight seconds flat in the restaurant kitchen. The kitchen staff always appreciates the show.
2. The piano can be played while standing up if the pianist's costume is not too low cut.
3. Always be on time for the job even if it means taking a "fucking helicopter."
4. Learn to live with jet lag.
5. Never stand next to a woman who is blonder or thinner.
6. Leave them wanting mo…
7. Performers are stupid, audiences are smart.
8. Audiences are stupid, performers are smart.
9. Lip gloss will stick to the microphone and make a big mess.
10. Presenters and promoters enjoy making speeches before the show, causing the audience to sink into a group coma. The smaller the town, the longer the speech.
11. The longer the song, the greater the odds that the singer will do something to screw it up.
12. When the singer forgets the lyrics, she will glare at the pianist, giving the audience the impression that the pianist has made a huge mistake. If the pianist glares back at the singer, the singer will try to get the pianist fired.
13. Waiters will always serve food at exactly the wrong moment.
14. The sound of overcooked peas being scraped off a plate with a serrated knife will most likely occur in the middle of a romantic ballad.

15. It's possible to tinkle in a cup if there is no toilet back-stage.
16. Fishnet stockings really hurt if one is not wearing proper full-rinky-coverage underpants.
17. Proper full-rinky-coverage underpants are a good thing, especially while doing the eight-second costume change in front of the kitchen staff (see #1).
18. The pianist will be blamed for anything that goes wrong.
19. The pianist will be given credit for nothing that goes right.
20. Never stop learning.
21. Never stop listening.
22. Throwing a flaming baton offstage into the parking lot will set the parking lot on fire *really* fast.
23. Never complain.
24. Never compromise.
26. Whimsy and imagination are the greatest gifts of life.
27. Never turn down a free meal.

Maybe I should have done the Ibsen, but I don't think so.

Don likes musicians. He asks for, listens to, and respects our advice. He pays us more than he pays the other performers, an oddity in the modern entertainment world. He says that musicians are on the top rung of the performing artist food chain, followed by writers, comedians, actors, dancers and singers, and slime molds, in that order.

"Look," he says. "You can take any schmuck off the street and teach him how to sing a song in three days. Maybe he won't be great, but he'll get through the song. Give that same guy a trumpet and watch what happens." In spite of what he says, Don admires many of the talented and seriously trained singers and dancers who pass through his ranks. It's mediocrity that he can't tolerate, in himself or anyone else. He doesn't have the time for it.

Those of us who work for Don learn how to protect him from himself. He's very good at choreographing his stage shows, not so good at choreographing real life. Because of his size, his Quasimodo limp, and his overuse of broad gestures, he's prone to small accidents, often leaving a trail of minor destruction in his considerable wake. Amazingly, he rarely hurts himself.

He cruises through Pittsburgh in his white Cadillac convertible, worships the sun from the deck of his beach-side shack on Nantucket Island, and composes songs at his kitchen table while his wife bakes bread and balances the books. When he's not performing, telling stories, or writing jokes, he's stitching original needlepoint canvases or painting colorful primitive images of places he loves. He creates jewelry from old beads, shells, and sea glass that he and his wife collect during their yearly jaunts to Sanibel and Nantucket Islands. He gives necklaces to those of us who work for him. They're half beautiful, half awful. Just like Mr. Brockett himself.

༄

We've just finished dinner at the China Bowl on the West Side of Manhattan. The table is strewn with leftover spareribs, dumplings, and moo-shoo shredded something. Don stands up to stretch and brushes the grains of rice from his suede shirt. Gucci, probably— the shirt, not the rice. As he bends backwards to ease the pain in his lower back, his needlepoint pants pop open and fall to his ankles. No underpants. His bad hips prevent him from bending over to pull up his pants.

There are six of us at the table and not one of us can help him. We are screaming with laughter. We guffaw until we turn purple. I wipe the tears of mirth from my eyes and look up. In Don's face I catch a glimpse of the boy he used to be—alone, a little sad, but searching for a way to turn his predicament into art.

He laughs too, harder than any of us, sits down, yanks up his pants, and calls for the check.

༄

Don's wife, Leslie, has perfected the art of being married to a man larger than life, sheltering his fragile ego while cultivating her own sense of style. She knits lovely sweaters, cooks up a storm, runs the business, and remains calm during the darkest of Don's tempestuous creative periods. Every year the two of them host a stunning Christmas party in their rambling Victorian home in the Squirrel Hill section of Pittsburgh. Don collects Santa Claus memorabilia, and Leslie collects crystal candlestick holders. Going to their home on Christmas is like stepping into a fantasy world of light and laughter.

Don and Leslie don't have children, but the two of them are show-biz midwives, getting their "kids" through the trauma of delivery so their talent can be born, safely, into the calloused and yellowed hands of the entertainment world. Working for Don is like boot camp, especially for a pianist. He screams and yells and rehearses us to death to prepare shows in ridiculously short periods of time. It isn't easy for me. I've just gotten my feet wet playing solo piano gigs where I get to make all of my own choices. All of the sudden someone else is telling me what to do. Change the key! Change the tempo! Change the line-up! Change your dress! I feel like a trained poodle in a silver gown. But that's show biz. Don gets me ready. Because of him, I learn how to concentrate, work hard, get the job done, and have fun. I even learn how to charter a helicopter so I can make my start time. No complaints. No compromises.

All of us believe he will live forever.

༈

My working relationship and friendship with Don will last for another eighteen years. On May 2, 1995, Don dies suddenly while having one of his typical everyday arguments with his loyal assistant Joe Delien. They had been planning and rehearsing his next Cabaret production, a musical satire called *Forbidden Pittsburgh*.

St. Mary's of the Point Church in Pittsburgh holds about 1,500 people, and it's filled to capacity for Don's funeral. The casket, decorated with a black top hat and a rhinestone-encrusted cane, is followed by Leslie, wearing a black dress and Don's bright yellow trench coat.

Don and Leslie's friend, Doug Nowicki, the Archabbot of St. Vincent's, says the Mass. Then Fred Rogers gives the eulogy. At the very end, when the audience—some might say congregation—is told to "go in peace," Dan Fallon, managing director of the Pittsburgh Public Theater, stands up and shouts "BRAVO, DON!" Everyone in the church—*Mister Rogers' Neighborhood* co-workers, family, friends, fans, and fellow performers alike—jumps to their feet. They shout and applaud and whistle for five minutes.

လ

There are hundreds and hundreds of Don's performers roaming the world. Most of us won't become household names, but all of us will know how to get the job done, with style. Rob Marshall will set the film industry on fire with his award-winning direction of *Chicago*. His sister Kathleen Marshall will be the toast of New York with her innovative and colorful choreography. Actor Michael Keaton, musical-comedy genius Lenora Nemetz, director Jamie Widdows, Tony Award–winning choreographer Rob Ashford, Chuck Aber—Neighbor Aber on *Mister Rogers' Neighborhood*—all of them are Pittsburgh kids who started out with Don. We're everywhere.

Someday we should erect a monument to Don's memory. The plaque at the bottom could read DON BROCKETT, PAIN IN THE ASS, HERO, TEACHER, FRIEND. The monument could be a mosaic of sea glass and glittering jewels, cast in bronze or carved from granite, or sculpted from a soft cloth like velvet or satin.

လ

Three weeks after Don's death, Don's show *Forbidden Pittsburgh* opens. The show is directed by Joe Delien, with help from dancer Danny Herman and musical director Michael Moricz.

On the emotional opening night, halfway into the first act, an enormous blue and purple iridescent butterfly approaches the stage of the theater tent where the show is being performed. The graceful butterfly glides into the amber glow of the spotlight, lands on the proscenium, and allows the star performer to cup it in his hands. The actor carries it to the door leading outside, raises his arms, and sets it free. The butterfly steals the show. The young cast watches, silently, as it flies away. The show goes on.

Don Brockett never could resist an encore.

Playback 1979

———

I run through the front door of the Redwood Motor Inn, plug in my microphone, and sit down at the piano. I love arriving at the job exactly on time. Being late is a drag, but being early is death.

There are three people sitting at the piano bar, eight or ten other people scattered at nearby tables. I start my Michel Legrand medley, and two of the ladies at the piano move to another table on the far side of the room, muttering that the music is too loud. I am playing as quietly as possible.

Tinkle tinkle tinkle tinkle.

There are mice that make more noise than this. I don't dare sing.

My sister crosses through the lounge on her way to the front desk, where she is a receptionist. She sees me and comes to the piano and points at her watch.

"Why aren't you playing?" she asks. "It's past five."

"I am playing. But Laverne and Shirley over there say it's too loud," I say, tilting my head toward the table where the two women have resituated themselves. They are slurping piña coladas and devouring a family-sized serving of buffalo wings. And they think I'm too loud.

"Why do they call them buffalo wings?" I ask my sister. She wants to be a veterinarian, so I think she might know the answer to this.

"Because you start to look like a buffalo if you eat too many of them," she says, and walks away.

My mind wanders as I think about buffalos. I like that word buffalo. It's fun to say. Buffalo. Buffalo. Buffalo.

Tinkle tinkle tinkle tinkle tinkle.

The restaurant manager, from across the room, begins making the international sign for "keep it down, the music is too loud." He starts back by the kitchen, waving his arms, parallel to each other, in a downward motion. He walks in my direction as he does this, periodically stopping to perform the *shush* motion with his finger in front of his big blubbery lips. I've been in the lounge piano business for three years now, and every manager I've worked with knows how to make this sign. Maybe they learn this in restaurant school at the same time they learn how to order cases of wine and big cans of lard. Maybe they all have the same mother, and they learn it at home. Who knows.

Everyone in the lounge is now staring at the blubbery manager and staring at me. If they didn't think I was too loud before, they do now.

I want to smack this guy.

Tinkle tinkle tinkle tinkle tinkle.

I'm not even playing a song now.

Mr. Blubberlips finally makes his way to the piano and stands there directly in front of me moving his arms up and down like the guy in the orange suit who parks airplanes on the tarmac of military airfields.

inkle inkle inkle inkle.

I am now playing with one finger.

"No problem, Mr. B.," I say. "I'll keep it down." Why can't I be more like Don Brockett? Why can't I call the Blubberlips a pissant and tell him to go stick his head in the lettuce bin?

Because it's a miracle that I have a job, that's why. I still can't believe people pay me to play the piano.

My brother sticks his head out of the kitchen door and waves. He works in the kitchen chopping vegetables, even though he hates wearing those checkered chef's trousers and Swedish clogs that never quite fit.

It's like a Rawsthorne Family hat trick at this place. My sister checks you in, my brother makes your salad, and I play songs for you that you can't hear. We are the backbone of the Redwood Motor Inn, minus a vertebra or two. I think my parents had higher aspirations for us than this.

The place is starting to fill up with the Friday after-work crowd.

Happy, happy, happy hour.

"Over here, Father Louie!" shouts a thin, dark-skinned man wearing a light blue leisure suit. "This one's empty!" Father Louie and his entourage of five priests clump through the bar to the tables on my right. They seem happy enough. They smile and wave at me like we're old friends. We're not old friends, or new friends. But I wave back.

I play "Amazing Grace." Medium loud. I don't think the manager is going to argue with a table of priests. Father Louie and Co. order drinks and bar snacks. It's Friday. Probably calamari or crab cakes. I don't think crab and cake are words that should be used together. I wonder if there is such a thing as a buffalo cake.

I once was lost, but now I'm found...

Two old people at the bar get up and start dancing. This is a first. I have never seen anyone dance to "Amazing Grace." I am having a nice moment. The dancers are probably in their late seventies or early eighties. The man has little tufts of white hair around his ears and holds his wife gently. She is wearing a navy blue chiffon dress with little pearl buttons at the collar and cuffs. Her hair is thin and tied together in the back with a girlish black taffeta bow. The two of them sweep across the floor like Fred and Ginger. The effortlessness of their gliding and sliding burns a picture into my brain that will stay with me always. I want to be like them when I am old. Just not here.

I finish the song and the two of them stand in the center of the dance floor, alone, and applaud. I feel obliged to stand and take a small bow. I'm transported to another decade, one where people are elegant and the musicians are acknowledged for their efforts.

I feel a tap on my shoulder. It is Mr. Blubberlips.

"I told you to keep it down!" he hisses into my ear. "I don't want people dancing or applauding during the cocktail hour. We save all that stuff for later when the band gets here."

"Oh my," I say. "I'm sorry. It's just that…"

Suddenly there is a commotion at the priest table. Father Louie is jumping up and down and doing an odd sort of dance.

"Is there a doctor in the house?" yells Blue Leisure Suit. "We need some help. Fast. Call an ambulance. Somebody do something."

Father Louie has his hand on his throat. He is choking. Goddamn crab cakes.

"He's choking!"

"He's choking!"

"He's choking!"

This phrase gets tossed around the lounge like a hot potato.

"Quick, Robin. PLAY something. Loud! Loud! Loud! " says Mr. Blubberlips. "Come on! So that the people don't notice the choking priest."

Some happy hour this is.

"He's not choking. He's talking. You can't talk when you're choking."

"He's having a heart attack!"

"Heart attack!"

"Heart attack!"

What do I play? Shit. I can't think of anything. I've already played my one religious number. Shit. I play "I Feel the Earth Move Under My Feet."

"Louder, louder!"

I am not distracting anyone. Even my brother clops out from the chopping station to see what is going on. Everyone is horrified and staring at Father Louie. Father Louie is on the floor.

Ooh baby, when I see your face, mellow as the month of May…

I can't do this. I quit playing. I can't possibly sing a Carole King rock song while a priest is dying on the floor, I don't care what that goddamn Mr. Blubberlips says. I can't bear to watch. I leave the lounge and go into the lobby where my sister is waiting for the ambulance to arrive.

I sit in one of the dark-brown pleather lobby chairs and listen while she answers the phone.

"Good evening, Redwood Motor Inn, Randy Rawsthorne speaking, how may I direct your call…"

The paramedics carry Father Louie out on a stretcher ten minutes later. "Some sort of diabetic shock," they say. "He'll live."

"Probably the buffalo wings," my sister says to me.

"Have a nice day!" she shouts to the paramedics as they push Father Louie into the parking lot. My sister seems obliged, as the official Redwood Motor Inn door person, to thank the paramedics for attending the happy hour. "We'll look forward to seeing you at the Redwood Motor Inn again sometime soon!" she shouts.

I return to the piano. Maybe I should play "Louie, Louie." No, that won't work.

I play "Fire and Rain" instead.

Woke up this morning and I wrote down this song. Just can't remember who to send it to…

Got that right, James.

The old people return to the dance floor. Mr. Blubberlips waves his arms at me.

Here we go again.

Part II

1980–1994

Travelin' Light

On a dazzling January morning I stand to the side of the parking bay as my father helps Lenny, my husband of six months, load the last of our suitcases, cartons, and bags into the back of the rental car. I'm supposed to be traveling light. Instead it looks like I've packed every square inch of the dark red station wagon with the leftovers of my youth. My mother is working this morning, but she has remembered, as usual, to pack sandwiches and make a thermos of coffee for our trip. Mom never allows anyone to go anywhere without Kleenex and sandwiches. You have to be prepared in case you start to cry or get hungry. Heaven help you if you take off for adulthood without a chipped ham and mustard on rye and the proper equipment for blowing your nose. I tuck the makeshift picnic basket under my arm. It is the kind of day—cold and shiny and cloudless—that makes me think I can go anywhere, accomplish anything, win any prize. I'm moving to New York City. But really, I'm just a big kid with a college degree, a tiny plastic-wrapped package of Kleenex, and a bag of sandwiches from my mother, trying to hold it together and act like I know what I'm doing.

"Well," my dad says to me as Lenny slams the gate to the station wagon, "I expect the next time I see you will be on Broadway."

He throws his arms around me. I've left home before—for summer vacations on Nantucket—but this time I won't be coming back. This is it. We take baby steps away from our parents from the moment we're old enough to walk. They're all in preparation for this last giant leap. The one we make when we're almost grown-up, but not quite.

I'm twenty-one years old. Over my dad's shoulder, I see my childhood home, solid and strong, its red bricks gleaming in the harsh glare of the early light. My father missed his opportunity to move to New York City because my mother was pregnant with me. I like to think it has all worked out for the best; he has a successful musical career and a rich family life. Still, he must wonder what would have happened if he had left Pittsburgh at the age I am now. I feel the chill of the day and the warmth of the sun, all at once. Maybe I'm going to New York City for both of us. Too much pressure, that thought.

Dad tells some jokes, we sip scalding cups of coffee from the thermos my mom has provided, another map is analyzed and discussed, Dad wishes us luck, and then it's time. Off we drive, with Lenny honking the horn and me hanging out of the window and waving until my Dad is just a wee figure standing alone in the morning light.

I've left my Baldwin behind in my mother's perfect living room. We're moving into an Upper West Side furnished sublet and have a six-month lease. Our plan is to find something of our own and then come back for the piano.

I've been to New York City exactly three times, to visit my dear Aunt Pinky who lives on West 85th Street. I adore my Aunt Pinky. She's funny and smart and knows all kinds of exciting show-business people like Bette Midler and Betsey Johnson and the entire cast of *Saturday Night Live*. On my visits she has treated me to rides in stretch limousines, exotic dinners in ethnic restaurants, and shopping excursions to stores where the salespeople have lavender hair and safety pins in their cheeks. For my sixteenth birthday I traveled to New York by myself to visit Aunt Pinky and her roommate, pianist Cheryl Hardwick. That year the two of them were working at the Continental Baths, a gay men's bathhouse that was open to the public for cabaret shows on Saturday nights. On the night of my birthday I got to sit in the press box and watch Peter Allen perform for a room full of half-naked men. Cheryl was playing the piano. Aunt Pinky was running the light board. Peter Allen was shaking his booty and singing "I Go to Rio." I was in heaven. That was the precise moment that I knew I had to move to New York.

This time I'm going as an adult. With a husband. Lenny looks just like Omar Sharif. I'd met him while doing a college production of *A Delicate Balance*, an Edward Albee play produced by the school in my senior year. Lenny, a thirty-one-year-old professional actor who had been teaching classes at the college, was a hot commodity on the all-female campus. When I first met him he was holding court to a gaggle of moony-eyed college seniors who were sitting cross-legged on the floor and hanging on his every word. It looked like he was auditioning girls for a harem. He smiled at me. I got in line.

Now we're married and we're going to have our very own Manhattan sublet. With a couch, a TV, and everything. If we ever get there, that is. Lenny and I drive and drive and drive that day.

"Are we almost there yet?" I want to ask, but then I remember that I'm an adult.

The Pennsylvania Turnpike grinds on and on, cradling us in the arms of its rolling hills and lovely curving stretches of nothingness until we're ready to scream. We stop for lunch at an Amish restaurant outside of Reading and enjoy the irony of being served biscuits and gravy by women wearing bonnets on the very day that we are moving to the mecca of sophistication.

Oh, you're really sophisticated, says Voice of Doom. *Aside from a wardrobe of black clothes, a working knowledge of Shakespeare, and a couple of years spent playing cocktail piano, there isn't much difference between you and the gal selling the apple cider outside Ye Old Restaurant. New York City! Ha! What are you thinking? You're a hopeless babe in the woods.*

But I'm wound up and full of anticipation and I don't pay attention. I'm conquering the art of coolness.

Later in the afternoon, just as the sun is setting over the Hudson, we spot the Manhattan skyline. The city—daring me with its jagged edges and perfect asymmetry—glows with a fury and excitement that is at once energizing and intimidating. I'm here. I'm ready. Bring it on.

Then I see the Viking. We stop for a traffic light on the corner of 57th Street and Sixth Avenue, and there, holding a spear, is a Viking. He is very large and is wearing a fur toga and a huge fur hat with horns. I am impressed. We don't have Vikings in Pittsburgh.

I forget about being cool and I scream at Lenny, "Look! There's a Viking!"

"Forget the goddamn Viking!" he yells. I'm getting on Lenny's nerves. I can't blame him. Eight hours in a packed rental car with a wife who gets car sick and refuses to read maps is enough to put anyone on edge.

"We have to find Columbus Circle," he says. "Where the hell is Columbus Circle?"

"How should I know?" I say. Imagine that. I don't even know where Columbus Circle is. "I'll ask the Viking."

The light changes before I have a chance. Lenny finds his way to 107th Street and Broadway. As the sky darkens the city becomes brighter. It begins to snow just as we're unloading the last of our bags. The snowflakes are huge—the size of a child's paper cutouts.

We return the rental car and then walk twenty blocks, hand in hand, back to the apartment. With the fresh dusting of snow, the city looks clean and innocent and safe, like a place where art and love can rule the world and nothing bad will ever happen.

Gypsy, Tempest, and Me

"Thank you, Miss. We'll be in touch."

"Thank you, Miss, but you're not the type we want."

"Thank you, Miss, but we're actually looking for a very special Taiwanese-looking girl who juggles and has Canadian citizenship."

"You're too pretty."

"Not pretty enough."

"Too old."

"Too straight."

"Too fat."

"Too skinny."

"Too tall."

"Too young."

Too, too, too, too, everything.

Why don't they just say, "Thank you, Miss, but you suck." We know that's what they're thinking.

❧

"I trained fuck dancer and they no give me no chance," says the beautiful Japanese girl who has been standing next to me in line.

"Fuck dancer?" I say.

"Fuck dancer. I very good fuck dancer but these big buttheads not ask me to fuck dance. They no interested in fuck dance."

"Fuck dance?" I say. After waiting six hours to be seen, we'd both been cut from an audition for a regional theater production of *Annie Get Your Gun*. Neither one of us has gotten a chance to say a word or sing a note. They just looked at us, gave us the *thank you, Miss*, and nodded toward the door.

"Yeah, yeah, yeah. Fuck dance. You know. Swing you partner round and round."

"Oh! You mean folk dancing?"

"Yeah, yeah, yeah. Fuck dancing."

"Well, you should be able to get some work doing that. Japanese fuck dancing. Now there's a specialty."

"Yeah, yeah, yeah. So why we get cut? We cream of crop. I too ugly or what?"

"No, no, no!" I say. "You're not ugly! Maybe you're just too short."

"You crazy. You twelve inch taller than me and you get boot too. Maybe we both ugly."

"Are you going to the *Barnum* audition tomorrow?" I have this crazy idea that if I'd been good enough for the real circus, then maybe the Broadway show about the real circus will think I'm good enough, too.

"Yeah. I go tomorrow. Maybe they need fuck dancer. Be there seven A.M. Big bitch line for Barnum."

꒰

I've been in the Big Apple for two months and have attended dozens of acting auditions. I've stood in more big bitch lines than I care to admit. And for what? I've opened my mouth exactly one time, and that was to say my name to a group of four sloppy, beer-bellied producers sitting at a tiny table eating egg-salad sandwiches. New York is proving to be tougher than I'd expected. I've been stuck in subways, lost in Midtown, and tricked by taxi drivers speaking unidentified foreign languages.

I've had my purse stolen twice and had my best winter coat ruined by a crazy lady at a bus stop who threw half of a barbecued chicken at me. I've played one piano job—a two-week engagement at the Newark Airport Holiday Inn. I took a job spraying perfume on snobby ladies in Bloomingdales but quit after I discovered that working the first floor of Bloomies' involves hand-to-hand combat, even if you are employed by Chanel.

Pittsburgh is starting to seem like a pretty civilized place.

I'm resting my swollen feet in my apartment one evening when the phone rings. It's Don Brockett. With a job. An acting job, sort of. The national touring company of his hit Off-Broadway show *Big Bad Burlesque* will be hitting the road. First stop, Boston. Don wants me to cover the female comedy roles. That means wearing some skimpy costumes and performing in the old burlesque sketches that are the crux of the show. What a thrill! A real job, at last. There's just one catch.

"You're gonna have to play the piano and strip."

"Excuse me?" I say.

"Look, the club in Boston is insisting on a stripper for the show. The stripper they wanted broke her ankle—she had some kind of bizarre act on roller skates—and they hate everyone else I've recommended. There aren't too many authentic strippers left. Ann Corio and Tempest Storm are still around, but they're booked solid."

"Aren't they, uh, seventy years old?" I ask.

"Yeah, but they're *good*," Don says. "They're artists. That's what the club wants. They want someone who can strip tastefully. You know, the old-fashioned way, like Gypsy Rose Lee. But they also want someone young. All the youngsters out there doing strip acts these days are completely raunchy. We've gotta get someone classy. No Coke bottles or livestock or dollar bills up the hoo-ha. See, that's where the piano comes in."

"Excuse me?"

"Like the song says, 'you gotta have a gimmick.'"

"You want me to play the piano naked?"

"No, I want you to start your striptease by playing something classical on the grand piano. Then the band will take over and you can get away from the piano and let it rip."

I have to think about this. I'm on the verge of saying no when I remember that my next paying job in New York is demonstrating a product called *Astonish, the most incredible pot polisher of the century.* The Astonish marketing team wants me to wear an apron with a British flag on it, stand for five hours a day in Macy's basement, and polish expensive French copper pans.

Sure, I'll strip. Why not?

"Okay. So let me get this straight. I'm supposed to go to Boston, play classical piano, and then stand up and take my clothes off."

"That's the gist of it, yeah," says Don. "You can get on the train tomorrow morning. We have four days until we open."

Two months after arriving in New York, I stand in the bedroom of our 107th Street sublet, preparing to leave. I stuff assorted books, music, shoes, and stage makeup into my largest travel bag. Lenny hovers on the other side of the bed and watches. He doesn't seem concerned that his new wife is about to become a stripper. I've assured him, and myself, that my strip act will be tasteful, a term not always synonymous with burlesque.

"It'll be fine," Lenny says. "They've got all those weird laws up there in Boston, you know. Unless you're working in the Combat Zone, you're not allowed to show anything that anybody wants to see. Don will probably have you strip down to a bikini and that will be that."

"Yeah," I say. "Don says this is a dinner theater chain that caters to the bridge club and after-church crowd on Sundays. The whole thing will be completely innocent, I'm sure."

"Maybe you could get tickets for my mother's Russian cousins." Lenny's relatives emigrated from Russia two weeks ago and are now living outside of Boston.

"Oh," I say. "That'll be nice when they report back to your folks in Pittsburgh. How do you say stripper in Russian, anyway?"

"Slutz-ky. I don't know. I suspect it's the same in any language." He laughs and turns on the television set.

Ironically, the film version of the musical *Gypsy* is on TV. I watch the movie as I pack and try to imagine what Natalie Wood would have done if she'd had a piano in front of her.

I sketch out the charts for the band on the train ride to Boston. I'll start out playing a Chopin prelude, segue into "Night Train," play a little something on the flute, and then sing "Hard Hearted Hannah," a number my sister and I used to sing when we were kids because we liked the part about "Hannah pourin' water on a drownin' man." How in the world I'll manage to take my clothes off while doing all of this is too much to think about. Don will have to figure that out for me.

వ

The Chateau de Ville dinner theater chain boasts four huge theaters scattered through New England. Our first stop is Framingham, Massachusetts. The place is the size of a small stadium and looks like a catering hall or a funeral home in Flushing, Queens—lots of fake crystal chandeliers, fountains, patterned carpets, and artificial plants. There are mirrors everywhere. The Framingham Chateau de Ville seats around eighteen-hundred people, and opening night is sold out.

I arrive in the middle of a rehearsal. There is a Steinway nine-foot grand on the stage, and the band is on a platform to the right. Don stands onstage barking orders to the lighting technician. Six beautiful girls wearing Donny Difonso elaborately jeweled corsets and headpieces practice a tap combination as Danny Herman, a twenty-one-year-old whiz-kid choreographer, counts off the steps.

"Hey Robin!" shouts Danny as he jumps off the stage and runs into the house to greet me. We've worked together in Pittsburgh and on the road. We're great friends.

"Hey, Danny! Your girls look swell up there. Uh—I won't have to tap dance will I?" I ask.

"Maybe for a couple of group numbers, but don't worry—we won't put any taps on your shoes. And there aren't too many turns. You know the drill. Swing your arms and smile. Mainly you're just here to get naked." He is grinning.

"Danny!"

"It'll be a piece of cake," he says. "Come on, let's get the crew to move the piano into place so we can start working on this. We don't have much time. The costumer is in the back sewing Velcro into everything so you can get out of your clothes fast. Oh, yeah! Ann Corio is here to coach you."

"*The* Ann Corio? Are you serious?"

"Yeah. She might be old, but man, does she know how to walk. Poetry in motion."

"Just like me, right?"

"Ha! Listen, you can pull this off. You're an actress and a musician, remember? You have the charts for the band?"

Danny turns back to the stage. "Hey everybody, look! The *stripper* is here!" he says. There are some wolf whistles and shouts, most of them from Don and his assistant Dave Wilson. I'm dressed in head-to-toe L.L. Bean with my hair scraped back in a ponytail. Hardly anyone's idea of an undulating exotic dancer.

Backstage on opening night I receive four dozen red roses, sent by three guys from the Chateau de Ville management team named Dino, Rocco, and Louie. They've sent the flowers because they've tipped off the press that a *concert pianist* is about to make her debut as a stripper, and they want the dressing room to reflect the excitement of the evening. Ha. I take a sip from my cold Dunkin' Donuts to-go coffee and stand in front of the mirror practicing how to take my bra off at the end of my big number. There are eighteen-hundred people in the audience—including tour buses from Bigbutt, Rhode Island, and locals from the Rotary Club—and they're all out there eating meat loaf and mashed potatoes, waiting for the show to begin. I can hear them buzzing and clinking their butter knives against their bread plates.

"Do I take my gloves off before I take off my corset? Or after? Corset first, then stockings? Does the bra get tossed into the piano or in front of it?"

"It doesn't matter," Danny says. "Just remember, the bra doesn't come off until the very end, and it has to be timed with the lights because if you actually show your knockers, you'll be, uh, in trouble."

"Make sure the lighting techie doesn't fall asleep up there."

"Oh, I don't think he'll fall asleep," says Danny. "The crew is really looking forward to this!"

"Danny Herman!"

"Fifteen minutes, Ladies and Gentlemen," says the stage manager.

There's a knock on the door.

"Time for a few questions, Miss Meloy?" says the hip-looking reporter hovering outside the dressing room. He is fully clothed. I'm wearing black fishnet stockings, false eyelashes, and a bathrobe. It's freezing backstage. I grab a jacket and put it on over my robe.

"Yeah, I guess that would be okay," I say.

"We've heard that you've never stripped before. Is that true?"

I look down and see that my jacket is on inside-out.

"Uh, yes. The girl who was supposed to strip tonight broke her ankle."

"And you're here to save the show."

"Let's hope it turns out that way, yes."

"Do your parents know about this? How will they feel about their concert-pianist daughter taking her clothes off in front of thousands of people?"

This is something I haven't considered. I haven't had time to call my parents. And this "concert pianist" stuff is getting on my nerves. Next thing you know they'll be referring to me as a Juilliard graduate.

"Five minutes, please, Ladies and Gentlemen!"

I guess I have to answer this guy's question.

"Oh, I don't think my parents will be upset. My dad is a drummer, and when I was little he played at the burlesque theaters in downtown Pittsburgh. My mom used to take us to the theater to pick him up after matinee performances. All the other little girls I knew had fathers who were executives, and you know when you're little you don't really understand the difference between executives and burlesque drummers. I actually thought that this woman named "Irma the Body" was my dad's secretary. She was about six feet tall and had three French poodles on a leash. I think she did an act with a boa constrictor."

"Really?" says the reporter, grinning like I've just given him the story of the century.

"You think I could make that up?" I say.

"Places, please!"

My number is about halfway into the first act. I wait in the wings. In spite of my multiple layers of clothing, I stand there shivering, mentally rehearsing the choreography and the sequence of the strip. Danny is behind me with his hands on my shoulders. The lights go to black, and three time-weathered comedians, authentic burlesque guys, scurry past me. The crew pushes my piano center stage.

Here we go.

Suddenly I spot the menacing silhouettes of two burly policemen with dogs. They're in the wings on the opposite side of the stage.

"Holy shit," I say. "Danny, why are there policemen over there? And dogs?"

"Oh, it's nothing."

"Don't say that! It's not nothing. You tell me the truth right now or I'm not going out there."

"Yeah, it's uh…"

"Danny, I mean it!"

"Ladies and Gentlemen, direct from the Juilliard School of Music and the concert stages of New York, Paris, Tokyo, and Nairobi, *Big Bad Burlesque* is proud to present the girl with the golden fingers, Miss Robin Meloy!"

Ha! says VOD.

Applause, applause, applause.

"They're there just in case," says Danny.

Applause, applause, applause.

"In case of what?"

The empty spotlight meanders around the stage, searching for me.

"To arrest you in case you show your tits. Now get out there!" Danny pushes me into the spotlight. I take a long luxurious bow, pose at the piano, and begin to play. I wait for Voice of Doom to harass me, but he's eerily silent—my fear of playing classical piano in front of an attentive audience diminishes as I face the prospect of having my breasts mauled by two German shepherds.

What have I gotten myself into?

I see Don teetering on a riser backstage next to the cops. I hope he's bribing them or telling them I'm a nice girl. I hope the lighting technician hits the switch on time.

ᘏ

I wind up the Chopin portion of my act and count off a nice slow stripper version of "Night Train." The band joins in and we're off and running. I would pay a million dollars to stay at the piano for the rest of the night, but I must get up and start stripping. Slowly, I work my way through the number—*rip!* There goes the jacket—*rip!* There goes the skirt—*rip rip rip!* There goes the black lace blouse! Now I'm standing in a blue spotlight wearing a corset, stockings, and some long fingerless gloves. So far so good. I get down to my bikini and I saunter stage right. Danny hands me my flute, right on cue. He has taped a little note to the mouthpiece that says "suck this." I turn to smile at him and he takes my picture. I balance center stage, playing the flute in my underwear and high heels. I look ridiculous and I almost laugh, but I don't. I sing "Hard Hearted Hannah," and when I get to the part about "leather is tough, but Hannah's heart is tougher," I look right at those policemen and practically dare them to come after me. Oh. Look. The dogs are wearing muzzles. The evening is taking a turn for the better.

Hey, check this out—I'm having fun!

Don howls with laughter. I hear him from the wings.

I let a man in the front row untie the bow holding my bra together in the back. His female relatives, including a woman who is probably his grandmother, cheer him on. The last chorus is ending and we're coming to the tag. This is the tricky part. I sing the last few bars of the tune and glide back to the piano, walking just the way Ann Corio taught me. I glance backstage and Don crosses himself. I look in the other direction and Danny covers his eyes with his hands. Playing a glissando with my right hand, I rip off my bra with my left, just as the lights go to black. Nobody sees a thing. Danny runs onstage, in the dark, with a robe, and pulls me back into my dressing room.

We laugh until we cry. Then we get ready for the second show of the evening.

The next day, one of the Boston newspapers runs a large color photo of me sitting backstage next to an impressive bouquet of roses. The headline reads:

ROBIN MELOY, STRIP DEBUT:

HER PARENTS TAUGHT HER WHAT TO DO

The Man on the Ceiling

*T*he crowded 57th Street rehearsal studio smells like sweat and I'm anxious to leave. I've been here all day rehearsing a Don Brockett industrial show for a private investment company. Word has it that the year's returns have "reflected an industry-wide downward spiral, caused by a decline in the interest rate on high-grade bonds, and a persistent inflation of wholesale and consumer costs." Which means that our client's party-going company has lost big barrels of money and we're being paid to help them forget.

I'm frustrated. I've been hired as a spokeswoman and pianist for this production, but I've also been asked to join the chorus for several dance numbers—something I'm capable of doing if there's no spinning involved. I've been struggling with the choreography to a difficult ballet sequence that I need to master before we fly to Los Angeles later in the week. I hate this. I'm an actor and a musician, but I can't seem to get a job that doesn't involve dancing. For this show a very tall fellow named Jerry will lift me onto his broad shoulders. After he sets me down I'm expected to execute a triple pirouette to the left and then exit to the right. At this afternoon's rehearsal I got it backwards and the *Corps de Ballet* trampled me as they stampeded off the stage.

Dancers are serious people. Earlier in the day Jerry told me he'd once kicked so high that he hit himself in the head with his own kneecap and knocked himself unconscious. Playing the piano isn't quite as perilous. I'm looking forward to tomorrow's rehearsal—I'll get to sit down and play.

"Is there a Robin Meloy here?" shouts the studio manager into the rehearsal room. "I have a long-distance emergency call for her."

My skin gets tight and my stomach flips. Grandma Curtis was scheduled for surgery this morning. Something must be wrong.

I accompany the studio manager into the lobby where 200 dancers preparing to audition for the Scandinavian touring company of *Cats* are stretching and warming up. Maybe a dozen of them will be chosen. I manipulate my way through the twisting bodies to the quiet of the studio office.

I hear my father sob as I pick up the receiver. I start to cry, anticipating the worst possible news. Gulping air, I compose myself. Dad explains that Grandma Curtis won't be coming home from the hospital—she has cancer of the pancreas. Maybe she'll make it through the next month, maybe she won't. No one knows. My mom and Aunt Jean are keeping watch at the hospital. They'll tell Grandma Curtis the truth when she awakens.

How do you do that? How do you tell your mother she is dying?

ॐ

Here is what I remember about my grandmother, Laura Curtis.

She loved music. Grandma was the only person in the family who sat for hours listening to me practice. She enjoyed hearing me play, even the mistakes. Her very favorite piece was the "Theme from Love Story."

"That is just the most divine song," she would say. "Play it again." So I did. Again and again and again. She was my best audience.

Big Green, the ancient Boardman and Gray Civil War–era piano that I played as a child, had once belonged to her. She played with gusto and style, showing up at our house to practice patriotic songs for her Daughters of the American Revolution and American Legion Auxiliary meetings. She played for her Sunday school class and other church functions—she was a sort of lounge pianist for the church-lady social set.

When I was a kid and my mother was working, Grandma let me eat the same thing for lunch every day. For two years I ate crab meat with melted Velveeta cheese on toast, and she never complained, not once. It was during our mealtime chats that I learned what it was like to have an adult really listen to me. Before returning to school for my afternoon lessons, we would watch *The Dick Van Dyke Show* on TV. We both loved the part at the beginning, during the theme song, when Dick would trip over the ottoman and almost kill himself.

Once, during my crab-meat-and-Velveeta phase, I hurried home for lunch and found my grandmother hard at work in the basement. Covered in soot, she was crouching in an alcove under the cellar stairs. She was cleaning out the furnace.

"Two dead squirrels, a pigeon, and a big old pile of Lord knows what," Grandma said, slinging a clump of feathery debris into the heavy-duty trash bag strapped around her shoulder. "Sorry about the crab meat being late, but I couldn't stand being in this house one more minute knowing how dirty that furnace was."

I had never thought about things being dirty on the inside, in places you couldn't even see.

Grandma's husband, Vernon Curtis—the man with the coin collection that paid for my Baldwin grand piano—died when I was young. I remember the funeral. Dignified men wearing military uniforms folded a giant American flag into an impossibly small triangle and handed it to Laura at the end of the burial service. Laura was left with a small inheritance, a fierce independence, and plenty of time to make lunch for her grandchildren. I never did figure out what had happened to that flag. I still dream about it.

Laura learned to drive shortly before her sixty-seventh birthday. Dad gave her lessons and managed to stay calm even when she made a left-hand turn into oncoming traffic and collided with a Pittsburgh Plate Glass truck. As far as I know, Grandma was the only person in the city of Pittsburgh to get three traffic tickets while on a learner's permit.

When she got too old to drive, she gave the car to me so I could get back and forth to my piano jobs. While I zoomed around town in her cute little Plymouth Valiant, Grandma became the queen of Pittsburgh's senior-citizen bus program. Almost every day, after drinking a glass of sweet white wine and eating her Meals on Wheels lunch, she trotted out to the bus stop and headed for destinations unknown. Courtesy of the Port Authority, she toured parts of the city that her own children had never seen. Sometimes she would have a goal in mind. If the Kroger's in Butler had a sale on Ivory Soap, she would spend five hours getting there and back just to save a few cents.

"It gets me out," she would say. "I need to get out."

Because she knew she was clumsy, she took a course in falling—learning how to relax, tumble, and roll with the ease of a seasoned stuntwoman. I had visions of her practicing—walking casually around her apartment and throwing herself over the ottoman and flipping onto her feet, just like Dick Van Dyke. She had trouble keeping her wig on her head when she took a spill, and that disturbed her. Once, at my senior recital at college, the eighty-year-old Laura took a dive down the sixteen red-carpeted steps of the university theater.

"Don't worry about me," she said as dozens of audience members rushed to her aid. "Just hand me my goddamn wig."

She waved a white hankie from her place in the audience whenever I was onstage. "I just want you to know I'm here. How else would you know?" Grandma Curtis never stopped smiling when she was in the theater for one of my productions or concerts. Once, when I was playing the title role in Sophocles' *Electra*, I turned downstage to deliver one of the play's tragic monologues and caught sight of my adoring grandmother sitting in the third row, grinning like a hyena. I managed to refocus just as Grandma started waving the hankie. But the theatrical moment, at least the one that Sophocles had intended, was lost. I got through the scene with only one giggle.

In the last church-directory photo taken of Grandma, she wore a snappy red ultra-suede pantsuit with a matching paisley scarf. She liked bright colors, fur hats, and the sparkling jewelry that her grandchildren gave her for holidays. Because of a painful nerve condition in her face, she fancied winter coats with fur collars that she could pull close to her in the biting wind that swept through Pittsburgh every winter.

In 1976, at the end of a Christmas Eve candlelight service at her church, just as the solemn congregation was singing "Silent Night" and marching together toward the vestibule, a candle-toting church member got too close to her fur collar and set it on fire. Grandma's good friends responded so quickly to the emergency that she never felt the heat of the flames. When she was hit from behind, knocked to the ground, and beaten by men wielding carpets and winter coats, she thought she was being mugged right there in the sanctuary of Brookline Lutheran Church. She said she didn't mind the damage to her best coat so much as she minded being wrestled to the floor and rolled in a rug, minus her wig, while the entire congregation looked on.

"I know how to drop and roll, thank you very much," she said. "If someone had simply screamed *Mrs. Curtis your coat is on fire* I would have been glad to comply. They really didn't have to tackle me like that."

Grandma was once rescued by the Pittsburgh fire department after she had been stuck in an elevator for six hours in ninety-degree heat. When they got to her she was sitting on the floor of the elevator in her underwear.

"I knew you would get here sooner or later," she told them as she stood up and brushed herself off. "I prayed to the Lord." She was still wearing her wig.

Grandma Curtis picked the winner of the Miss America contest almost every year. She also liked to watch a television show called *Dance Fever*. She claimed she had an excellent eye for talent.

She believed in God, in looking good, and in keeping an open mind, no matter what.

‿

My mother assures me that Grandma will live for a few weeks and tells me that I should go on to Los Angeles, do my show, and then come to visit later. I ignore my mother's instructions. Lenny and I rent a car and drive the eight hours from New York to Pittsburgh.

I arrive at the hospital expecting the worst, yet I'm unprepared for the sight of her. She looks like an ancient baby—toothless, innocent, and translucent. Her wig balances on a Styrofoam form on the table next to her bed. She sleeps. I retreat to the waiting area where I sit with my sister and cousins and cry.

"What in the world are you doing here?" Grandma asks me when she awakens. "You've come a long way. All the way from New York. Imagine that." She gives me a half-smile.

"I wanted to see you, Grandma. How are you feeling?"

"I'm okay. I'm going home." She points up. "There's a man up there. A man on the ceiling. He's coming for me and I'm going home. There is light there." She smiles again and drifts away. I want play the "Theme from Love Story" one last time for her, but I don't get a chance. She dies later in the night.

As we prepare for Laura Curtis's memorial service, which is called a victory service by the Lutheran Church, I ask my mother if Grandma had talked to her about the man on the ceiling. It's a beautiful image—being lifted into the warm light of heaven by a man beckoning you from above.

"No," says Mom. "But there was a man on a ladder over her bed repairing a light fixture the day before she died. A janitor, I think."

"The face of God is everywhere," Grandma had always said to me. "You just have to look." In her last hours, she had found serenity in the countenance of a South Side Hospital maintenance man, changing a light bulb and beckoning her home.

In Laura's heaven, her hair is perfect and she uses her best china. She tumbles and rolls and never gets hurt, she treasures the words of the children around her, and she listens to the "Theme from Love Story" as many times as she likes. Grandma's heaven is like her earthly days, with a few small improvements.

After the cremation and burial of Laura's ashes in a plot next to Vernon's grave, I say good-bye to my family and fly to Los Angeles. I play a song on the piano, speak about investor confidence, pirouette to the left and exit to the right. As I return to the stage, a member of the audience muffles a sneeze with a white handkerchief. Jerry, the muscular dancer, lifts me onto his strong shoulders. I look up and feel the warmth of the rose-tinted light on my face. I laugh, and begin to sing.

She hears me, she sees me. She'll be with me, always.

The Waterbury Blues

*T*here's a drink called a Blue Hawaiian. Anyone drinking a Blue Hawaiian has the potential to do something insane during the course of the evening. Men indulging in this drink, for instance, have been known to strip down to their shorts and start doing the alligator dance on top of the bar. I don't enjoy this. Women drinking Blue Hawaiians have a tendency to sing "Summertime" in a very high key halfway through my second set.

The drink—generally served with a slice of pineapple, a very long straw, an ancient maraschino cherry, and a paper decoration resembling a little umbrella—is the color of Scope mouthwash mixed with blue day-glo paint. It's a popular drink in Waterbury, Connecticut, not necessarily a town associated with exotic tropical cocktails. I'm the lounge pianist at the Holiday Inn, which advertises me on a big billboard in the parking lot:

NOW APPEARING! ROBIN MELOY—ALL YOU CAN EAT
SHRIMP SCAMPI $5.99, BLUE HAWAIIANS, 2 FOR 1.

There's a one-legged spinet in the corner of the bar. I keep the extra leg in the corner to use as a weapon. This is necessary one night when I'm accosted by an overzealous member of a

Triple-A baseball team who is drowning the sorrows of a lost game in a Blue Hawaiian.

What's he thinking? *Gee, we lost 16 to 0, guess I'll go drink something blue, do the alligator dance, and attack a piano player.*

I have to poke him in the stomach with the spare leg.

We have lots of regulars in the lounge. Dutch and Roy-Boy, Clark the newspaper man, and Dennis and Maryanne, two special-needs young adults. Dutch is old and decrepit, wears one of those tall Russian fur hats, and has long yellowed fingernails. He and Roy-Boy, a Pillsbury doughboy look-alike who claims to be Dutch's nephew even though no one believes him, sit silently at the bar and stare morosely into space until I finish a song. Then they cheer violently, take a drink, light cigarettes, and resume the death watch. Clark is pleasant enough, but he drinks himself silly every night and recounts the same story to anyone who will listen, something about a Xerox machine and a women in his office named Katrinka who once sat on it. Dennis and Maryanne always order Blue Hawaiians, then the fun begins. They bicker—yelling childlike insults—and throw Pepperidge Farm Goldfish and ice cubes at each other until the bartender calls their chaperon to come pick them up.

There's a man at the bar named Koko who plays chess against himself and gets really depressed when he loses. Occasionally a group of deaf adults comes into the bar. They sit right in front of the piano and hold their hands against the soundboard so they can feel the vibrations.

What, and leave show-business?

I learn to like my clientele, unusual as they are. This is a pretty good job as far as cocktail-piano gigs go. Or at least it's a good job for me at this particular time in my life. Lenny and I, having survived the move to New York City, have decided to separate. We're still friends, but he has moved out of our apartment and into his own place. I'm okay about this, really I am, even though I feel stupid for not trying harder to keep us together. But I'm on the road all the time and there's not much I can do. I stay in New York City Sunday through Wednesday, then drive ninety miles back to Waterbury late Wednesday afternoon and play through the weekend. The Holiday Inn pays me well, feeds me, and gives me a nice big double Holiday Inn room with an orange floral bedspread and Norman Rockwell prints on the wall. I keep all of my piano things here, even when I'm not working, so I never have to carry much back and forth to the city. I have a constant supply of friends visiting from New York. Waterbury isn't East Hampton, but it's an okay hangout.

There's a small outdoor pool and a fabulous thrift shop a few blocks away. The thrift shop is one of those great places where everything smells musty. It's a veritable treasure trove. The really hip stuff is rolled into tiny balls and shoved into the store's hidden corners. A successful visit means crawling around on the floor, a lot of sneezing, and brushing away the dust bunnies from the knees of my jeans, but that's the price I happily pay for a silk nightgown from 1926 and a pink tweed Chanel skirt for a dollar. On one outing a shipment of sixteen black cashmere priest coats arrives just as I do. I can't imagine, short of a massacre at the seminary, why the Catholic Church is giving these coats away. I buy five of them for two dollars each, keep one for myself, and distribute the other four to my ex-husband, my ex-boyfriend, my current boyfriend, and a great guy named Mark who wants to be a serious actor but keeps getting high-paying jobs appearing as Spider-Man in shopping malls all over the East Coast. All of us wear our priest coats around town, thinking we look like we've just stepped out of Bergdorf Goodman. Maybe we do.

 ✧

I practice in the mornings in the bar, which reeks of stale cigarette smoke and the sickeningly sweet smell of pancakes being served at the breakfast buffet next door. One Thursday morning during a practice session, I hear a terrible sound coming from the restaurant. I stick my head through the door and I see an old man choking, holding his throat, and about to drop to the floor from lack of oxygen. The waiters are running away with horrified looks on their faces. No one is helping the poor guy.

The manager screams, "Look out, he's gonna puke!" Then the manager races out of the restaurant.

The choker's wife starts punching him in the chest, which instinct tells me is not the proper procedure for the Heimlich maneuver. Ah, shit. I've got to help, I've got no choice. I push the wife out of the way, catch the choker as he's falling to the ground, jam him in front of me and start applying forceful upward pressure on his diaphragm. How come I'm doing this? Shouldn't the manager or a waiter be taking care of rescue missions? I thought every hotel and restaurant employee was required to take a first-aid class and learn how to do the Heimlich. Apparently not. So how come I know this stuff? Maybe I've spent too much time hanging out in hotel kitchens with nothing to do but read the First Aid Chart. I've learned a lot from those graphic illustrations. Here is a tip for choking restaurant guests: Look for the nearest musician. We're the only ones who have read the chart.

I keep working on the guy. It takes a couple of tries, but finally a piece of pancake flies out of his windpipe. It's like an Aunt Jemima air-to-surface missile. Two dignified businessmen stretch back in horror to avoid being hit by the offensive flying object, which lands right on their table, next to the syrup dispenser.

There's a slow, uncomfortable exodus of customers, which results in a traffic jam by the front door. I stand there, frozen, in a classic post-trauma position. I'm good in emergencies, but lousy when they're over.

"Chuck," says the wife. "I told you to put your goddamn teeth in this morning. You can't eat a goddamn pancake without your goddamn teeth." She pauses, shakes her head, and looks at me. "Hey," she says, jabbing me in the shoulder and grinning, "aren't you that piano girl?"

Chuck the choker, who looks to be about seventy-five, has attempted to eat his pancakes by gumming them. He makes an unintelligible wheezing reply to his wife, lights a cigarette, and resumes eating his breakfast. I sort of have to admire a toothless guy who can simultaneously eat a pancake and smoke a cigarette thirty seconds after a brush with death. The restaurant is now empty. The waiters have fled, the other customers have left in disgust, and the manager, who has turned an odd shade of green, is out by the front desk calling an ambulance, probably for himself.

I can't believe that neither Chuck nor Mrs. Chuck manages to thank me, but if he's the kind of person who won't put his teeth in before going to a restaurant, then most social niceties are beyond his reach.

I never want to see another pancake again as I long as I live.

∿

I write a lot of songs—sad songs with country-western lyrics about falling in and out of love. Something about Waterbury—the thrift shops, the weird and lonely customers, the deserted quality of the town square on weekend mornings—inspires me. There's so much I don't understand about music, about life, about love. I'm twenty-three years old and living alone—anxious about the future but looking forward to each day and whatever mystery it will dump on the third floor of the Holiday Inn.

I play at the Waterbury Holiday Inn for several years, on and off, between acting jobs and summers on Nantucket. The last week I play there, Dutch dies. I tie a black ribbon around his barstool. We drink a toast to Dutch and follow it with a moment of silence, which is, in Dutch's case, very appropriate, since he never said anything at all.

Two years later, while on location for a film, I return to the hotel just to see if things have changed. Some of the waiters and front desk staff are the same. The lobby has been renovated, and there are lots of big plants in the restaurant. The bar has new carpeting—green with little clusters of yellow and red stars—and the Rockwell prints have been replaced by Georgia O'Keefe posters. I spot several of the old customers. One of them is drinking a Blue Hawaiian. There's the piano, under a small blue spotlight, looking as if the evening's entertainment is a little late but will be showing up at any moment. A piano leg is propped in the corner, about where I had left it after hitting that baseball player in the stomach. I can't decide if it feels like I've never played here at all, or if it seems like I've never left. Nobody recognizes me. I sneak out of the bar the same way I sneaked in two years earlier—just another young woman passing through the hotel on her way to somewhere else.

Yellow Bird

SEEKING ATTRACTIVE FEMALE PIANIST / SINGER, 25–35,
FOR THREE-WEEK FEBRUARY ENGAGEMENT IN LUXURY
CARIBBEAN RESORT, EL RANCHO HOTEL, PETIONVILLE, HAITI.
GOOD SALARY, ALL EXPENSES PAID.
CONTACT DODO MARTIN AT DM CASTING.

*T*he ad is in *Backstage*, a New York City show-business news-paper. I don't know much about Haiti. I mean, I know it's a sun-drenched island somewhere in the Caribbean, full of hard-working poor people and governed by a dictator named Baby Doc Duvalier.

"You're perfect for this job!" says Spider-Man Mark. "You have to apply, you just have to!"

Who am I to argue with Spider-Man? I've just spent two years at the Waterbury Holiday Inn lounge with its blue cocktails and mentally disabled customers chucking goldfish at each other. Playing the piano in a Third World country shouldn't be much more of a challenge. It might even be a step up. I submit a photo and resume, wondering if my blond hair and light skin will be an advantage or not. I'm not too surprised when the casting agency calls me for an audition the following week. Ads for singers, dancers, and actors always attract thousands of applicants, but as soon as the term *female pianist* is introduced, the field narrows to about a dozen women.

"Three-thirty on the twenty-fourth of January, Sigma Sound Studios," I repeat as I write everything in my date book. I hesi-tate. "Will someone from the agency be there as well?" I ask. The last thing I need in the middle of a busy week is a run-in with a creepy hotel owner looking for an easy way to meet women. This doesn't just happen in the movies. One year after moving to New York City, I had been forced onto the roof of a very tall building where the producer of a play I was reading for tried to talk me into having sex with him. When I resisted, he pushed me up against a brick wall and rubbed himself all over me. Sickening. When he let go with one hand to pull down his zipper, I kneed him in the balls and ran down thirty-six flights of steps before escaping onto Third Avenue. I spent the entire night crying and throwing up.

These days I'm not taking chances. No meetings alone with strange men.

"Yes, of course someone else will be there," says the woman from the casting office like I'm making a stupid request. "Dodo Martin will be there to assist him."

The afternoon of January 24, 1984, is miserable—cold and steely gray and rainy. I've wasted away the early part of the day with my half-boyfriend Thomas at his loft on Nineteenth Street. Thomas paints pictures of oceans and sunsets, the type of paintings people buy to match their sofas or wallpaper. Since separating from my husband I've been working hard at being alone without being lonely. But I'm not very good at it. I like having a man around. I recently found out that Thomas has been continuing an affair with one of his "art" patrons, a wealthy and well-preserved woman in her seventies, a real Victorian piece of artwork herself. Just last summer, while I was staying with Thomas at his summer home on Nantucket, the art patron, whose family seems to own half of New England, had a thirty-foot sailboat delivered to Thomas as a birthday gift. I'd given him a tiny handmade needlepoint pillow. I keep seeing Thomas, but I know deep down inside our relationship is finished, unless of course the heiress dies, but I don't think that's likely to happen soon. We never discuss any of this.

When I leave Thomas's loft that afternoon, it begins to rain sideways, blowing my umbrella inside-out before I even get it open. Normally, I have excellent taxi karma, but this is an exceptionally rough day. Cars and trucks and jeeps with loud sirens and flashing lights speed by, splashing water and sludge everywhere. I get soaked by a speeding Con Edison van that drives too close to the curb. "You big fat idiot," I yell at the driver, which doesn't do a bit of good.

Finally I run across Sixth Avenue and tackle a taxi just as another passenger is exiting the rear door. "Good luck," she says, which strikes me as an odd greeting. I climb into the back seat, and the driver hands me a card that says he is deaf and that I need to write down my destination on a piece of paper. I ask him for a pencil, but he doesn't hear me, and it takes me forever to find one in my bag—my hands are stiff from the cold. The driver gets impatient and starts groaning at me.

I'm wearing a cute little black dress with pink tights and pink high heels. In the taxi I manage to remove the rain splatters from my legs using spit and the lining of one of my mittens. January in New York City is such a drag. I repair my smeared eye makeup and brush my hair, which is long—almost to my waist—soaked, and sticking to my jacket.

Well, aren't we looking fabulous today? says Voice of Doom. *Like you have a chance of landing this gig? Ha! Silly girl. Silly, silly, silly girl!*

I ride the elevator up to the eighth floor of the studio building. Bending over, I adjust my twisted pink tights. After several years of auditions in New York, I'm an expert at doing last minute touch-ups in elevators. Just before the doors open I stand up and throw my damp hair back over my shoulders. It is my favorite *Charlie's Angels* move.

"You're late, Miss Meloy," says the efficient Dodo Martin. "We were expecting you fifteen minutes ago."

"Sorry. Rain, heavy traffic, sludge, deaf taxi driver, no pencil, the usual. Is this a problem for you? I mean that I'm late?" At this point I just want to go home and take a hot bath. I remove my sopping jacket.

"No; one of the hotel owners is waiting in studio four," says Dodo. "But I have to run, I'm expected at RCA in five minutes.

The receptionist will show you back to the studio. Wait—look up, you've got something there." Dodo jabs an unnaturally long fuchsia-colored fingernail at my eye. "There, got it. Good luck. The hotel owner liked your photo. You've got a shot at this. Should be a good gig. Who couldn't use a little sunshine in the middle of February? Wish I could go myself. I've seen pictures of the hotel and it's gorgeous, just gorgeous." She picks a stray blond hair off of my shoulder. The way she's poking at me, I feel like a lice-infested chimp.

"*Ciao*," says Dodo.

People named Dodo shouldn't say *ciao*.

"*Ciao*," I reply. Jeez. Girls from Pittsburgh shouldn't say *ciao*, either.

The elevator doors close and off she goes. I hope she gets my cab driver.

The receptionist takes me back to the studio. Auditions are big adventures. I never know what will be waiting for me on the other side of the door.

⏴

On the American Airline flight to Haiti, the Americans sit in the front of the airplane, the Haitians in the back. At least that's what it looks like to me. A sea of laughing black faces in economy, a smattering of serious pallid ones in first class. There's a big commotion in the back as the Haitians load king-sized packages of Pampers and Tide laundry detergent into the overhead compartments. One man struggles past me carrying hubcaps; another carries a basketball in one arm and a large bag of pillow stuffing in the other. As we're being offered champagne, orange juice, and stylish magazines on thick glossy paper, I look over my shoulder. Complete chaos breaks out as the storage spaces fill up. One woman, unable to find a place to stash her giant carton of Bounty paper towels, sits on them and hopes the flight attendant won't notice.

I'm young and spoiled and can't imagine visiting a country where you have to take your own paper towels and hubcaps. But on the other hand, I've never seen so many *happy* travelers. There's an air of celebration onboard—I hear songs, laughter, and whoops of sheer delight. The flight from Kennedy to Port-au-Prince takes four hours. As we approach the island the mood grows somber, but when we touch the ground the Haitians break into wild applause. They're glad to be home.

I'm glad to be anywhere that isn't Waterbury. In my carry-on bag I have a round-trip ticket and a contract for $1,000 a week.

I step onto the scorched tarmac, and the heat of Port-au-Prince hits me like a wall. Soldiers with machine guns patrol the airfield, and three musicians wearing big straw hats stand by the door to the terminal and serenade us with "Yellow Bird." I say *merci* and toss an American dollar into their pot. On the exterior wall of the terminal, I spot a large poster with my picture on it. It's a press photo of me that makes me look like a fashion model, which, in real life, I do not. People will be disappointed when they discover I'm not a dead ringer for Kim Bassinger. Inside the building the walls are lined with the same poster, the same picture.

Yellow bird, up high in banana tree.

Yellow bird, you sit all alone like me...

I thought that song was Jamaican. Huh.

I look up at the little TV over the immigration desk. There's my picture again. And the announcer is saying something in French that I can't understand—I hear my name and the words *chanteuse*, *ce soir*, *merengue*, and *taboo*. There are wild drums playing on the soundtrack of the commercial. My fingers start to tingle.

A pretty young white woman waves from the other side of the immigration glass. I have no idea who she is, but I wave back. Just then, an Official Haitian Man wearing aviator sunglasses and a dark-blue suit grabs my arm, whisks me past the security officers, and leads me through immigration.

"Hi!" says the young woman. She is American and is wearing a bright orange shift with matching Chanel sandals and bag. Her hair is a weird shade of orange, and her skin has a sun-baked orange-ish cast to it. But in spite of all of her orangeness, she is attractive. "I'm Stacey," she says. "I'm the manager of the club. Let's get you back to the hotel so you can rest. We're sold out for tonight. Your opening act goes on at, like, eleven. You play at, like, midnight." She turns on her orange heels and starts walking away.

"Uh, wait a minute. My opening act?" I say, chasing after her. We're being escorted by officials through the hectic Customs area. Two scrawny brown chickens race by me. I want to stop and stare at the disarray around me, but our entourage hustles forward out of the terminal and into the parking area.

"Cocktail piano players don't usually have opening acts," I say.

Stacey is walking three feet ahead of me, barking orders in Creole. *"Ou est le? Le est la? La-bah? Ou la-bah?"*

The language sounds like one big song. *La, la, la, la, la, la, la.* I suspect she's looking for our driver.

"You're really lucky. We've got Tabou Combo, Superstars," Stacey says to me over her shoulder. "They're a sixteen-piece merengue band and they're, like, really super-hot right now."

"A sixteen-piece *merengue* band? I'm supposed to follow them? But I'm just one woman playing a piano. This defies every rule of show business logic."

"Not down here, *cherie*," says Stacey. "The locals can have merengue any day of the week. But you are a novelty." I hope I'm not being billed as a snake dancer. That might be dangerous in the land of voodoo.

I scoot into the back of the black BMW sedan with Stacey. The air-conditioning is a blanket of ice, and I shiver. Jean Louis, our skilled driver, winds his way through the back streets of Port-au-Prince, past Baby Doc's palace. As we stop behind a *tap-tap*, one of the brightly painted open-bed trucks that serve as Haiti's public transportation, a woman in a light green dress pounds on the window of our car. She is carrying a small wailing child.

"What does she want?" I ask Stacey.

"Oh. She wants, like, money." Stacey says, with a dismissive wave of her hand. "Or she might just want to, like, sell you her baby. Just look the other way."

᠕

I go for a swim and eat dinner—pumpkin soup and a tomato salad. The hotel is pretty, built into the side of a mountain that looks down over Port-au-Prince. The main building encircles two huge kidney-shaped pools. Behind the quiet garden that borders the casino is my bungalow. I recline in the rattan chair on my terrace and listen to the silence. The evening air is dense with the perfume of the flowers—there's jasmine, bougainvillea, and hibiscus everywhere I look—and my eyes grow heavy. I pull the crisp white cotton duvet over my legs and start to drift off.

> *...up high in banana tree.*
> *Did your lady frien' leave da nest again,*
> *Dat is very sad, make me feel so bad,*
> *You can fly away, in da sky away,*
> *You're more lucky dan me.*

I jerk awake. It's the Yellow Bird trio from the airport. They have two gigs—the airport and the Hotel El Rancho. I smile, wave, and give them another dollar. I can't tell if they're very young men or very old men. Between the three of them they have about seven teeth. They play endless choruses of "Yellow Bird" and then leave.

I bathe in the big red granite tub and dress for my job in a white evening gown and silver sandals. I step outside.

Crossing the stone bridge over the pool to the nightclub, I feel the vibrations of the bass and percussion coming out of the nightclub. The ground shakes and the pulse of the song wafts through the dark violet sky. The stars are out—there are so many of them! And the lights of Port-au-Prince twinkle, distant in the valley beneath me. I pass a long line of people waiting at the door, and some of them ask for my autograph. This is the first time I've been asked for my autograph, and it makes me feel like a movie star.

Working the door is Jean Louis, the man who had driven me to the hotel.

"*Bonsoir*, Madame Robin," he says. He snaps back a red velvet rope and I enter the club.

~

I can't believe the scene. At least a hundred frenzied dancers jump up and down to the music in such perfect time that they appear to be moving as one unit. Tabou Combo is on fire, working the crowd and stirring up so much rhythm, so much soul, so much *groove*, that I feel a need to jump into the circle of throbbing bodies. I want to dance, too! I don't know how to merengue, but it looks easy—a lot of rhythmic leg humping, sweating, and fun. Just as I'm getting ready to leap into the party, Stacey grabs me from the other side.

"No no no! You need to stay back here and hide," she says. "I want you to make, like, an entrance."

I almost forgot. I'm here to work.

Merde. I have to follow Tabou Combo, Superstars! I can't do this. I don't know what I had expected in Haiti, but this isn't it. I figured I would be playing in an intimate lounge area, secure behind a grand piano, with a couple of French-speaking Arab guys sipping island drinks and making passes at the waitress and me. That I could have handled. Following a sixteen-piece merengue band and a hundred sweaty dancers by getting up onstage and playing my simple rendition of "Skylark" is a different story. Oh God, I've even planned to start with a flute solo.

Hey you, white girl! says the Voice of Doom. *You're really in over your head this time. They gonna HATE you and your white girl music.*

"Stacey, I don't think I can do this." I have to shout over the music. "These people are gonna hate me."

"A plate of what?" she yells.

"THEY'LL HATE ME!"

"You'll be fine. We'll have the band announce you. Now stay put behind the bar and wait until you hear your introduction. Jean Louis will escort you to the stage. Be careful what you touch back there—there are a lot of weird diseases in this country."

I'm not sure what to do with this piece of information.

I hide behind the bar, sitting on a case of wine, and suck on a chunk of pineapple. Okay, I'll do it. I'll go on and play exactly what I've planned.

Play dat funky music white girl! What are you, out of your mind? says VOD.

What do you have to lose? says Voice of Reason. *A career? You hardly have one. Your reputation? No one on Haiti knows who you are. Your pride?*

Well, says VOD. *That's certainly up for grabs.*

࿓

"Et maintenant, mesdames et messieurs, j'ai l'honneur de vous présenter la chanteuse et pianiste américaine, Mademoiselle Robin Meloy, de New York City!"

I must admit, there is something thrilling about hearing myself introduced in French.

The Haitians don't throw papayas at me. They listen, which throws me off at first, but I get used to it after a few nights. Maybe Stacey is right; they just need a break from all the dancing. Tabou Combo invites me to a practice session under a thatched roof up in the mountains. It's the Haitian version of a garage-band rehearsal. We work out a few numbers together, which I love— I'm not just one of the boys, I'm one of the Haitian boys. I learn to merengue and have many partners ready to join me in the pounding dance of humanity that breaks out on the nightclub floor every weekend. The trick is to dry off in time to play my set.

The owner of the hotel shows up two weeks into my engagement, surprised that everything has gone so smoothly without him there. Typical. What can go wrong? I've been playing a beautiful Baldwin concert grand piano that is tuned every day.

"This piano! It isn't in the right position for the lights. I'll move it," Owner-man says. We're in the nightclub, alone.

"Wouldn't it be easier to refocus the lights?" I ask.

"Not in this country. First I'd have to find the lighting technician. Then I'd have to make an appointment that he wouldn't keep. Then I'd have to find him again."

"If you get a ladder for me, I could refocus the lights. I know how," I say.

"No no no. I'll just move the piano. Don't worry. I can handle this."

There are two things I've learned in life: one is to never argue with a man when he tells you *don't worry, he can handle it*; the other is that whenever a man says this, something disastrous is likely to happen.

Owner-man tries shoving the piano, but it doesn't budge. A concert grand is very large, about nine feet long and extremely heavy. He lunges at it. It moves about three inches and then the rear leg gets stuck on a crack, breaks off, and *boom!*—the piano crashes to the marble floor. My heart stops, just for a second.

I'm stunned. "Look at that," I say, staring in astonishment at the mess on the floor. "Another management-instigated broken-piano-leg catastrophe." He smiles at me, and my heart stops again.

When Owner-man invites me to dinner that night, I should say no, but I don't. He is, after all, the boss.

Never ever, never ever, never ever have dinner with the boss, says Voice of Reason.

But I can handle it. I fall in love with Owner-man and will spend the next six years commuting to Haiti once a month.

Nice Work If You Can Get It

"*S*orry, Miss, if you don't have an appointment then you'll have to leave. Mr. Ellis is busy." The dark-haired woman in the purple dress is seated behind a desk that looks like an airport control tower. She is half receptionist, half pitbull, although she looks a little like one of those troll dolls that I used to have as a kid.

"Okay, I understand," I say. "Look, would it be all right to leave a picture and résumé for him?"

The phone is ringing.

"Well, yeah, that would be—just a minute—hellojerrykravatentertainment susanspeakingmayIhelpyou?" Her voice is a combination of Betty Boop, Nell Carter, and one of those little yapping dogs that never shuts up. She could have starred in *Cujo*. "One moment please," she says into the phone as she presses a complicated series of buttons and transfers the call.

"So maybe I could write a note to Mr. Harlan Ellis; see, I'm a piano player and I've heard that he is the right agent…"

Ring, ring, ring.

"Sit there, but you can't stay. Jerry Kravat Entertainment is a very busy place. And Harlan Ellis is a very busy man…hellojerrykravatentertainment susanspeakingmayIhelpyou?"

Harlan Ellis. What a great name. In my short career I've worked for Pete Frank, Sammy Scott, and Rick Lester. Most agents seem to have two first names. Maybe Harlan Ellis will be different. He has two last names.

Ring, ring, ring.

This is a busy place. Uninvited, I sink into a beige velveteen modular sofa, the kind that makes you feel swallowed alive, and start writing my note to Mr. Ellis as Susan glowers at me from her control cubicle. This morning I attended an audition for the Broadway musical *Nine*. They rejected me after the second round of singing. I'm wearing a tight black dress, seamed stockings, and heels that make me six feet tall. All dressed up and nowhere to go, I thought I might take advantage of the outfit by toddling over to see Harlan Ellis, the agent who books most of the hotel piano gigs in Manhattan. I'm getting tired of doing the Waterbury-Haiti shuffle and think I'm ready to try to get some piano work in New York City—the Big Apple. I want to wake up in the city that never sleeps, especially since I'm paying for an apartment here. Everyone I know who is connected to the hotel music business says that Harlan is the guy to contact if I want to work in Manhattan. So here I am.

"I told you, you can't stay, Miss!" says Susan. There is a picture of Frank Sinatra hanging over her head. I swear his eyes are moving. "If you'd like to leave your picture with me, fine, but you can't just sit here in reception. This is a professional entertainment agency…*yip, yip, yip, yap, yap, yap*…"

Too bad. My feet are aching and this sofa is great. I would kill for a cup of coffee and a muffin but I'm being booted, all six feet of me, from the cozy confines of the agency's modular pit, "an area normally reserved for clients, not musicians," Susan tells me.

As I hoist myself out of the pit, Susan is called to another part of the office to handle some sort of entertainment agency emergency. Entertainment agencies are prone to emergencies. There's frequently a hysterical mother of the bride or a hyperventilating food-and-beverage director on the phone ranting about problems that haven't yet occurred. Right now, for instance, I'm overhearing a heated discussion about whether to hire an accordion player with a string section, a mariachi group with a girl singer, or a jug band. Must be an ethnic society wedding in West Virginia.

"I want you out of here in thirty seconds," Susan says to me. She scowls one last time, then scurries from her station like a crab on the beach running away from an incoming tide of demo tapes. "Leave your picture on the desk but don't touch anything!"

I've lived in New York long enough to know that if I leave my photo and résumé with the receptionist at an agent's office, it will be unlikely to see anything other than the inside of the trash can, but what else can I do?

I'm teetering next to her desk, bent over, writing Mr. Ellis's name on the photo when a voice behind me says, "Hi. May I help you with something?"

"Yes," I say. "Maybe you can. I play the piano. And I sing a little."

"Perfect," he says. "Come into my office and sit down. I'm Harlan Ellis."

Wow, that was easy.

"And I'm Robin Meloy. I was just writing a note to you. That secretary of yours is like the Gestapo."

He laughs. I laugh. "She's just doing her job," he says. I notice a huge stack of cassettes on his desk. There are photos of famous musicians and singers strewn across the surface of a nearby table.

You don't belong here, says VOD. *You're really out of your league this time, dear.*

I look long and hard at Harlan Ellis. He's good-looking and well dressed. I listen to him talk. He seems really smart, and he has a sense of humor. He asks intelligent questions and is interested in my semi-intelligent answers. In about ten minutes I know that this guy is a shining light in the black hole of agents. Sign me up.

We talk for an hour. There's a piano in the corner of his office. I expect him to ask me to play.

"No, no, no," he says. "I can see by your résumé that you tend to hold onto your jobs for long periods of time. That means you're doing something right. I'll have you come in for an audition sometime, just to hear you play a little. But these auditions don't mean much. You can't audition for a three-hour piano job by playing a couple of razzle-dazzle tunes for a committee of executives."

Two weeks later he invites me to an audition for a job in Sweden. Sweden! Several of the big Scandinavian resorts want American piano music, and since there is no built-in musical reservoir of American piano talent on that side of the Atlantic, they import pianists to Sweden for three-month stays.

"Harlan, I came to see you because I want to work in New York," I say. "I'm tired of traveling. Last time I checked, Stockholm was not located in one of the five boroughs."

"I know, I know," he says. "I have something in mind for you here in town. I just have to hear you play a little. Come and play a couple of tunes. No big deal."

I'm very nervous on the day of the piano audition. I want to make a good impression on Harlan. There are six pianists there that day, all of them women. One woman looks like a truck driver and plays a Rachmaninoff concerto. The next one performs a great medley from *West Side Story*, but she's wearing no makeup and is having a very bad hair day—you might even say she's having a no-hair day, since her head is shaved on one side. Then there is the *Rhapsody in Blue* girl. Later I'll discover that there's always someone, at every audition, who plays *Rhapsody in Blue* perfectly. Where do these people come from? Oh. Right. Juilliard. Another woman, more seasoned than the rest of us, sings a couple of jazz standards in a deep smoky voice that sends shivers down my spine. But she has a nasty attitude and sneers and snarls at everyone in the room in-between songs, like she's way too good to be auditioning for anything less than a recording contract with Blue Note.

Now it's my turn. I'm very intimidated. Feeling like a complete wimp, I get up and play and sing an old Janis Ian tune I like called "Jesse." Then I do a couple of standards—"Misty" and "Wave." I try to sing in tune and play all the right notes, and smile.

That was the lowest, says VOD. *You're gonna be in Waterbury for the rest of your life.*

ᘔ

I'm offered the job in Sweden. I'm shocked. I don't take it, but I'm tempted. I'm beginning to understand something about the music business: Playing one of these cocktail piano jobs isn't just about the music. Based on sheer musicianship, anyone of those other six women should have gotten the gig. Style plays a more important role.

Harlan doesn't mind when I turn down the job in Scandinavia. I can tell he's looking out for me and what I want to do. I trust him. The following month—true to his word—he books me at the Grand Hyatt Manhattan at Grand Central Terminal, playing a cocktail-hour job from five to eight Monday through Friday. I've seen the last of Waterbury and the Blue Hawaiians.

What can I say about a guy whose favorite song is the Tony Bennett rendition of "Once Upon a Time"? I could say that he's sentimental, that he's an incurable romantic, that he's got excellent taste in music. I could say all of those things about Harlan Ellis, and I'd be right. Harlan is a matchmaker—connecting the people who make music with the people who need music.

A skilled entertainment agent provides a client experience, authority, and expertise in recommending talent—solo musicians, bands or groups, musical revues, and headliners. If the agent has done his job correctly, the client is happy, everyone gets paid, and the client calls the agent again when he needs more music.

In addition to finding the right act for the job, a good agent functions as a barrier between the musician and the client. Harlan Ellis has a soothing effect on difficult customers. Many enter his office flustered and unsure of what they want, but they leave confident that they're in capable and caring hands. And Harlan maintains a roster of diplomatic performers who are expert at dealing with emergencies and pressure on the job. He knows who to send. Everyone lives happily ever after, most of the time.

Artists aren't the easiest business partners. Some are divas. Some are hypersensitive, and some get cranky and temperamental when things don't run smoothly. But as long as a degree of professionalism is maintained, Harlan copes with—and even enjoys—the broad range of artist eccentricities.

"I've always had an affinity for working with creative people," Harlan says. "I think I understand them. So often they fail to realize that talent alone isn't enough, and they either hate the business side or they're just plain bad at it. I'm happy to give them my advice. Sometimes they listen."

Harlan has carved a career by respecting his musicians and his clients. He's a smart guy, so yes, I listen to his advice. But he listens to me, too—my songs, my dreams, my plans. It's an even exchange. For the next decade, I'll work for Harlan and he'll work for me. We're a good team.

Marble Fountains, Velvet Caves

"*E*xcuse me, Miss, but are you a Juilliard student?"

"No," I say, and I smile as politely as I can. I've been working in Manhattan for three weeks, and already I've been asked this question several times. People like the idea of a struggling Juilliard student working her way through college playing the piano in a cocktail lounge. But I'm not a Juilliard student, or a student anywhere else for that matter. I'm twenty-five years old, I've been out of college for four years, and this is what I do for a living, thank you.

And just to set the record straight, this "hire a Juilliard student" thing is a big fat scam. I've heard of middle-aged club-date musicians passing themselves off as Juilliard students, running ads to entice the society ladies, then showing up at posh parties where they can drink buckets of expensive scotch and hit on the wealthy and gullible matrons who believe they've employed an ensemble of diligent and deserving prodigies.

The Grand Hyatt is my first piano job in New York City, and I'm proud of it. The hotel is renowned for its music. At any time of the day or night, commuters can walk out of Grand Central Terminal into the hotel lobby and hear the most beautiful sounds. The Hyatt lobby features music during breakfast and lunch. And seven nights a week, guests can hear some of the finest jazz in New York City, played by alternating trios. Trumpet's, a little velvet jewel-box lounge tucked away in the corner of the vast marble lobby, employs two shifts of pianists starting at five every evening and continuing until midnight.

My regular job is back in the cocktail lounge, but I also sub for Earl Rose, one of the lobby musicians, who maintains a busy composing and performing career in addition to his hotel piano job. Earl's shift starts at eight in the morning, so subbing for him means a packed rush-hour subway ride into the hustle and bustle of Grand Central Terminal. Businessmen and women in dark suits lay their expensive briefcases on the piano and wait to meet their breakfast appointments by the entrance to the restaurant. Sitting down to play a gig at 8 A.M. is a novel sensation for me. The lobby smells like a day beginning—coffee and bacon, shampoo and aftershave, clean laundry and shoe polish.

The tones of the Steinway in the lobby carry into the various restaurants, but if you're not in the mood to spend eighteen dollars on an omelet or a glass of wine, you can just sit in a comfortable lobby chair and listen, free of charge.

Mixed in with the business crowd are the Lobby People. Although the Hyatt lobby—which looks like it's been carved out of the side of a mountain in Tuscany—is swarming with hulking security guards, it boasts a fair number of crazies and other misfits: street people in passable clothes, rich people who are out of their minds, the obsessed, the bored, the lonely, the drooling, the slightly insane, the very insane, the great unwashed, the proselytizing born-again whatevers, the prostitutes, and the prostitute-seeking inebriated fools carrying Hermes briefcases. They sneak in, usually unnoticed by the crack security agents who spend most of their time barking into walkie-talkies from the employee cafeteria—when they aren't lurking by the entrance to the hotel commenting on the breast size of any female under the age of fifty. The Lobby People don't all show up at once. But when I play in the lobby, I can always count on two or three of them, in various stages of lunacy, staring me down from the edges of the polished granite surrounding the piano. The Lobby People keep me on my toes.

❧

One morning when I'm subbing for Mr. Rose, an unshaven man wearing layers of ancient clothes and smelling like too many years of cheap wine and bad luck approaches the piano. He has that look in his eye, the look of a worn-down Veteran of Life who has the ability and the desire to take out anyone who crosses his path or plays a wrong note.

"I hate this music," he hisses.

I'm playing "How About You?"

I like New York in June, how about you...

"I hate this music," he says again, this time much louder. His face is turning red.

I look around the lobby. Is there a security guard watching?

I like potato chips, moonlight and motor trips...

"I HATE THIS MUSIC!!!!" he screams. By this time his face is swollen and scarlet. I swivel my head, still playing, desperately looking for security.

I like it, how about you?

I take an early break and scoot away from the piano. The Veteran of Life circles a rubber tree, sticks his head between the giant leaves, and rants about the music—even though I've stopped playing. I retreat to the employee cafeteria, where I find three security guards eating heaping plates of lemon meringue pie.

❧

"I just can't take my eyes off your ankles," says Irma.

Irma is a regular Lobby Person. She wears a long skirt, black oxfords, and a babushka. I'm on a first-name basis with her. Irma and her brother Roy show up, every day, to hear whoever happens to be playing in the Hyatt lobby. Roy is a big man—a former pianist. When he approaches me he swoops down on the Steinway like a hawk gliding in for a landing. His daily uniform is a dark red jacket and a white shirt—gray from age, but clean and pressed. Sister Irma looks like the Kathy Bates character in the movie *Misery*. She is quite frightening. Every chance she gets she stares at my ankles. At the Hyatt the Steinway is on a marble landing, and the Lobby People sit a few feet beneath the piano, leaving my ankles directly at eye level. I start wearing long skirts, but I have nightmares about Irma showing up with a sledgehammer.

I'm not the only pianist in town being followed by Roy and Irma. Roy has a complete listing of every musician's schedule and does an admirable job of putting in appearances at all of our gigs and keeping us informed about who is working where. I could live without his axe-murderer sister, but Roy himself is both a weird and welcome fixture in the lobby, perched on a leather sofa, dishing out embarrassing applause and annoying gossip about other players. He's a pest, chasing after me on my breaks, insisting that I spend my twenty minutes of free time discussing the chord changes to a Michel Legrand song or listening to his play-by-play description of a gig he played in 1956 with a trombone player named Schmoozy. Roy drives me crazy. But he's there, a constant force in a transient lobby-world. I can count on him.

‮ى‬

One day a guy sits next to the piano—right next to it—with his penis hanging out of his Bermuda shorts. And the worst part is, he doesn't even know it. Even I don't see it at first, and I have pretty good exposed-genitalia radar.

The guy—who has bright red hair and a full beard—is very fat. He sits with his hands folded on his big belly, talking to a group of college students about Jesus and God and how we should ignore the temptations of the big city and lead good Christian lives. I'm half-listening to his prattle as I play a new composition of mine. Maybe he's a minister from one of those states where they think it's perfectly acceptable to enter a Manhattan hotel lobby dressed for a day at SeaWorld. He starts quoting Bible verses. His shorts creep up his chubby thighs, and, bingo, out pokes Mr. Penis from the hem of his right leg. I can't believe my eyes. No one notices except for me. The students don't notice, the host of the restaurant doesn't notice, the other Lobby People don't notice, even Roy doesn't notice and he notices everything. I don't want to stare, but I can't help myself, and I keep looking over there to see if he has tucked it back in.

I'd like to tell a waitress, but I'm pretty new here and I don't want to make a bad first impression or, worse yet, appear to be naive. I mean, who knows? This is New York City. The Big Time. Maybe this is a common occurrence. Mr. Penis and his flock stay for an entire set, and even pray together in a circle, before they head off to tour the USS *Intrepid*.

ↄ

Trumpet's, the elegant cocktail lounge in the back of the Hyatt lobby, has a different character from the bustling, slightly dangerous atmosphere in the main lobby. You can't walk into Trumpet's without buying something, so that eliminates most of the Lobby People. But the paying customers can also do some ridiculous things, especially the ones who like to balance a vodka martini in one hand and an illicit love affair in the other.

I play at a very busy time—rush hour on work days—and Trumpet's, named after Donald Trump, is the perfect place for commuters to get drunk enough to face the train back home to Westchester or Greenwich or one of those places with lawns, little puff-ball dogs, and wives wearing twinsets and pearls. Fortunately, Trumpet's is very dark and smoky, which is a good thing because there's an abundance of adulterous activity going on at the booths in the back. Just last week I witnessed the Bobbing for Apples at Table Twelve Incident. Or, as one of the stylish Australian men drinking in the lounge that night said to the bartender, "Look at that mate, blowjob right over there in the corner! Now I know why you Americans call it *happy hour*."

This kind of thing never would have happened in Waterbury or Pittsburgh.

The Steinway is between the bar and table area. Everyone ignores me. At first it bothers me that no one even bothers to say *hello what's new you're doing a nice job*. I think it's my fault, that I'm too loud, or too soft, or maybe my material is all wrong. And then, about a month into the gig, I have one of those lightbulb moments. *Not one of these people has come to hear me.* They've come to talk, to get drunk, to flirt with each other, to do business, to bob for apples. It doesn't matter if I play Gershwin or Elton John or Mozart. It only matters that I stay out of the way of their original intentions, playing with enough presence to be heard, but softly enough to be ignored.

Oh. Now I get it. I'm like the flowers, or the paintings on the wall, or the subtle indirect lighting, or the crystal tumblers. I'm like the pretty waitress, or the cocktail nuts, or the votive candles on the tables. I'm like the marble floor or the Persian carpet, the velvet loveseat, or the single rose placed on the podium by the door. I'm one element of the atmosphere in this room. I'm not being paid to perform. I'm being paid to enhance the ambience. A huge weight has been lifted from my shoulders.

I stop trying to entertain my customers. Instead, I allow them to entertain me. I keep playing, but I quit singing. There is something humiliating about singing to a room full of talking people. I'm a better pianist than vocalist, so my decision to only play isn't difficult. Now that I don't have to concentrate on lyrics, I can listen to the drama going on around me. This will keep me sane. From now on, I'll be the audience. Everyone else can be the show.

Playback 1984

*I*t's five o'clock. I flick the switch for the spotlight over the Steinway, check my makeup in the little mirror tucked behind the supply room door, and adjust my bra strap, which keeps slipping out the side of the sleeveless gold satin dress I am wearing. There's a cockroach on the side wall where I hang my coat. I smoke a cigarette, reapply my lipstick, and head for the piano.

The room is almost full. I see a few familiar faces. Look, there's James, the nice guy who is always running to the men's room to wash his hands.

Oh, Sam's here, too. We think he might be a secret agent because we can't figure out where he works and he speaks foreign languages we've never heard. Our latest theory has him working for the local government of a small island in the Maldives.

Drat. There's the Booger Lady. Not a highlight in my evening. She always sits right behind the piano and coughs, spits, and blows her nose so hard that I think one of the trains from Grand Central is pulling into the lounge. Then she rolls her little wet tissues into balls and stuffs them into her empty glass and ashtray.

I say hi to Melissa, a gorgeous waitress who changes her hair color with every new boyfriend, as she scoots by with a tray of smoked almonds. Pam, my good friend and favorite bartender, is busy slicing lemons and limes.

I float into the first chorus of "Moon River."

James, the obsessive hand-washer, heads for the restroom.

The conversations improvise a contrapuntal line to the Mancini tune.

"Fuck you Bernie, fuck you. I told you I wanted British racing green and you just had to get red. It's so cliché…" says the blonde woman with the bad perm seated at table three, right next to the piano. Her date, or husband, or whatever he is, is wearing an Armani knockoff black-on-black-on-black double-breasted suit. He almost disappears into the darkness of the room.

"The guy at table fourteen wants to buy you a drink," says Melissa. "The one with the beard and the glasses with the tape on them. Can you play something from *Chorus Line*? Oh man, oh man, oh man, did you see? The Booger Lady is here. I am *not* touching her old noserags tonight. Last time she was here I almost got the plague."

"Hey Miss, we need another round," says a chubby man in an orange cardigan sweater. He has three chins.

"Keep your fuckin' pants on," says Melissa under her breath.

"If you'd ordered green we would've gotten green," says table three. "I know you ordered red just to bug me. If you think…"

Booger Lady speaks: "Is there a non-smoking section in this bar? I'm suffocating. The smoke makes my allergies flare up."

honk sputter cough.

I'll say.

"So don't tell her. Serves her right," says a woman to the man with his hand on her ass as they pass me. She trips, catches her foot on the sound system cable, and knocks the boom-stand microphone into my teeth. I'm not singing anymore, but I use the mike to make announcements. I check to see if any of my porcelain veneers are damaged. No. Good. Shit, that hurts.

"I absolutely refuse to be seen in a red car. It's so tacky."

Can't forget, won't regret, what I did for love…

Laughter explodes from the bar. Oh look, Billy Martin is here.

"Miss, can you play 'Moonlight Sonata'?" says the guy with the tape on his glasses. There are smoked-almond crumbs in his beard. He waves a ten-dollar bill in front of me.

I play something that sounds like "Moonlight Sonata."

Billy Martin slugs the guy sitting next to him.

The manager runs over to the piano. "Quick, Robin, play something."

"But I am playing something. This is 'Moonlight Sonata' in case you don't recognize it."

"Well play something different. You know. Fast. Loud. So the guests don't notice the fistfight. I'll call security." Management only wants me to play fast and loud when there is an emergency and they want me to serve as a distraction.

There is nothing I can possibly play that will distract a roomful of inebriated people from watching two grown men, one of whom is a celebrity, pummel each other onto the red carpet that leads into the lounge.

I segue from "Moonlight Sonata" into "In the Mood," a transition that would have appalled both Beethoven and Glenn Miller. I am quite proud of myself.

honk honk cough cough sputter spit.

The Booger Lady is warming up. I think I can feel a fine mist of whatever is coming out of her mouth settling on the back of my neck. Maybe I should learn "A Foggy Day in London Town."

James heads for the restroom again.

A busload of Japanese tourists walks around the fistfight and into the lounge, They smile and take pictures of me. The Japanese bow toward me. I do my best to bow back while continuing to play "In the Mood." They bow again, I bow again. I should know better than to start bowing to a group of Japanese—I might end up in an all-night bowing duel. By the time the Japanese leave, Billy Martin and his sparring partner are joking. They embrace each other and order another round.

I play "You've Got a Friend."

honk honk sputter sputter spit cough cough.

"Miss, I need a clean ashtray," says the Booger Lady.

"In your fuckin' dreams," mutters Melissa.

For some odd reason I start playing "Old Cape Cod."

I hear Sam the Spy instructing Pam on the proper way to cut tropical fruit. See? That's exactly the kind of thing a spy from the Maldives would know.

James returns from the restroom, inspecting his fingernails.

"Miss, I really need a new ashtray. And can you take this empty glass?" The Booger Lady is getting testy. Melissa ignores her, puts her nose in the air, and leaves the lounge.

An eight-year-old girl wanders in from the restaurant and stands next to the piano. "You play like a princess," she says. I play a song from *Sesame Street*, but I don't think she recognizes it. She leaves with her grandmother, who casts a backward glance at the coughing Booger Lady before dragging her granddaughter out of harm's way.

I play an original tune, or the chords to an original tune for which I have not yet composed a melody. It sounds nice.

What time is it, anyway? Pam walks by with a giant bucket of ice and the warm smile of a woman who really likes her job. The general manager of the hotel gives me a wave and goes into dinner with a group of men wearing L.A. Lakers warm-up suits. They are very tall.

cough sputter spit hack.

Melissa returns to the lounge from the ladies' room, where she has borrowed a huge pair of industrial-strength rubber gloves from the housekeeping staff. She pulls on the gloves and proceeds, very dramatically, to clear the Booger Lady's table. Too bad she couldn't find a gas mask. The Booger Lady blows her nose into a fresh tissue and requests a new bowl of cocktail nuts.

It's twenty minutes to six. I end the set with a Debussy Arabesque and get the hell out of there.

All the Sad Young Men

Sing a song of sad young men,
Glasses full of rye,
All the news is bad again so,
Kiss your dreams goodbye.

—Alan Bergman, Marilyn
Bergman, Norman Luboff

"Why do they call it a fake book anyway? Is it for fake piano players?" says Michael the waiter. "That would be good for me."

"You play the piano?" I say. It is five minutes to five and I'm standing in the kitchen of the Omni Park Central, eating spicy corn chips and drinking a coffee while leafing through an old fake book for ideas. My gig is a five-hour marathon, six days a week, and I need material.

"Yeah, I played a lot while I was growing up," he says. "It was like therapy for me. Saved me from having to try out for the basketball team. I either had to learn an instrument or play a sport, my parents said." He is carefully arranging flowers into the individual bud vases that will be placed on each table in the lobby cocktail lounge.

"Too bad there wasn't a florist club at your high school. You would have been a hit," I say.

"Fat chance, darling. There was only one florist in my hometown, and she was strictly a carnation-and-chiffon-butterfly kind of gal. I used to collect the butterflies whenever my mother got an arrangement. I decorated the ceiling of my bedroom with them. So tell me about this fake book thing."

"It's called a fake book because it gives you just the basics of the song. Just enough. Then you can fake your way through it," I say.

"So how do they decide which songs to put into the fake book?"

"They pick songs that people want to hear. You know, popular songs, standards, that kind of thing."

"But you never play with music in front of you."

"Yeah, I try to avoid having music on the piano. My teacher always said it was unprofessional and most improper to play solo piano in public with music in front of me. To this day I swear a bolt of lightning will come out of the sky and strike me dead if I dare to perform with a piece of music on the stand."

"So why lug the fake book around?"

"In case somebody waves a twenty-dollar bill at me and asks for a song I don't know. For twenty bucks I'm willing to risk the lightning bolt. I might be professional and proper but I'm not stupid."

"I don't know, honey. Some of these titles look suspicious," Michael says as he thumbs through the book. "Like this one. 'Turkey in the Straw.' Has anyone ever asked you for that?"

"No. But Thanksgiving is coming up. You never know."

"Or here's a real classic: 'The Rambling Wreck from Georgia Tech.' Or what about 'The Livery Stable Blues'? Or 'Too Fat for the Chimney'? Who plays this stuff? Oh wait, this is good—'Born to Hand Jive.' How are you gonna play that on the piano? Look! A whole section of marine-animal songs. Here's 'Flipper.' And check this out. 'The Theme from Sea Hunt'! I'll bet that's a popular request on the cocktail piano circuit. Ha!"

"Maybe if you had a cocktail piano gig at SeaWorld?" I'm half serious.

"God I used to love that *Sea Hunt* show. Nobody ever looked better in a wetsuit than Lloyd Bridges. I learned to swim because of that show."

Petra, the manager, rounds the corner. "Uh, Michael, the flowers? It's ten past five!" He loads the thirty vases, each one containing a fragile stem of snow-white Friesia, onto a tray. On his way past the white Kawai grand, he takes a extra spray of blossoms out of his apron pocket, and places it on the piano.

The Omni Park Central is an older hotel between Fifty-fourth and Fifty-fifth streets on Seventh Avenue. Right before I started playing at the Omni, the lobby was gutted and redone in white marble. The furniture is white, the reception desk is white, the Kawai grand is white, and Lord knows I'm white. The management team has even asked me to wear white dresses. They're doing their best to make some sort of theme statement with the interior decorating, but I can't imagine what it is.

There I sit, night after night, right smack in the middle of the lobby, looking like I've blown in from the Alps. My piano is about twenty yards away from the revolving doors that lead to the grit and grime of the city streets. Michael calls me Heidi on Seventh.

"He's here! He's here! He's here!" Flustered, Michael runs to the piano around tables and chairs, briefcases and Louis Vuitton travel bags, all the while balancing a mixed green salad and a Chardonnay on his tray. "He's here!"

"Who's here? Calm down, your face is all red," I say. I continue to play "Memory" from *Cats*, the hit song of the decade.

"Lloyd Bridges. Do you believe it? Where's your fake book? Get the fake book! Get it! Get it now! It's your chance to play 'Sea Hunt'!"

I'm caught in the frenzy. Lloyd is checking in at reception. He's wearing a white suit—someone must have tipped him off—and he's very tan.

"The book is in the back, Michael. Next to Hector's station. Go get it. Fast. Before Lloyd splits. Hurry up!" Michael drops his tray on the piano and races to the kitchen.

"Here," he says, out of breath. "Page 134. 'Theme from Sea Hunt.' You go for it, girl." Michael walks to edge of the platform, strikes a spokesmodel's pose and announces: "Mr. Lloyd Bridges, we welcome you to the Omni Park Central. Here is a song prepared by our lovely pianist especially for *you*."

I play "Sea Hunt." Not very well, but I bang it out. Mr. Bridges nods and points in my direction. He seems totally unimpressed.

"*What?*" says Michael. "Like every piano player in the world plays that song for him? He's lucky anybody even knows who he is. You'd think he'd at least come up here and thank us in person or send us a drink or *something.*"

"Maybe he didn't recognize it. I played it pretty badly. If I had known we were going to have a *Sea Hunt* moment, I would have practiced." I stand up. It's break time.

"Honey, even I recognized it and I haven't seen the show since 1975." He casts a disdainful look in Mr. Bridges' direction. Sitting at the piano, Michael looks at the fake book and takes off his glasses. He plays the first four bars of 'Sea Hunt' and flips backwards off the piano bench, just like Lloyd used to do off the side of the boat when he was about to go battle a shark in dangerously deep water.

ॐ

"Table two wants to buy you a drink, honey. That fab-looking guy in the navy blazer," says Michael.

It's almost nine o'clock, time for my last break of the evening. I'm ready for a glass of wine. "Okay," I say to Michael. "The usual. Do I have to sit with him?"

"Don't know, darlin'; he says he wants to book you for a party. It wouldn't kill you talk to him for a second. Looks like he's got some money."

"Michael, everyone here has money, except for us."

"Testy tonight, Missy Robin?"

"Tired. Just tired." I've been playing five hours a night, six nights a week and going to acting classes during the day. I need a vacation.

I finish the set with "Long and Winding Road" and go to table two. The man sitting there springs to his feet.

"I'm Reginald Thomas Simpson," he says as he holds the chair for me. We exchange a few banal pleasantries, and he asks if he can book me for a party at his penthouse.

"That shouldn't be a problem," I say. "You can contact my agent and he'll take care of the details."

"Can't I work with you personally," he says. "Without the agent?"

"I'm sorry, Reginald, I'm under contract." Not true, but I decided long ago to always use the agent buffer as a security system. "But do call Harlan Ellis, my agent. He's a great guy. Thanks for the wine. Hope to see you again!" I give him Harlan's card and return to the piano for my last set, not thinking too much about Reginald, just wanting to go home.

"You'd better get some sleep, honey," says Michael. "You're looking awfully pale. If you get any whiter you're going to just fade away in this room."

On my way out of the hotel I notice Reginald across Seventh Avenue, leaning against a building and smiling at me. I scoot down into the subway station where the train is waiting. As it pulls away, I see him again. This time he isn't smiling.

ॐ

"Robin, you've got mail. I left it on the piano."

"Me? Mail? Okay, thanks." I've taken a few days off to fly down to Florida with my boyfriend. I'm not as tan as Lloyd Bridges, but I've gotten a little color. The sunshine has done wonders for me. I open the letter.

Oh, God. "Michael, check this out!"

"Fan mail?"

"Not exactly."

The letter says ROBIN YOU WILL DIE. The letters have been cut out of newspaper print and pasted on a plain white sheet of paper.

"Wow," says Michael. "This is like a bad movie."

"Who put this here?" I ask him. My palms are sweating.

"No clue," he says. We look at the envelope, hoping for a clue. But it's blank.

"You know what, honey? I think I'd better call security."

I start my first set with "Windmills of Your Mind." A security guard comes to the piano to pick up the letter, makes a couple of jokes about it, and leaves.

Later that evening, as Michael and I are pounding out a four-hand version of "The Ben Hur Chariot Race March," I look up and see a street person enter the lobby from the Seventh Avenue revolving door. He lurches towards the reception desk and waves a stained rag in small circles around his head. The lobby bustles with late check-ins and frazzled business people rushing off to important places. No one looks at the homeless man—they avoid his stares and step over and around him like he's just another hurtle on a New York obstacle course. The man shuffles in a wide arc around the cocktail lounge. Suddenly he stops, crouches down low on the white marble floor, looks directly at me, and grins. It is Reginald. The sophisticated and elegantly dressed man has vanished. He's dressed in a torn and filthy coat and layers of dirty sweaters. He's wearing old ragged slippers and his skin is sooty. He has foam in the corners of his mouth. But the grin is the same.

We are coming to the big finish of our "Chariot Race March." A handful of people, Michael's customers, are sitting close to the piano cheering us on.

"Michael, that's *him*," I say as we play the last chord. The beginning of an anxiety attack creeps under my collar. I'm sure that Reginald, with his multiple outfits and maniacal smile, is the author the death threat. Michael runs to call security, but by the time they arrive, Reginald has disappeared.

"Darling," Michael says. "Looks like you've got yourself a stalker. How dramatic!"

࿐

I'm the house pianist at the Omni, but Michael is the real entertainment in the lobby. He tells jokes to his customers and sings songs with me accompanying him. Whenever we get a chance, we play one of the four-hand pieces we've rehearsed. The guests adore him. I adore him.

In Michael's free time he serves meals at a Manhattan soup kitchen. He also donates his time to GMHC, Gay Men's Health Crisis, a non-profit group in Manhattan. The city has been ravaged by AIDS. We fear it will get much worse. At GMHC Michael persuades gay men to be tested for HIV.

One week he misses five days of work. I can't reach him at home and I'm worried. Nobody at the Omni has heard from him. Finally, on the sixth day, he returns.

"What's going on with you?" I ask.

"Meet me by the telephones on your break," he says. There's a private area upstairs, by a bank of public phones. I race up there after my first set.

"I'm sick," he says. "Full-blown AIDS." He starts to cry. The marble floor beneath me feels like it's vibrating. One of the pay phones begins to ring.

"I thought I was in the clear. I haven't had a partner for nine years. I didn't even bother with an HIV test because I've been celibate for so long. I live like a fucking nun. Here I've been out counseling other men to be tested when I should have been tested myself. How stupid is that?"

I embrace him and we cry together. I can't speak. I can barely breathe.

The pay phone keeps ringing.

He pulls himself out of my arms and squares his shoulders.

"No one here can know about this. They'll fire me. And if I lose my health insurance I'm doomed. I'm going to fight this. I've already contacted the NIH and put myself on the list for experimental programs."

Ring, ring, ring.

Michael picks up the phone and says, "Fuck you, fuck you, fuck you." He slams it back down.

I sob. I want to be strong for him, but I can't get it together.

"Honey," he says. "It'll be okay. Looks like we both have stalkers. We just have to wear them down."

We return to the cocktail lounge. I play. He works the room, shuffling back and forth with kir royale and chicken satay. He sings and plays the piano with me and fills the lobby with his tragic optimism. Watching him tonight is like watching a ray of sunlight, the kind that catches you by surprise and dances around your living room on an otherwise cloudy day.

ॐ

It's early November and Reginald continues to make appearances in the lobby.

"What fashion statement is he making today?" Michael asks. "Dumpster or Brooks Brothers? Do you think he carries that paper bag in his Gucci briefcase, just in case he wants to change his look midday?"

Reginald T. Simpson, whatever he's wearing, is clever enough to avoid being caught. He sneaks into the lobby, stares at me, waits for a waiter to call security, and then runs out of the hotel before they arrive. Not once in three months has any member of the security force actually seen the guy. Some nights Reginald lurks outside of the hotel, waiting for me to leave. I always know when he's there. He hides in the shadowy recesses of the Carnegie Hall entrance, and I can feel his eyes burning through my heavy winter coat as I hurry along Seventh Avenue. I stop taking the subway home. I take cabs. One of the waiters, Michael usually, escorts me out of the hotel and waits until the taxi door closes behind me. I'm terrified that Reginald will jump into another cab and follow me. Taxi drivers don't pick up street people, but they do pick up Caucasian businessmen wearing good suits. I breathe a sigh of relief on the nights when Reginald wears his ragged clothes.

"Not a thing we can do, Robin," says Bill, the chief of hotel security. "We can't touch him unless he actually attacks you on hotel property. Sorry."

"Do you think you might post a guard in the lobby? I mean, wouldn't that be a good place to have a guard anyway? I know you guys come through the lobby every so often, but this Reginald guy has been coming in every night for months and you've never even seen him."

"You have to call us, Robin, the minute he arrives."

"But your office is a two-minute walk away from the piano. Reginald bolts as soon as he knows he's been spotted. It takes him five seconds to get back onto the street."

"Look, our hands are tied. There's nothing we can do but wait until he does something nasty on the property. Then we'll nail him."

"That's reassuring," I say.

"Sorry."

Two nights later, just as I'm playing the bridge to "As Time Goes By," Reginald appears at the piano, on my left side. He leans over me. His body is rigid and he stinks like raw onions, rotting meat, and mildew. I turn away from him and try to escape from the right. He grabs my arm and pushes me back against the wall. Then he holds up a large closed umbrella and shoves the point of it against my throat.

"I'm gonna fuckin' kill you." His voice is rough and strained.

The umbrella doesn't have any fabric on it. It's just the handle, the spokes, and the point, which is sharpened to a spike. I'm unable to move or scream for fear of being impaled. There are scores of people around me and no one is paying any attention.

Please. Someone. Look. This. Way.

Michael spots me from across the lobby, throws his tray to the floor, and races towards the piano. Just as fast, Reginald drops his umbrella and escapes out the side door. I don't know what to do—I'm out of breath, frozen with panic. But I feel an urgent need to finish the song I'd been playing when Reginald attacked me. I sit back down at the piano and resolve the cadence. The chord hangs for a second, then I bolt for the kitchen. I sink to the floor and sit there, shaking, until Michael packs me into my woolen coat. He escorts me into the darkness on Seventh Avenue and stuffs me into a taxi.

༉

Two weeks later I return to the Omni in a Valium-induced daze.

"I'm leaving," Michael says to me. "I'm going home to Wisconsin. My parents will help me with money. I need to be able to get back and forth to Washington for these treatments and tests."

"When are you leaving?"

"Next week."

"It will be terrible here without you."

"Yes, darling," he says. "It will be dreadful. Abysmal. Devastating. But I suspect you'll all deal with it. Here, I saved something for you." He takes me in the back, and there, next to a stack of booster seats, is the stick umbrella. He has tied little pink ribbons around each bare spoke.

"Michael," I say. "That's *awful*."

"Well that's the beauty of it, honey. It's art. A little too big for your coffee table, but I'm sure you can make it work somewhere in that gorgeous apartment of yours. Now stop sniveling and go play something pretty."

Reginald doesn't come into the hotel on my first night back, but I sense that he is outside, somewhere, waiting, waiting, waiting. At ten o'clock, just as I'm finishing my last set, Bill, the security chief, shows up at the piano.

"I'm sorry about what happened," he says. "We'd like to make sure that you get into a taxi safely tonight."

"Yeah, well, Michael's been seeing to that for the last few months, but I think it would be a good idea for you to take over," I say. "I'll go and grab my coat."

I kiss Michael goodbye and push my way through the revolving doors. Brooks Brothers Reginald, in plain view, stands just across Seventh Avenue, holding his briefcase.

"That's him," I whisper to the security guy.

"Where?"

"Over there. In the suit."

"I thought he was supposed to be a street person," he says.

"Sometimes he's a street person. He changes his clothes. I've told you all of this before." Reginald jumps off the curb and into the traffic. I panic. He bounces off a taxi cab and continues walking. Toward me.

"Shit, He's coming. Fuck. What should I do?" From across the wide street I see the intensity in his eyes. He looks right at me and ignores the honking horns and screeching brakes. He begins to run.

"He's gonna kill me. What should I do? Please tell me what I should fucking do." I stand frozen, staring at Reginald running toward me. I want to move but I can't.

"Turn around and walk into the hotel," says the security man. "We can't grab him unless he's in the hotel. Listen to me! Walk real slow and go into the hotel. Let's hope he follows you."

"I don't want him to fucking follow me!"

Bill pushes me toward the hotel, hard. "Trust me. Now go."

I set one foot in front of the other and force myself to look straight ahead. I hear the hollow echoes of the voices and laughter around me and a vague *thump thump thump* of Reginald's footsteps as he draws nearer and nearer. I walk, in slow motion, through the door. Now Reginald is directly behind me. There is a whirl of movement as Michael, who has been waiting inside the lobby with four security guards, grips my arms and jostles me away from the door.

"Get out of here fast, honey. You don't wanna see what they're gonna do to this guy," says Michael. I turn to look just as one of the guards snatches Reginald. I manage to close my eyes just before they knock him to the ground.

ॐ

The cognac laps against the sides of the oversized snifter. An hour or so has passed. Michael comes into the bar, his face ashen. He is breathing hard.

"Those security guards are total thugs," he says. "What do they do when they hire these guys? Go to Rikers Island to recruit the senior class of convicts?"

There is blood on his shirt.

"Michael, are you hurt?" I ask.

"No, honey. I just got a little involved in the tussle out there. This is Reginald's blood. He was on the floor and they were still hitting him. Kicking him, even. Someone had to get them to stop."

"Oh, Michael."

"Yeah, do you believe that? Me. In a fight. Someone should have sold tickets."

"Where is Reginald now?"

"Oh, he's upstairs being questioned and printed and photographed. All of which would have been possible without the pummeling in the lobby. I don't think he'll be hanging around here anymore."

A waiter brings me another cognac. I give it to Michael and it's gone in one gulp.

"So. I think tonight was my farewell performance," he says. "I intended to stick out the week, but I'm too tired. Plus the Steven Seagal act tonight would be a tough one to follow."

We're quiet for a few minutes. Beneath the loosened collar of his shirt I notice the outline of a lesion.

"It's not fair, Michael."

"What do you mean it's not fair? That I'm sick? Or are you talking about Reginald? He's sick too, you know. None of it's fair. But I'm lucky, honey. I have a family who loves me. I have an entire collection of Bette Davis movies. I have friends and music and flowers, and chiffon butterflies on my bedroom ceiling. I have a place to go. Not to worry."

As we say good-b ye I touch the sharp contours of his smooth face. He's still a boy, really. He puts me in a taxi and balances on the curb as the cab pulls away, a brave young man in a black leather jacket, leaning into the cruel winter wind.

I know that I'll never see him again.

There's a Small Hotel

There are hotel lobbies and then there are hotel lobbies. As the Marriott Marquis, the huge hotel overlooking Times Square, is being erected, I have a premonition that I'll play there. I've been reading articles about the construction of the hotel and the marvelous atrium lobby that will be its dominant feature, and I'm sure they will place a piano right smack in the middle of it all.

For the last year I've been doing my Heidi on Seventh stint in the all-white decor of the Omni, playing substitute gigs in the lobby of the Grand Hyatt, and doing acting jobs whenever I get them. Each day, as my taxi traverses the streets of Midtown, I gaze up at the growing tower on Broadway and Forty-fifth and wonder just how long it will be before Harlan calls to book me there. It isn't that I love the building or that I've got a thing for the Marriott Corporation. I don't want to work there, really. But I know that I will.

I get the call on an afternoon in late August, 1985. I'm in Haiti for the week, trying to escape the heat of New York City. It is so sweltering and loathsome in Manhattan this year that even a third-world country close to the equator is an improvement. When Harlan phones, I'm reclining next to the pool, reading *Life Is Elsewhere*, and drinking dark rum with lime juice.

"I'm holding the audition in two days," he says. "It's a great job. They're going to need at least four pianists—two five-hour shifts seven days a week."

"Harlan," I say as I light a cigarette. "I can't make it back for the audition. I've been, uh, waylaid." He laughs. I've had too much rum this afternoon. "Do I have to audition? I mean, can't you just give the guys in the suits a picture or something and talk them into hiring me? Come on, Harlan, you're the agent! You can do it. Tell them—what?—that I'm down here playing for generals and dictators and that I can't get out of my contract until exactly one day before the gig starts, or Baby Doc's thugs will shoot me. I don't care, tell them anything, but please don't make me fly back early."

"Okay, I'll see what I can do. But I can't promise anything. I've got about thirty piano players showing up for this audition."

"That's an even better reason to stay away," I say. "The suits won't even know who is who." I hate piano auditions. A bunch of hyper piano players trying to vibe each other isn't my idea of a good time. In real life, most pianists are friendly people who respect each other and the art and craft of making music. But put us all in a room together, competing for the same job, and the audition monster rears its two-faced head, transmuting us into show-biz lunatics prancing around behind the piano like four-year-olds trying to get our parents' attention.

"Look at me I'm the bebop guy!"

…My analyst told me that I was right out of my head…

"Look at me I can play Gershwin!"

…than any Russian play could guarantee…

"Look at me I can sing Janis Joplin songs plus songs people want to hear!"

…Isn't it rich?…

"Look at me I was a former Miss Texas and now I can play three chords!"

…Almost heaven, West Virginia…

"Listen to this I can sing in Latvian and Portuguese!"

…Olha que coisa mais linda, mais cheia de graça…

"I'm a Juilliard graduate—really a concert pianist—but I need a job!"

...*Hallelujah, Hallelujah, Hallelujah, Hallelujah, Hal-le-lu-jah!!!!*

"Check this out I only know obscure songs you've never heard!"

...*The carpet needs a haircut, the waitress is on fire...*

"Vatch dis, I come from old country and I zing zongs of new country!"

...*Zummertime, und ze livink iz eazy...*

"I'm too cool to smile!"

...*Smoking, drinking, never thinking...*

"I'm a starving artist and I need a break!"

...*Gone, love is never gone...*

"Pay attention now!"

...*When we're out together dancing cheek to cheek...*

"Here comes the big finish!"

...*It's up to you New York, New York!*

༄

I don't feel like subjecting myself to another piano audition. It's humiliating. The same thing happens every time. The other pianists play better but I get the job because I'm polite and wearing a nice dress. It makes me feel guilty.

"So, can you do it?" I ask Harlan.

"Okay," he says. "I'll let you know what happens."

I add a new rule to my list of piano player dos and don'ts: Never ever audition for a piano job. Say you're busy working, even if you're floating around a pool on a raft with a drink holder on each side.

Harlan calls back three days later. I'm sitting in the same lounge chair. This Barbancourt Rum is like a hallucinogenic drug.

"So," he says. "You've got the gig."

"I figured as much."

"You wanna do three days a week, or four?"

"Give me five."

And that is that.

The Marriott Marquis hovers over Times Square like a giant spaceship, but when I enter the ground-floor level there isn't much to see. Oh, there is the standard marble floor (where do the hotels in New York City get all that marble, anyway?), and there are little men in fancy uniforms with fringe on the shoulders. They hold open the doors and say *welcome to the Marriott Marquis have a nice day* with thick outer-borough accents. But the lobby? Nowhere to be seen. The clever designers have placed the lobby on the eighth floor, a practical scheme for keeping the street people out of the lounge area—a feature that does not go unappreciated by me. After my episode with Reginald, I'm relieved to have the piano far away from the street.

In order to access the lobby, you must pass the scrutiny of the Highly Trained Security Team situated on the ground floor. Well, that's good. The Highly Trained Security Team looks very official with their bordeaux jackets, secret-service-type earpieces, and multiple television monitors. Once you're past the Highly Trained Security Team, you have to wait forever for an elevator. Or you can ride the escalator, winding and climbing up through the bowels of the hotel, past the Broadway theater and floors of ballrooms, convention halls, and administrative areas, until you arrive—*plop*—in lobby-land. And what a lobby it is—a spectacular expanse of metal and leather and empty space that soars so high it makes you dizzy to look up.

The Marquis boasts five restaurants and two lounges. Two of these outlets are revolving. If you live in New York, what you want, at the end of the day, is to sit still—I enjoy a good sunset as much as the next guy, just not when I'm spinning around. But I've underestimated the appeal of the *ever-changing panoramic view*, especially to tourists. Harlan has promised me that I will not be playing in the revolving Broadway Lounge on the eighth floor, or in The View restaurant on the top floor. He knows I have a problem with motion sickness and has assured me that I will be sitting perfectly still at the piano in the Atrium Lounge, on the lobby level.

The piano, a Yamaha conservatory grand, stands off to the side of the atrium, surrounded by ficus trees and huge beds of white flowers that are already starting to turn brown around the edges. I introduce myself to the waitresses, most of whom are miserable because of the unfortunate uniforms they've been forced to wear—full-length black skirts slit up to the hoo-ha, white polyester sleeveless tops cut down to you know where, black belts and gloves trimmed with rhinestones, and, as if that isn't enough, a little black hat that looks like something you'd see on an organ grinder's monkey. I've read somewhere that the Marriotts are practicing Mormons, but after I see these outfits, I begin to wonder. Marie Osmond wouldn't be caught dead dressed like this.

The ceiling of the atrium stretches up to the sky, fifty floors above the lounge. The glass elevators zoom up and down, and the passengers' faces press up against the windows as they streak, Jetson-like, through the atrium. The Marriott surprises visitors not with its design—which isn't unique—but with the audacity of its location, right in the middle of Times Square. Looking at the absurd amount of open space, it's easy to forget this is a Manhattan hotel. In spite of the Marquis Broadway theater downstairs, the catchy New York names on the menus, and the droves of unemployed actors working as waiters and waitresses, I feel like I'm somewhere else, in another city's fantasy of New York. The gentrification of Times Square is in the early planning stages, and the Marriotts are foot soldiers in the battle to turn the area into a family entertainment mecca. Sitting there at the Yamaha, I'm on the front line.

༄

Dozens of giant ficus trees—rumored to have cost tens of thousands of dollars apiece—form a green umbrella over the Atrium Lounge. New York isn't a ficus tree kind of place. The trees agree: two weeks after we open, they begin shedding leaves. Autumn in New York. The falling leaves drift by my piano and they aren't red and gold. They're brown and dusty and they land in the piano and crunch when they bounce on the strings. It's quite a predicament—a spanking-new hotel lobby that looks like it needs a good raking. Management appoints housekeeping workers to stay on top of the crisis, twenty-four hours a day.

"Shitty leaves," mutters Carolyne as she coasts by the piano. Carolyne wears the standard Marriott housekeeping uniform—a variation on the French maid theme—and big white fluffy slippers. I don't know if the slippers are a fashion accessory or a medical necessity, but either way, she has a nice gliding motion on the marble floor. She looks like she's skating. She carries a giant broom and dustpan. What she needs is a leaf blower.

"This is the thirteenth time I've been around this lobby in the last hour," says Carolyn as she coasts by the piano with a nifty little crossover step. "Shit. Whose idea was it to buy these shitty trees?" She stuffs the last of the leaves into her trash bag. Then she looks over her shoulder as more dead leaves begin to fall. "Shitty leaves. They oughta just chop down the shitty trees." And off she skates, broom in hand. This goes on for weeks until the trees are completely bald. The hotel hires a new firm to replace the old branches with artificial ones. Another ficus crisis averted.

The sound of the music in the Marriott is marvelous. With all that empty space above me, I can play and play, full-out, no holding back, no managers giving me the international sign for *keep it down*. What a joy! In the lounge itself, listeners sit close to the piano. People who want to talk with friends or review quarterly sales reports sit far away. It's an immense area with deep leather chairs and sofas.

Hotel guests report that they can hear the piano, clear as a bell, all the way up on the top floors. The balconies around each floor open onto the atrium; reasonably high railings planted with philodendron prevent people from falling over. Occasionally guests lean out stories above me, and I can see their little heads silhouetted against the midday light that pours through the windows. They wave or sing from high above. Some of them, teenagers probably, throw ice cubes or paper airplanes.

One weekday afternoon when I arrive for work, one side of the lobby has been cordoned off and covered with black drapes. Several of the waitresses, monkey hats akimbo, cluster in the corner and sob. The manager on duty hustles me to the piano, where I'm instructed to *play so that the guests don't notice the dead body behind the black curtains*. A traumatized waitress tells me that some poor soul has thrown himself from one of the sky-high balconies into the pit of shedding ficus. Thank God I wasn't playing at the time of the jump. Playing after the incident is bad enough. I look around at the people reading newspapers, chatting with each other, and sipping cappuccinos. Do they know what has happened? Do they care?

What do I play in a situation like this? Nothing is appropriate. Choking priests, heart attacks, fistfights, suicides—all lounge musicians, sooner or later, will be expected to play the sound-track for some kind of disaster. Look at those poor guys playing in the Titanic band. Better to have tunes ready that no one knows. At least then the customers won't sing along.

꒰

The piano is close to the entrance to the restrooms, so I find myself inadvertently conducting a study of post-restroom etiquette. Here's a fact: One out of two men exiting the men's room checks his fly after he is out in public. You can do your own research on this. It's astounding. You'd think these guys would check before leaving the toilet area, but no. From my piano perch I observe several fly-checking methods, my favorite being the discreet Little Finger Under the Belt Buckle maneuver. But some gentlemen just spread their legs, look down at themselves, and tug away.

The women have their own set of problems. Often, right in the middle of my set, some poor gal will saunter out of the ladies' room with her skirt tucked into her pantyhose. Or worse yet, dragging a piece of toilet paper on her shoe. These things concern me. Once I watch, helpless, as a woman in her seventies gets into the glass elevator and exposes half of her rear end to 200 Volkswagen salesmen drinking beer in the lobby. I play "Cheek to Cheek" and try not to stare.

One of the Marriott's most unusual features (for stylish peo-ple "in the know") is a fashion boutique operating inside a restroom on one of the lower floors. Maria, a housekeeper in charge of cleaning the public toilets, has set up shop in the toilet stall for disabled people. Shopping at Stall for the Handicapped is one of my favorite break-time activities. Maria, whose clothing comes from unknown uptown sources, hangs her high-ticket items from the metal rails inside the cubicle. I hustle into the restroom on my twenty-minute breaks, try on a bunch of clothes, and end up with designer dresses at rock-bottom prices. Maria never gets into trouble—there's a rumor that many of the female managers are also shopping at Stall for the Handicapped. I'm Maria's in-house model. She sends me out to the piano in an outfit, and a third of the waitresses order the same thing.

"Where'd you get that, Robin? It's fab-u-lous! Bergdorf?"

"No. Stall for the Handicapped."

"Should have known. Maria has the very best things. Think she has it in a medium?"

"Maybe. I saw one just like it in butter-colored silk hanging on the back of the toilet door. Maybe it's a medium."

When a disabled person shows up, Maria clears her racks of silk skirts, cashmere coats, and leather pants from the toilet stall. She works hard to make it look like a routine cleaning job. Sweating, she emerges from the cubicle with enormous trash bags stuffed with designer outfits, smiles at the person in the wheelchair, and says, "There you go, honey, nice and clean, just for you."

Everyone loves Maria. She's my favorite person at the Marriott. During a five-hour shift I have four twenty-minute opportunities to visit her in the ladies' room. It adds up. Often on my breaks I'm obligated to remain in the cocktail lounge and chat with a customer, but whenever I can—*swoosh!*—I disappear to Maria's restroom. I kick off my shoes, sit in a big pink upholstered chair, and do needlepoint while she chatters at me in her delightful New Jersey–Puerto Rican accent. Maria knows exactly what to say; she's a counselor, a giver of strength, and a comedienne, making me laugh with stories about her grown daughters and her bus-driver boyfriend. She's my pocket therapist, my fashion coordinator, and my friend. And she manages all of this while scrubbing toilets and sinks for the nose-in-the-air ladies who barely acknowledge her presence as they throw a quarter into her tip jar.

I see Maria get mad exactly one time. It's a Wednesday afternoon, matinee day, and a group of boisterous Midwestern women sitting next to the piano begin to tell dirty jokes. All four of them are quite heavy, which doesn't stop them from ordering platters of deep-fried mystery tidbits. They've skipped the matinee, having determined that sitting in the lobby and getting sloshed on strawberry margaritas is a lot more fun than seeing Peter O'Toole in *Pygmalion*. They're plastered, roaring with glee, and practically falling out of their chairs. One of them tells a joke about a parrot in a whorehouse. I wonder if their raucous laughter travels up to the thirty-seventh floor the way the piano music does.

"Shit!" screams one of the ladies. "Oh no!!!!"

"What?!" the others cry.

"I just peed my pants."

The ladies howl. To them this is the funniest thing that has ever happened in the history of civilization.

I keep playing. Joy, the waitress, bolts to the piano. "What's going on?" she says.

"Lady at table two just peed her pants," I say. "That's a first."

"What the fuck is wrong with these people?" says Joy. She huffs and stomps away to report the catastrophe to her manager and the three other waitresses who are lurking around the bar waiting for the five o'clock rush. They huddle in the corner, working on a plan to deal with the incident.

In the meantime the ladies, who have already paid their check, get up to leave. There is a puddle the size of Lake Michigan on the chair, and it goes *drip drip drip* onto the marble floor. The guilty party has a huge wet circle on the back of her lavender pantsuit, but she doesn't seem to mind.

I'm playing "All the Things You Are." As the ladies exit one side of the lounge, a handsome older man enters from the other side. He stares at me and smiles, bobbing his head in approval and looking around the deserted lobby to make sure that he is noticed. Well. With all these empty chairs in the lounge—there must be fifty or sixty unoccupied seats—he makes a beeline to the one covered in urine. He's so busy smiling and nodding that he doesn't see, or smell, what he's about to get himself into.

Surely he will realize that he can't sit there.

Surely a waitress or the manager will guide him to another seat.

But the entire staff is involved in their meeting about how to clean the chair. They are unaware of our new guest.

He pauses. Then he begins to sit down.

"NOOOOOOOO!" I scream as I jump up from the piano bench. The poor guy, who is hovering between standing and sitting, nearly has a convulsion as he jerks himself around and does a little Gumby dance to stop himself mid-sit. Joy gets him to another seat. God knows what she tells him.

The next thing I know, poor Maria is being dragged out of the restroom to survey the chair in question.

"It's only number one," says the manager, whose name is Jeff. "She didn't do number two. At least I don't think so. Joy, did she do number two, or just number one?"

"How the hell should I know?" yells Joy.

"One," I shout to Jeff from the piano. "She just did number one." I play "Here's That Rainy Day."

Silence. Maria is warming up for a fight.

Go Maria, go!

"And?" says Maria.

"Well, could you, you know, clean it up?" says Jeff.

"I'm not in charge of cleaning the lounge. I clean the restrooms."

"Yeah, well, I know, but it's, it's, it's…"

"Go ahead and say it, mister. It's piss. And you think that I am in charge of all piss-related cleaning activity. You got that wrong. When someone leaves a glass in the bathroom I don't call no waitress to clean it up. I do it myself. Same thing applies here. The customer peed in your outlet, you deal with it. What do I look like, the fuckin' pee-pee lady? I don't clean up no one's pee-pee unless they do it in my restroom. Got it, mister?" She pokes him in the chest with her yellow-rubber-gloved finger.

I am very proud of Maria.

Jeff, using a broom handle, jostles the chair to the side of the lounge, back behind the service area where no one sits. The next day when I arrive for work, the chair squats in the corridor, still wet, with orange warning tape crisscrossed over the top. Management will probably have it incinerated.

☙

There is more to life at the Marriott than restroom activity. For instance, I'm engaged in a battle to protect the piano. A brand-new Yamaha conservatory grand costs tens of thousands of dollars. It's in everybody's best interest to take good care of it. Isn't it?

One year into the gig, the piano is pushed from one side of the atrium to the exact center of the lobby. Good. Now I won't have to watch the zipper parade marching out of the men's room. Plus the new position will make for a better sound in the atrium—the music will be more balanced. But the relocation has nothing to do with acoustics. A few days after the piano has been moved, I arrive at work to find the Yamaha completely covered with food. It's not a piano any longer. It's a brunch buffet.

I sit down to play as people line up behind me. I'm playing underwater—the piano is closed up tight in order to accommodate the impressive spread of food—and I can't hear myself. There's a giant silver coffee urn on the piano. The guests serve themselves miniature prune danishes, french toast, and eggs benedict—complete with dripping hollandaise sauce—onto giant plates decorated with the Marriott logo. Each of the hot dishes on the piano has a little Sterno flame underneath it, keeping the contents warm. There's no protective covering on the piano. There's no protective covering on me, for that matter. You put a bunch of hungry Evangelical tourists from Macon, Georgia, around a grand piano covered with seven variations on the egg-and-cheese theme, and someone is going to get hurt.

I play my first set, feeling like a short-order cook.

"Hank, do you want the crepe with cheddar or mozzarella? Hon, could you play that song about the cats?"

"Mozzarella. No cheddar. I hate cheddar."

Memory, all alone in the moonlight…

"No, I mean the song about the cats."

"That is the song about the cats."

"No, the other one."

I smile. I nod. Then I improvise a weird melody, one that I am temporarily calling I HATE CATS.

"That's the one. Did you say cheddar or mozzarella, Hank?"

By then, Hank is on to the blueberry pancakes. I look behind me. There are twenty people lined up, balancing their super-sized plates and checking their watches. They're going to have to eat real fast if they want to make the matinee performance of *Phantom of the Opera*.

"Coming through, coming through!" says Patrick the bus-boy. He carries a huge pan of fried potatoes. The crowd parts, and directly over my shoulder he dumps the tray of sizzling potatoes into the big warming dish on top of the piano.

"Hank, come back! They got potatoes!"

I take a break, escape to the bathroom, and weep. My lovely Manhattan atrium piano job has been ruined. I might as well be working the breakfast shift at the Neptune Diner in Astoria, Queens.

ॐ

I fight the brunch-buffet battle with great gusto, and little success. It takes me several months, but I persuade the Food and Beverage Manager—a large man who looks like a pigeon and thinks that music is something that interferes with food—to close the piano brunch-buffet before I arrive each day to start my shift. I convince him that he needs to buy a protective covering for the Yamaha, unless he is willing to spend a small fortune on a new piano. We go back and forth on this issue. See, he wants the customers to know they're getting their food from the top of a grand piano. He thinks this is a clever idea. The only covering he agrees to is clear Plexiglas, cut precisely to the shape of the instrument. Fine. Well, not fine, but it's better than nothing. The cover, which is completely rigid and extremely cumbersome, must be carted in and out of the storage room each day. Poor Patrick is in charge of this unnerving task. Because the cover is clear, it's almost invisible. He must negotiate his way through the crowded hotel lobby with a seven-by-five-foot piece of see-through Plexiglas. Patrick's chore gets more complicated when there's a midget in the lobby, because he has a midget phobia. Patrick refuses to turn his back if there's a midget in the vicinity. Walking backwards with that giant Plexiglas cover is very tricky. I watch from the piano as guests take cover behind the fake ficus.

"Listen," I say to Pigeon Man. "Here's a novel idea. Instead of using the piano for all that food, how about a table?"

Never offer common sense to a Food and Beverage Director, says Voice of Doom. *He'll spit at you. And then he'll want revenge.*

Just Beyond the Garden Wall

*T*he dictator of Haiti, Baby Doc Duvalier, is invited to hear me play at the El Rancho Hotel in Petionville. He declines the invitation—the streets of the nation's capital are overflowing with determined rebels gearing up for a revolution—but he sends several other palace officials and thugs in his place. I see them at the bar, wearing dark glasses and gold chains that sparkle on the black skin of their muscular necks. They stuff themselves into the cushioned rattan chairs, smoke French cigarettes, and bark orders at the nervous hotel workers. Although Owner-man has a good relationship with the government, the very idea of Baby Doc terrifies me. I've heard stories and read reports of the way his henchmen have tortured and murdered thousands of innocent people because they posed minor threats to his regime. The USA tolerates and subsidizes Baby Doc's corrupt government because of Haiti's proximity to Cuba. Duvalier wants his people to stay poor and illiterate, so little of the American money designated for humanitarian aid or education ever reaches the poor Haitian families I meet. Duvalier pockets the funds, and the American government pretends not to notice.

In 1985 I play the cocktail hour for a New Year's Eve party at the hotel. It's a stunning event, with 300 wealthy and influential

Haitian guests seated poolside under a star-studded charcoal sky. A popular Haitian band performs, and there's a fashion show featuring expensive clothing from exclusive Petionville boutiques. There's a seven-course meal and dancing on the wooden platforms constructed over the swimming pools. Dozens of hotel workers serve the party-goers endless bottles of French champagne. I sit on a balcony with Owner-man and watch the fireworks light up the sky over Port-au-Prince.

The next day I travel to the end of the hotel driveway to witness a Haitian New Year's Day ritual. Every year, on the first of January, Duvalier and his slobbering team of privileged military officers drive through the streets of Port-au-Prince and Petionville hurling big wads of cash from the windows of their luxury automobiles.

Owner-man warns me not to go to this event—he says it's too risky—but I decide to go anyway. Jean Louis—the hotel driver, security guard, and massage therapist—insists on coming with me, whether to protect me or to grab a few *gourdes*—the local currency—for himself, I'm not sure. There are thousands of people lining the main street where the procession is to take place. I spot some of the hotel workers with their children, and they wave at me.

Jean Louis instructs me to hide behind a garden wall.

"You can see from here, Madame Robin, and if there is any shooting you will not be harmed." There are five-year-olds and elderly people out in the street. I feel coddled and white and embarrassed that I have to hide behind a wall.

"Why should there be shooting?" I ask. "Isn't this a happy celebration?"

"*Oui*, but people are angry. They want Baby Doc out. But still they come for money."

Suddenly a large Mercedes jeep with a flashing blue light speeds past the crowd.

"Now it begins," says Jean Louis. I hear machine-gun fire from the distance. The crowd grows silent, and they crane their necks to see the entourage of black Mercedes jeeps that approach our part of the street.

"Stay back. And be careful," says Jean Louis as he races to join the other Haitians. Music blares from speakers on top of the cars. A rainstorm of *gourdes* pours out of the sunroof of each jeep. The occupants of the cars hide behind tinted glass. The crowd screams and cheers and there is much gunfire, most of it going into the air. Frightened, I hold my position behind the wall. Children and their parents scramble onto the street—grabbing and clutching at the *gourdes*, narrowly escaping the heavy tires as the jeeps speed by. I count almost thirty of them and shudder when I realize that Baby Doc himself is in one of the vehicles—covered with gold jewelry and fat from years of gourmet meals—throwing money with one hand and shooting a machine gun with the other.

It's over in less than a minute. I see a small boy lying on the side of the street. Oh, God. He hasn't been run over by a jeep, but trampled by people—his own neighbors or family, perhaps—scrambling for the money. I watch as he picks himself up and is attended to by three older boys, each clutching small wads of bills in their bony fists. Hidden by the garden wall, I brush the dust from my face and walk back to the hotel so I can play piano for the well-dressed guests arriving for a New Year's Day lunch.

Prisoner of Love

(Always a Bridesmaid, Never an Inmate)

Some women are magnets for disaster. In the course of one year my friend Liz Chipnik is wounded by a sniper hanging off the roof of her apartment building, kidnapped at gunpoint by masked men while coming out of a Midtown nightclub, beaten up by the police in a case of mistaken identity, and robbed three times. She's had an astonishing streak of bad luck, and that's not even counting the car accident and the grease fire in her kitchen.

I can't explain my friendship with Liz. We don't have much in common. She's a dancer, I'm a musician. Before her run of bad luck started, we lived together for one year on the road while we were doing a Brockett show. We shared take-out fast food and traded stage-makeup tricks when we weren't bickering about which guy in the cast was most likely to be straight.

Liz is very pretty in a hard-ass sort of way, with curly strawberry-blond hair and a tight little body in perfect shape from years of performing. She has a butt that looks like two tennis balls. She's a great tap dancer, with a perky smile and a snappy attitude. But she has got the world's largest black cloud hanging over her sweet little head. The cloud gets larger and more ominous every hour. I know this, because she phones me twice a day to complain.

Liz seems to enjoy a lot of drama in her life. There's a major upheaval when a bisexual janitor named Tony tells Liz that it just isn't working out and much trauma when her next boyfriend—a doctor she had met during a hospital stay—dumps her. But then she starts dating a new guy named Jimmy Chang, and life, for me anyway, becomes very calm.

Now she only calls me when Jimmy gives her a new toy and she wants to brag about it. On Valentine's Day he gives a her a gold necklace with her name spelled out in diamonds. Even her last name. Elizabeth Mary Katherine Chipnik, it says. That's a lot of diamonds. Liz is very secretive about what Jimmy does for a living. I just assume he is an importer of Chinese art or something. Or something, is right.

One sunny Memorial Day, my half-boyfriend Thomas and I are invited to a picnic at Jimmy's Jamaica Estates house, or mansion, as Liz likes to call it. Jamaica Estates is an Emerald City of huge fancy homes located incongruously in the middle of Queens. Wow. This Jimmy Chang is very rich indeed, and I'm impressed. The sprawling Tudor-style house is stunning. We approach the back garden entrance and hear a growl coming from behind an iron gate. Before we have a chance to retreat, an enormous rottweiler leaps over the gate and tackles Thomas, who has a platter of mozzarella and tomato salad balanced in his arms. The dog is wearing a muzzle. But still. What disarray: Thomas in his white linen jacket, covered with tomato goop, scrambling around on the ground trying to get away from the snarling dog. Jimmy races out of the house. He sees the tomato goop and thinks Thomas is bleeding.

"Liz, get my gun; I'm gonna shoot this fuckin' dog," he says.

What a way to start a party.

We get the mess straightened out, and Jimmy takes Thomas upstairs to change his clothes. After putting Rover back on his chain, Liz escorts me to the garden where seven men wearing black suits and sunglasses stand around a grill staring at big pieces of sizzling meat.

"Hey guys!" says Liz. "I want you to meet my friend Robin. She's a piano player at the Marriott in Midtown! This is Armando,

Enrico, Big Sammy, Lucky Lenny, Hank the driver, Charlie the Tuna, and Mo." I shake hands with each of them and say *pleasure to meet you* and *how do you do* while they grunt at me. I'm wearing a big white wide-brimmed straw hat.

"You all can chat while I go and mix up a batch of Mai Tais," says Liz.

"Well that's something unique," I say. "I've never had a Mai Tai outside of Trader Vic's. I'd make them myself at home but I'm always running out of gardenias. Ha, ha, ha, ha."

They stare at me.

"So. Charlie the Tuna," I say. "That's an interesting name! How did you get it? Are you the one who never gets caught?"

Silence.

This is like trying to hold a conversation with the Martin Scorcese version of the seven dwarfs. I feel silly, so I remove my hat. There, that helps.

"You know, there is nothing I like more than a nice tuna steak," I say. "Have you ever had grilled tuna? It's really quite delicious."

No reply.

"So. How do you know Jimmy and Liz?"

They glare at me.

"Okay!" I say, throwing my hands up in the air with a little too much enthusiasm.

"So."

Anyone up for a chorus of "Kum-Bye-Ya"?

"Do you guys speak English?" I say.

"Yeah, baby, we speak English," says the man named Mo.

I have this really annoying habit of babbling like an idiot in uncomfortable social situations. I've inherited this trait from my mother. For some unidentified reason I believe that it's my duty to fill up every awkward social silence with inane chit-chat. This skill serves me well in the cocktail lounge, but it doesn't encourage sophisticated adult conversation with a committee of hit men hanging around a barbecue. I'm lucky I don't get whacked and thrown on the grill.

Thomas returns from the house and informs me that there is no furniture and there are dead-bolt locks on every interior door.

"Yeah, well, be careful what you say out here," I whisper to him. "That Charlie the Tuna guy is one mean bastard."

"What about Mo?" says Thomas. "He looks nice. I'll talk to him." Thomas thrives on predicaments like this. He doesn't care if no one listens to him, he just rambles on and on about the Albanian Air Force or the mating habits of hornets or the complete works of Vladimir Nabokov. I knock back a Mai Tai.

⌇

Three months after Jimmy has been arrested and sent to Rikers Island without the possibility of bail, he pleads guilty to possession of large quantities of cocaine and heroin. While Jimmy is awaiting his sentencing, Liz arranges a meeting with me at a diner in Hell's Kitchen on the West Side of Manhattan. She lives a few blocks away in a fifth-floor walk-up on Fifty-second and Tenth.

"What do you mean you're marrying him?"

"Keep your voice down, will you? We're being watched," Liz says.

The only one watching us, as far as I can see, is a street person named Carl, who is a feature of this particular diner. Carl likes to walk into the diner, sneak up to your booth, and blow his nose directly onto your table. When you leave in disgust, Carl eats your food.

"Jimmy loves me. I love him. People get married when they're in love."

"Not when one of them is in a maximum-security prison, for God's sake. Liz, look, Jimmy treated you like shit when he was a free man. He's a drug dealer. Even you admit he's guilty. The headline in the *Post* said COKE KING KONKED!"

"Keep it down, would you!" she hisses.

Carl now has one eyebrow raised and is looking in our direction.

"No, he didn't treat me like shit. He bought me those fur coats. And the widescreen TV. Let's not forget about that!"

"Yeah, well, what about the other girlfriends? Guess you won't have to worry about that now, will you?"

"Look, if we get married before he is sentenced and sent upstate, we can have congenital visits."

I choke on my scrambled eggs. "Don't you mean conjugal visits?" Although I like the idea of congenital visits.

"You know what I mean. I mean—don't make fun of me." Her eyes fill with tears.

"Okay, okay. I'm sorry. If this is what you want, I'll support you."

"Thank you," says Liz. "See, we have to do this fast. The sentencing date could be any time in the next two weeks. If we're not married by then we don't qualify for the—what is it?—conjugal visits and I won't get food stamps and state support if I get pregnant."

Oh brother.

"I'd like you to be my maid of honor."

Silence.

"Oh—uh, thank you. I'd be honored. Who is the best man? Charlie the Tuna?"

"No, he got arrested last week."

"Oh," I said. "What about Mo? He's nice."

"No, that won't work. Mo is dead."

"Somebody shot him?"

"No. Natural causes."

"Oh."

"Champ will be Jimmy's best man. You know, Jimmy's brother Champ Chang."

"Oh, that's good. Yeah, Champ."

"I have a really big favor to ask you."

Another one?

"Will you play the piano and sing at the wedding? The theme from *Ice Castles*. You know, it's called 'Through the Eyes of Love.' That Melissa Manchester song."

Oh God.

∽

The day of the wedding I'm in a fashion quandary. I have wardrobe solutions for a large assortment of odd situations, but this one has me in a tizzy. No stripes, that's for sure. I put on a conservative charcoal-gray pantsuit and a light pink blouse. I throw a floral scarf around my shoulders because I'm sure the fashion mavens who write those wardrobe dilemma columns would recommend a *cheerful accessory*. I apply lipstick with a hint of shimmer. There. Perfect.

I have to be at Liz's apartment at six in the morning. I played my piano gig at the Midtown Marriott last night, and I'm tired. When I arrive at Liz's place, the mother of the bride answers the door.

"Hi Mrs. Chipnik," I say. "Well, today's the big day."

"My little girl, all grown up and getting married," she says to me. "I can hardly believe it. Wait till you see her. She looks just beautiful."

Right on cue, Liz steps out of the bathroom.

"Ta-da!" Liz says. "What d'ya think?"

Liz is wearing a full-length beaded gown—aquamarine silk with silver sequins and beads of rhinestones and pearls. The dress is cut very low in both the front and the back, and it has a fishtail train. She paid a ton of money for it, but I think it looks just like a Donny Difonso hot-glue-gun glitter gown from a Brockett production. Liz's hair has been lacquered into a perfect helmet, and she's wearing so much makeup she looks like she has been spackled. All in all, it wouldn't be a bad outfit for representing an Eastern European country in the Miss Universe contest. But for an early morning wedding ceremony at a maximum-security penitentiary, she's a tad overdressed.

"It's perfect!" I say. I've made up my mind to have a good attitude about this. It is, after all, her wedding day.

Liz's mother bursts into tears and says again, "I can't believe my baby is getting married." She doesn't say, *I can't believe my baby is getting married in a prison and will spend the next twenty-five years of her life having sex in a penitentiary trailer somewhere in upstate*

New York. Mrs. Chipnik is ignoring the whole prison feature of her daughter's wedding.

The phone rings. "That must be the limo," says Liz.

"The limo?" I say.

"Yeah. Jimmy used his contacts on the outside to get us a limo." She winks at me. " 'Nothing but the best for my baby,' he told me."

"Listen," I say to Liz's mom. "Are you sure you don't want to go in my place? I mean, you could be the maid of honor. Why not?" Liz gives me a killer stare.

"And just who then would play the piano?" she asks. "I'm only allowed to take one person, and you're it! You're the maid of fucking honor and you're goin'. Oh please, Robin, don't let me down when I need you most."

"You girls just go ahead and have fun." says Mrs. Chipnik. "I'll see you at the reception."

"The reception?" I say.

"I'll tell you later," says Liz. She throws her full-length silver fox coat over her shoulders and pushes me out the door into the hallway. The paint is peeling out here and it smells like urine.

We stomp down five flights of steps with me holding Liz's train. Parked at the entrance to the Hell's Kitchen apartment building is an extra-long white limousine—the kind you normally see on music videos about gangsta rappers. I look up to make sure there aren't any snipers on Liz's roof, then I get Liz and her gown situated in one of the white leather seats and pour myself a straight vodka from the limousine bar.

We stop to pick up Jimmy's brother Champ. Champ Chang is a handsome guy. He's wearing a very nice dark suit. He presents Liz with a big bouquet of red roses.

"Here," he says. "These are from my brother." I find this touching, but I'm worried that there could be a nail file or a razor blade hidden in the baby's breath. I have another drink.

"We're here already?" I say as we arrive at the security station for the bridge that leads to Rikers. Our car doesn't have pre-approved security clearance, so we're not permitted to drive across the bridge. The only choice is to get out of the car and wait for the prison bus. It's an overly invigorating twenty-five degrees outside, and windy. I'm glad I'm wearing pants, but sorry I don't have Liz's big fur coat to keep me warm. Liz frets about her hair. I worry about her makeup, which is starting to crack around the edges of her face. Champ takes off his coat and puts it gently over her head, covering her ears.

"Don't do that! You'll fuck up my hair!" she yells.

The bus arrives. It's packed with women and children going to visit their incarcerated husbands, fathers, brothers, and sons. All of them are black. Liz climbs onto the bus with me holding her train and Champ carrying her flowers and purse.

"Look, Mommy! Vanna White!" says one little girl to her worn-out mom. The mom just stares straight ahead.

I read all about Rikers Island at the library last week. I wanted to know what I was getting myself into. Rikers is located on a former garbage dump across the river from Manhattan, next door to LaGuardia Airport. It isn't just one jail, but a complex of ten separate jails housing over 15,000 inmates and accommodating schools, ball fields, medical clinics, a bakery, a beauty salon, a barbershop, a bus depot, and several chapels. The Rock, as it's called by inmates and staff alike, is a clearinghouse for federal and state penitentiaries elsewhere in New York State. On average, an inmate stays at Rikers for about two months before being moved to another prison or set free. About 100,000 inmates pass through the high-security gates of The Rock each year. I don't have any Rikers statistics for bridesmaids or wedding pianists.

ॐ

We arrive at Jimmy's prison. Liz—in her fur coat and evening gown—clutches her bouquet of roses. We register at the security desk with a nasty-looking woman who tries her best to be compassionate. She informs us that the wait will be several hours. The priest on duty this morning has been delayed, she tells us. But we're not given a reason for the delay.

Telling jokes and stories, we sit in the orange molded-plastic chairs in the waiting room. Champ's English isn't great, but he keeps up, laughing and pretending to understand what we're saying. I try, really I do, to keep the mood upbeat and airy, but there's no escaping the fact that we're sitting in a prison waiting room with a bride who is dressed for a wedding at the Golden Nugget. Liz goes to the restroom every thirty minutes or so to check her hair and reapply her lipstick, which means that I have to follow her so I can hold her train. Some of the little kids in the waiting area make a game of counting the pearls on her dress, and their exuberance makes me sad. They don't see anything strange about sitting in a prison waiting room. Many of the kids know the guards by name, and they're all experts on the vending machine in the corner, begging for quarters from their moms when lunch time rolls around. I get in line with them at the machine—so far today I've had a cup of coffee and two shots of vodka, and I'm dragging. Liz and I sit in our plastic chairs and share a bag of chips while Champ goes to check on the delay. Miss Nasty at the desk isn't any help at all.

"You just gotta wait," she says.

As two hours turn into four turn into six, the surreal atmosphere begins to get to me. Liz paces. I follow her—carrying the train—but I can't stand this a second longer. I march over to Miss Nasty and yell through a little speaker area built into the bulletproof glass.

"Look," I say. "We've been here six hours waiting for the priest to show up so he can perform this wedding ceremony for my friend over there. The one in the green, uh, evening gown. Could you please tell me what the delay is? The bride is getting depressed."

"Oh, is she now?"

"Well, yeah. I mean the whole thing is depressing if you ask me, and I tried, I really did, to talk her out of it, but…"

"And who are you, exactly?"

"Well, I'm the maid of honor. And I'm also the piano player."

"The piano player?" Miss Nasty finds this very amusing. She chuckles for a good ten seconds. "Hold on, honey. I'll see what I can track down."

Thank you very much. I lean against the glass wall while she makes a series of phone calls, each time mentioning that the "piano player" for the Chipnik-Chang nuptials wants to know what is taking so long.

"Well, honey," Miss Nasty says to me. "You just have to tell that bride to come back next week on Wednesday. The priest is at a burial."

I'm defeated. I slink back to the orange chairs and break the news to Liz.

"WHAT?!!!" she screams. She jumps to her feet and begins to howl. Yowl. Wail. Bray. She's hysterical. The sobbing causes a thread on her dress to break, and pearl and rhinestone beads pop off the silk and skid across the floor.

Ping, ping, ping, ping!

Hundreds of them.

Kids chase the beads and Liz chases the kids. She falls to her hands and knees, attempting to grab the beads before the kids can get to them. She hollers at the children. I chase her around the room, holding her train, a useless task at this point because she's throwing a big fit and nothing I can do or say will get her to stop. Champ follows the two of us. He thrusts the flowers at Liz—like that will make her feel better—and she flings them across the room. She collects all the beads, dropping them one by one into a brown paper sandwich bag that one of the mothers has given her. I drag her into the restroom so we can wash her face, which is streaked with rivers of mascara and lipstick.

"Look at you!" I say. "Is this what you want to look like on your wedding day?"

"B-b-but it's not my wedding day. We'll have to come b-b-back next week."

Oh my God. I'll have to do this again next week?

"Oh no we won't," I say. "You stay here and wash your face."

I slam through the restroom door and almost knock Champ to the floor. How does a guy who weighs 115 pounds get a name like Champ? Champ has been hovering outside the ladies' room waiting to see if everything is okay. He has retrieved the roses.

"Wha?" he says. Champ never says what with a "t."

"Here's wha," I say. "We're getting this friggin' wedding over with today if I have to perform the ceremony myself. Does it have to be a Catholic priest? Or will any old guy in a black robe do the trick?"

"No matter," says Champ.

"Good. No matter. Now go buy Liz a Snickers bar. I'm gonna go straighten this out."

&

"Okay, here's the deal," I say to Miss Nasty. "We'll take anyone you've got to perform this ceremony. Priest, minister, judge— there have got to be a couple of judges lurking around here somewhere—we'll take anyone who can legally marry my friend here. Maybe you can do it. Look," I whisper into the speaker box. "I'm desperate. I can't go through this again next week. She's nuts."

"I noticed," says Miss Nasty. I glance back at Liz. She slumps in her chair while Champ massages her shoulders. "Okay, I'll see who I can find. But you'll have to wait."

So we wait some more. I have a headache as big as the Bronx and I'm starving. Champ spent his last quarters on the candy for Liz. I try to get one of the officers to change a twenty-dollar bill for me, but he can't, or won't. One of the moms sitting there takes pity on us and gives us a bag of pretzels.

"It's always like this," she says. "You have to come prepared to spend the day."

Finally, they call our names.

We pass through several security stations and leave all of our belongings with one of the guards. The flowers don't make it past the first checkpoint. I worry this might trigger another

Chipnik fit, but Liz holds it together. My heart pounds as we're escorted beyond the metal detectors and into the actual prison.

Boom! The big steel door closes behind me, just like in the movies.

I expect to see—what?—a cellblock and a chain gang of men wearing striped uniforms and little hats. But it's so sterile here. We're in a large foyer that could be in a school or a hospital or any other normal place. Jimmy Chang, the groom, is escorted through the door by five guards. One of them is an enormous woman with flared nostrils and blue eye shadow. Jimmy wears a black Armani suit that Champ had delivered to the prison. I'm shocked—there are no handcuffs, no leg shackles, no nuthin'. Jimmy winks at Liz and struts toward us. His arrogance is obnoxious. The chaplain, or judge, or whatever he is, asks for a few minutes alone with the bride and groom. Champ and I scoot to one side. The guards are less discreet.

"So," says the chaplain, turning back to Champ and me. "I'm assuming you two are the witnesses."

We introduce ourselves as we walk down a long hallway to the chapel. The chaplain explains the ceremony. Liz stays with Jimmy and the guards.

"I'm the pianist for the ceremony," I say. "When should I play the music requested by the bride?"

"You're the *pianist?* Hey Horatio, did you hear that?" he yells to one of the guards up ahead. "The bride brought a pianist."

"Excuse me," I say. "Why does everyone think this is so funny? You know I'm just trying to help out here and make the best of a bad situation and I know it's not a real wedding in the traditional sense but she's my friend and I want to make it nice and…"

The guard unlocks the door to the chapel. It's a large auditorium.

"There's no fuckin' piano," says Liz, like it's my fault. "Now what? You'll have to sing the song without music."

A cappella? I'm horrified by the thought.

They all stare at me.

"Fine," I say. "Let's get this show on the road."

You're really in deep shit now, says Voice of Doom. *You're quoting your mother.*

So here we stand: the convict, the bride, the chaplain, the maid of honor, the best man, and five Corrections officers. I'm about to faint from hunger. When it's time for my song, I recite the lyrics to "Through the Eyes of Love" as poetry. There are certain lines I won't cross, and singing a Melissa Manchester song a cappella in a maximum-security prison is one of them.

After the ceremony, the guards, Champ, and I retreat to the back of the auditorium so that Mr. and Mrs. Chang can have some time alone in the front row. We sit in a line and watch them while they do Lord knows what up there. I make small talk with the female officer—but all I can think about is food.

"So," I say. "How is the meal service here at Rikers?" From the size of her I figure she might enjoy talking about food. "Do you, for instance, have a special meal for the inmates on Thanksgiving?"

"Oh yeah," she says. She's got a raspy voice, like she has been smoking two packs of Camels a day for the last twenty years. "Turkey and stuffing and mashed potatoes. The works. Even had pumpkin pie this year. With whipped cream."

Silence.

"And what about, say, the vegetarian inmates?"

"Fuck 'em. They all eat meat if they hungry enough." I can't tell if she's serious or not.

Oh God, I just want to get out of here. Hurry up, Liz. I know this is your honeymoon, but ten minutes is long enough.

"We do serve a nice tossed salad and fruit cup, though. Everyone likes that," says the guard. The whole time she talks she has her eyes focused on Liz and Jimmy, who are going at it like a couple of horny teenagers at the drive-in. We can see the tops of their heads bobbing up and down, up and down.

"And I think the lasagna we make is vegetarian. Made with them spinach noodles, you know, the green ones."

I consider bribing the guard to bring me a meal.

Twenty minutes pass. Finally the happy couple finishes doing whatever they're doing, and the entire group rises and files out of the auditorium. Liz kisses Jimmy one last time, and off he goes with the five guards.

Boom! The door slams behind him.

Liz bursts into tears. Again.

"Why, why, why? she cries, banging her head against the wall. "Why do these things always happen to me?"

I want to slap her.

By this time it's six o'clock. I'll never make my seven o'clock start at the Marriott. So I call Bob Dawson, another pianist, from a pay phone in the waiting room.

"Bob," I say. "Can you cover for me tonight? You're not gonna believe where I am."

"Don't tell me you're in Haiti again. You were just there last week."

"No. Worse. I'm on Rikers Island."

"Jesus Christ," he says. "Jesus fuckin' Christ. Did you do something wrong or do you have a gig there?"

"A little of both. I'll explain later. Can you cover for me?"

"Yeah," he says. "If you can cover for me tomorrow. I just booked a last-minute private party at the Iranian Embassy."

"No problem. Don't get taken hostage over there."

"Same to you."

You know, I thought that playing the piano was a safe career choice. But it's not. Not really.

I wish I could say I went home and ate a huge dinner, had a hot bath, and fell asleep in my nice warm bed with Lucky the cat curled up next to me. But I have to attend the wedding reception. As maid of fucking honor, it's my duty.

I've never been to a Chinese wedding reception where the groom isn't present because he's serving a prison sentence, so I'm not sure what to expect. I assume it will be a solemn occasion. Sad. Tragic. Pathetic, even.

Wrong. Wha? Wrong. There are seventy-five people at the Chang house, all of them Chinese except for Liz, her mother, and me. It's one swingin' party. The food is fabulous. I don't understand any of the conversation, but I'm too busy eating to care. When I'm called upon to make a toast, I'm unprepared, but I vamp for a few minutes and then paraphrase a line from an Emily Dickinson poem about tranquil blossoms on tortured stems. I figure the Asians will like the flower imagery.

Liz looks at me like I've got a lettuce leaf on my head and says, "What the fuck is that supposed to mean?"

A five-tier wedding cake with butter-cream frosting and little pink rosebuds is rolled into the middle of the living room, and Liz, all by herself, cuts the first piece. Balancing on top of the cake is a teeny-tiny bride next to a teeny-tiny groom. I look closely to see if anyone has tied teeny-tiny shackles on his teeny-tiny feet.

The wedding is the end of the road for Liz and me. I can't take anymore trauma-drama. Liz is nervous about being gunned down on Tenth Avenue by South American drug lords, and I, frankly, don't want to get caught in the crossfire. I feel guilty for cutting her out of my life, but enough is enough. I wonder what will become of her. Perhaps she really will visit Jimmy once a month, trying to get pregnant in a trailer on the prison grounds of Sing Sing or Attica. Or maybe Liz will scamper away with Jimmy's money and move to Hong Kong, where she'll reside in a luxury high-rise with Champ, lots of television sets, and the Chang extended family. Maybe she'll enter a witness-protection program, move to a small town in Oklahoma, raise twin Chinese daughters, and teach tap lessons to nine-year-olds at a local dance school.

Or maybe she'll decide to be happy. Anything is possible.

Playback 1989

"Hey Bob."

"Hey Robin."

"How'd it go this afternoon?" I ask. Bob is a piano player, and we trade shifts at the Marriott every now and then.

"Okay," he says. "Big hit before the matinee, then deadsville for a few hours. Same as usual. I have to go. My girlfriend is freaking out at my apartment. Last night she slashed one of my paintings with a butcher knife. I'm afraid she'll go after the Steinway next. I locked the box, but you never know."

Bob keeps his Steinway in a Whisper Box—a big soundproof container in the middle of his living room. His neighbors complained about the noise, so now his grand piano lives in a box. The things we put up with to live in this city.

Maybe he should lock his girlfriend in a box. I like Bob. The poor guy has terrible luck with women. I don't get it. He's talented, he's handsome, and he's straight.

"See you tomorrow?" I say.

"Yeah, assuming Carmella hasn't hacked me into little pieces."

Never date someone whose name sounds like an ice-cream flavor.

I sit down at the piano. Then I notice. Uh-oh. All around me are groups of men with models of dentures on their tables. Upper plates, lower plates, and some full sets. They look like those chattering teeth that kids play with on Halloween.

I play "The Way You Look Tonight."

"Hi Robin," says Joy the waitress.

"What's going on here?" I say.

"Dentist convention. Some sort of seminar on implant technology. They've been here drinking all afternoon. One guy bit me in the ass with his denture model. Be careful when you smile. I've already had two guys try to sell me veneers."

I play "Smoke Gets in Your Eyes."

Maria the housekeeper comes to the piano. "Meet me in Stall for the Handicapped on your break," she says. "I got in a new shipment of mink-trimmed sweaters."

The dentist sitting next to me holds an X-ray of a skull up to the light.

"What color is the fur?" I ask.

"Brown, black, beige. I got everything."

It's cold in here. I could use a sweater.

"*STAND BY FOR EVACUATION!*" booms a voice that sounds like God speaking. This is the emergency evacuation system. It malfunctions about once a month. The tourists look alarmed. The New Yorkers order another round.

I play "Will You Still Love Me Tomorrow."

STAND BY FOR EVACUATION!

"My friend wants to ask you if you once played in the Waukegan Holiday Inn," says one of the dentists, who is yelling over the alarm that has started to *whoop, whoop, whoop* in the background.

"You mean Weehawken, New Jersey?" I say.

"No Waukegan. Bernie, what's that state in Waukegan?"

"Waukegan isn't a state, you prick."

"Look," says the dentist. "Bernie's from Chicago, and he swears he saw you at the orthodontia suppliers' trade fair last year. He wants to sing an Elvis tune with you."

STAND BY FOR EVACUATION!

"Here. Take this." He gives me a dollar with his room number on it. Or maybe it's Bernie's room number. Who knows.

I play "Love Me Tender."

Bernie stumbles over to the piano and holds up his dentures. He claps the uppers against the lowers in time to the music, making the teeth sing to me while trying not to move his lips.

Rove me render, rove me rue, rever ret me ro.

The things a girl will do for a dollar.

Jennifer the high-rent hooker walks in. She is wearing a tight blue leather dress and a pair of black stiletto-heeled boots.

The ships on her hips make my heart skip a beat.

Jennifer wiggles into the lounge, takes one look at the crowd, and waggles out the other side. Better try the Hilton, Jennifer. A team of security guards follows her. It gives them something to do. Gee, I like those boots.

I wonder what she charges.

Oh, look, there's Tina Louise, Ginger from *Gilligan's Island*. Man, does she look great! She has the same hair as she did on the show, and she is wearing a fur coat. I'll bet she has on one of those movie-star dresses underneath. She smiles at me. Heads are turning. Bernie puts his teeth down on the piano. He is stunned by her loveliness. Or maybe he is just a big *Gilligan's Island* fan.

The pre-theater crowd arrives. There are no seats because the dentists are clinging to the big leather tub chairs like they are life rafts. They're savoring the last precious moments of their collective implant-conference high.

I play "Yesterday."

Four well-heeled middle-aged women wearing important dresses haul their beaten-down husbands through the lounge. One of the men is looking over his shoulder as Jennifer slithers down the hallway.

"Miss! Miss! Miss!" says one of the ladies. Her hair is dyed an unnatural shade of reddish-purple. Eggplant-ish. "We need a table! We need a table!" But she bellows into the air. Joy is serving drinks to Bernie and his teeth, and the additional waitresses are busy making espresso for the other dentists. The manager is on a break.

"We need a table!" she says to me. "And where is the bathroom?"

I hate it when people treat me like an information desk.

I stop right smack in the middle of the song, stand up, and direct her to the bathroom. I sit down and pick up where I've stopped.

I said something wrong, now I long for yesterday-ay-ay-ay...

Tina Louise has gotten a table. Wouldn't it be nice if the Professor and Maryanne showed up too?

I play "Try to Remember." Bernie has his teeth sing along.

Rollow, rollow, rollow, rollow, rollow...

A dozen men in tuxedos walk across the lobby, followed by two brawny firemen carrying huge axes. I love the axes.

I finish a last chorus of "Try to Remember" and chase after the firemen.

"What's the problem?" I ask. "Is there a fire?"

"Naw," says the bigger of the two. He is very handsome in his big boots and metal helmet. I am sucker for a guy in uniform. "False alarm," he says. "Nice music. I was listening from upstairs. Hey, is that Ginger in the lounge?"

I want to ask him what he's doing later, but I don't. I can't hit on a guy when he is drooling over Ginger, for heaven's sake.

I take the escalator down to Stall for the Handicapped and buy myself a mink-trimmed sweater for ten bucks.

Purple Hibiscus

"What do you mean, you're not flying today?" I say. The Chalk's Airline counter man at the Opa-Locka Airport looks out the window and squints at the bright white sky.

"I have to be there by tonight," I say. "It's crucial."

I'm trying to get a flight to Cat Cay, a private island in the Bahamas. Don Brockett has booked me to play there for two weeks. Don, his wife Leslie, and the other performers are flying into Miami on a private jet from Pittsburgh. There is no airstrip on Cat Cay, so Don and his entourage will be picked up by one of the island yachts and transported over to the island. Because I'm coming from Haiti I'll have to take a commercial seaplane over to Cat. I've never flown on a seaplane before, and I'm a little nervous about it.

"These winds are blowin' way too high for us," says Counterman. "No way we can fly safely in this weather. Can't land a seaplane on water this choppy. Nope."

"Oh, no," I say. "Well then, I'll just have to take a boat or something. Is there a charter service in the area?"

"Yep. But you won't be able to take a boat either. They got the warning flags up. No go, Miss. Not today, anyway. You come back tomorrow. Things'll be calmer then."

"But I have to get there tonight!"

"You got an emergency or something?"

I don't know how to answer this question. Most people would not consider a piano gig an emergency. But Don Brockett expects me to be there on time to play the job.

"Yes," I say. "Yes, it's an emergency. To me it is, anyway."

"Talk to that fat guy over at the phone booth. He's got an emergency on the same island, and he said something about chartering a helicopter. A chopper can fly easier in this weather than a seaplane."

"Thanks!" I say. I look across the room. A morbidly obese man wearing a natty blue blazer and freshly pressed chinos is hanging up the phone. Wow. I had no idea Brooks Brothers made clothing that large.

"Hi," I say. "I'm Robin Meloy. I understand you're trying to get to Cat Cay this afternoon."

"I'm Billy Berg," he says. He gives me the once-over, as if he's being hit on by the local Opa-Locka hooker. We shake hands. He's got fat on his knuckles, and his palms are cold and clammy. Normally I would run the other way, but Billy Berg is my only hope for a flight. I give him my most seductive damsel-in-distress smile.

"Nice to meet you, Mr. Berg," I say. "Some weather, huh? Did you have any luck with the helicopter?"

"The commercial services won't fly," he says. I detect a New York accent. "But I found an emergency rescue helicopter to take me. Why?"

"Do you think I could come along? See, I'm a pianist and I'm supposed to play on Cat Cay tonight for a party hosted by the president of the island association."

Billy Berg's teeny-tiny eyes, surrounded by great mounds of cheek and forehead fat, light up.

"I mean, I'll be glad to pay my share of the flight."

"My dear," says Billy Berg. "It would be a pleasure to have your company. I'm applying for membership on the island, and I'm sure the president will be thrilled to have me deliver his pianist in a helicopter." He claps his chubby hands with delight.

Funny what people will do to get where they want to go.

We walk, or rather we're blown, over to the helicopter terminal, where a pilot wearing a bright-orange suit waits for us. I'm right behind Billy, using him as a windscreen. The helicopter is tiny, with lots of open space where the doors should be. It's a rescue vehicle, equipped to carry stretchers. A worker named Vicki runs out of the terminal, trying to look official. That's an odd thing about Florida. None of the officials looks very official. You can't wear a kelly-green blazer and expect people to take you seriously.

"Uh-oh," she says when she spots Billy Berg. "You're gonna have to weigh in."

I don't know what Billy weighs, but I weigh 120 pounds and the pilot weighs at least 170. She instructs me to sit on the same side as the pilot. Then she piles all the luggage on our side as well.

"Gotta balance this baby or she'll tip right over. Here's your life jacket," she says. "Put it on. Now."

"Now?" I say.

"You never know. Better to be prepared."

Billy Berg and I slide the big yellow life jackets over our heads. I buckle mine around my waist. Billy slips his waist straps into the pockets of his navy blazer. I'm fascinated by his blazer. There's enough lightweight wool gabardine in that one jacket to outfit the entire freshman class at Brown.

"Now look," says Vicki. "In the event of an emergency, uh, water landing, you will unbuckle your seat belt, jump out, *then* pull the cord. Repeat after me, unbuckle, jump out, pull cord."

"Unbuckle, jump out, pull cord," Billy Berg and I squeak. We sound like the Alvin and the Chipmunks.

"Again. Unbuckle, jump out, pull cord."

"Unbuckle, jump out, pull cord."

"Again. Unbuckle, jump out, pull cord."

"Unbuckle, jump out, pull cord."

Alright already.

Vicki makes us practice jumping out of the helicopter, but I think she's really checking to see if Billy Berg can fit through the passenger-side exit.

"I can't swim," says Billy Berg as he heaves his way through the opening. He lands delicately on his Gucci-loafered feet. "Maybe I should call my wife before we leave. If this chopper goes down and I'm found dead, washed up next to a blond piano player, she'll think I was up to no good. Are we anywhere near the Bermuda Triangle?"

"Let's go!" says the pilot. "Wind is pickin' up." Vicki straps us in, and up, up, and away we go—the fat man, the piano player, and the emergency rescue pilot in the orange suit. As soon as we're up in the air, I relax. The flight is smooth and graceful—beautiful, even. Billy Berg white-knuckles the strap hanging down from the roof. He yells at me from the front passenger seat, but with all the helicopter racket, I can't hear a thing.

꒩

Cat Cay is fifty nautical miles from Miami. The island has a spacious marina and hosts some of the largest yachts in the U.S. Registry. Membership on the island is determined by a board of directors that meets six times a year. Once an individual is "selected" for membership, he must pay a $25,000 initiation fee along with a $10,000 annual membership payment. Splendidly appointed rental housing is available only for members and sponsored guests. That's what I am, a sponsored guest. Or maybe I'm hired help. Either way, I'm an outsider.

There are no automobiles permitted on Cat Cay, and most of the guests transport themselves in golf carts. There aren't very many places to go: the Cone Bar for drinks, the Victoria Restaurant for more drinks, and then, if you're feeling like a drink, the Nauticat Restaurant and Lounge, Bu's Bar, or the Haigh House Bar for a nightcap. Most of the members of the Cat Cay Club are WASP-y Republican high-society types, the owners of big homes, big businesses, and big bar tabs.

We've been hired to keep the president's guests entertained for two weeks. I play cocktail piano whenever there's a piano handy—on yachts, in the restaurant, in the bars, at private homes. We're scheduled to perform one big theatrical cabaret show at a sit-down dinner for seventy guests and do a couple of numbers with the Lester Lanin Orchestra out of New York at a big hula-dula dinner dance at the end of the two weeks. For the rest of our stay on the island, we're expected to show up everywhere and be entertaining.

These people are lovely, really they are. Considering we're a ragtag bunch of struggling-artist Democrats with several homosexuals in our ranks, I think we fit in quite nicely. But I can't shake the feeling that we're here as token bohemians—gypsies paid to titillate imaginations without threatening notions of *the way things should be*. Our group doesn't drink nearly as much as they do, but we follow the dress code and show up—with cautious enthusiasm and carefully coordinated resort wear—to every gin-and-tonic pool party, champagne brunch, and Bloody Mary breakfast our hosts offer. We tell amusing anecdotes, conduct sing-alongs, and allow the rich right-wing titans of industry to think they're being given a privileged peek into our flamboyant artistic lives. It's hard work.

To blow off steam, we go out and race around in the golf carts.

Dave and I, tired of driving from bar to bar to pool to bar, go exploring. Dave is Don Brockett's assistant, a handsome young man with a hearty sense of adventure and a great wardrobe. We commandeer a golf cart and drive past Windsor Downs, the pristine golf course; the tennis courts; and the Olympic-sized swimming pool. We come to a long path lined on both sides with purple hibiscus, drive past a couple of sheds that hide the garbage bins from the delicate eyes of the island members, onto a dirt trail, through thick jungle vegetation, and into a clearing.

"Vultures!!! Holy shit, Dave. We need to get out of here, fast. Those birds look like vultures."

"Oh, my God," says Dave. "I thought vultures only lived in Africa. There must be a thousand of them." Actually there are about fifty, but that's still a lot of vultures.

In his hurry to get away from the menacing flock of birds, Dave mistakes the golf cart reverse gear for forward. We lurch up onto a big boulder and hover over the ground, our wheels spinning as the vultures begin to surround the golf cart. We look like Fred and Wilma Flintstone, out for a drive in Death Valley.

"This is excellent, Dave," I say, trying not to panic. "We're going to be pecked to bits by vultures. This is supposed to be a luxury island. We're here for two weeks, and now look at us. Stranded on a rock with giant birds of death threatening to eat our eyeballs. Nice work."

"I didn't do it on purpose. You try driving this thing. It's bad enough that I have to drive on the left. These damn foreigners. Why can't they drive on the right like everyone else?"

"Dave, we're on a path in the woods. Not a four-lane highway. And we're down here with a bunch of Americans, for God's sake."

"Okay. Sor-ry. Maybe we should call for help."

"Are you kidding? We're on the ass end of the island and it's cocktail hour. No one will hear us. I think I'm scheduled to play for dinner tonight. But they'll be so squished by then, they'll never notice I'm missing."

"Here's the way I see it," says Dave as he smooths out the wrinkles in his white linen pants. Dave can be very analytical when necessary. I'm surprised he doesn't take out a notebook and start making lists of pros and cons. "We can sit here and rot and wait for an inebriated CEO to find our bones, or we can get out of the cart, get it down off this boulder, and try to drive it back to Bu's Bar."

"I'm not getting out this cart, Dave." The vultures stare, just waiting for one of us to make a move.

"Think this through, Robin. Vultures don't eat live people, just dead ones. We're still alive. They won't be interested in us. Plus I heard the club is serving grouper for dinner tonight. And key lime pie. And if we don't get back soon, we'll miss it."

That convinces me. I jump down out of the cart.

"Shoo, shoo, shoo!!!" I say. The vultures just stand there like lawn ornaments in a George Romero zombie film.

"Shoo, shoo, shoo!!!" I say again. The birds cock their heads, unimpressed by my flailing arms. Dave shoves the cart off the rock. We zip out of there, race into Bu's Bar, and tell the bleary-eyed crowd about the vultures.

"You never know what you'll run into if you stray too far from the golf course," says the president of the island association. His speech is slurred and he's wearing bright yellow pants with little lizards embroidered on them. He winks at me. "The world can be a dangerous place. How about a little drinky-poo?"

"Ahhh," whispers the Bahamian barman. "I see you meet our island turkeys. Dey live back there. Wild turkeys. Dey could fly away, but dey too dumb."

The golf cart gets us into lots of trouble. Our third night on the island we're scheduled to attend a cocktail party at the president's house. Dave and I drive the cart over to Don and Leslie's beachfront apartment. The cart is designed for six passengers, but we can squeeze seven onboard. Don, wearing a snappy pair of Nantucket-red pants and a sailor-cloth shirt that laces up the front, lumbers out to the cart with Leslie, who is dressed in a batik-print caftan. Barb Russell, David Pressau, and Danny Herman run across the manicured lawn and jump onto the rear-facing back seat. We're ready to go. Dave, once again intending to drive backward, shifts the cart into forward, hits the gas, and knocks Barb, David, and Danny onto the gravel driveway.

"Jesus Christ, Dave," says Don, growling. "You don't know how to drive this thing. This is a car for big babies in diaper-pants—how could you screw it up? Let me drive, for God's sake."

We change places, with Don grumbling and David and Danny brushing away the dirt from their evening clothes.

"I'll be right back," says Barb. "I gotta get a Band-Aid."

"We'll be late for the president's cocktails," says Don.

"Fuck the president, my knee is bleeding," says Barb.

"You know, we finally get a job where they don't make us come in the back door, and we're late," says Don.

"Yeah, well, being treated like a guest is hard work," says Danny. "Can't we just eat sandwiches in the employee cafeteria or something?"

"The employee cafeteria is on Bimini," says Don.

Barb hobbles back to the cart.

"Okay, Don, are you straight on this forward and reverse shit?" she asks.

"Nothing to worry about, Milady. I'm at the helm," says Don. We pull out of the parking bay and drive 200 yards to the president's house.

It's a beautiful home, right on the beach, surrounded by palm trees, exotic bushes, and peachy flowers that complement the dusky Bahamian sky. Our hostess, the First Lady of Cat Cay, stands in front of the garage door awaiting our arrival. She's wearing a lemon-yellow Bill Blass sleeveless evening gown, and she looks stunning.

"Don, Leslie, kids!" she says, doing the queen's wave with one hand and balancing a highball glass with the other. "How delightful that you're here!"

"Okay, kids, everybody wave and smile!" Don whispers. "Leslie, get a picture of the First Lady."

"Hiiiiiiiii!" we all say, in unison as Don pulls up to the garage door.

"Don't park here. Park out by the charger," says the First Lady. "That way you can tank up your cart while you're at the party!"

"No problem," says Don. "Hey, love that dress! Is that a Bill Bla—"

He throws the cart into gear and hits the gas pedal, but instead of reversing, we lunge forward, pinning our hostess to the garage door and throwing David, Danny, and Barb back onto the driveway.

Barb, who is picking gravel out of her knees for the second time in ten minutes, says, "Now might be an excellent time to get that picture of the First Lady, Leslie."

I uncover my eyes, and there is our gracious hostess, stuck between the cart and the garage door. Amazingly, she's not injured, but she's trapped, with the headlights of the car pressing into her Blass-clad thighs. She has a smile frozen on her face and her hand remains in a waving position.

"Maybe somebody should go get the president," says Don. "We need to unpin his wife."

The First Lady, regaining control of the situation, sips her drink. "Don't worry," she says. "This happens *all* the time."

"What drug is she takin'?" says Barb. "I want some."

"Maybe I should just move the golf cart," says Don.

"NOOOO!" we scream in unison. "Get her out of there first."

The president rounds the corner. "Don, Leslie, kids! So nice to see you!!! Hey everybody, the kids are here! Now what's this I hear about you pinning my wife to the garage door? Heh, heh, heh…"

"Hello dear," says the First Lady with a girlish laugh. "Just a little, uh, problem with the gearshift thingy. Perhaps you could get me unstuck so I can serve the cheese ball." A crowd gathers in the driveway.

"Anyone got a Band-Aid?" says Barb. Everyone laughs.

"What I need is a drink," I say.

"No problem!" say three men at once as they run off to fetch a vodka and soda.

The president, Dave, and Danny push the golf cart back and free the First Lady.

"My goodness, that was exciting!" she says as she limps over to the terrace.

"Are you okay?" Leslie asks.

"Oh, I am fine, fine, fine. But I could use another drink."

"What's she drinkin'?" says Barb. "Get me one."

"I'll just park the golf cart," says Don.

Silence.

We all turn around to watch. Barb dives into the bushes.

Don, looking back over his shoulder, shifts the car into forward and drives through the garage door, putting a large hole in the white wooden paneling.

Everyone laughs. They think we've staged the whole thing.

"You kids are just a riot!" says the president.

I meet and greet and go to the living room, take a slug of my vodka, and begin playing the white piano.

ᢒ

Doctor Love and the Bahama Cats, a Bahamian band from Bimini, has been shipped over to play with Dave and me as we welcome weekend guests who are just arriving in their yachts and seaplanes. We do one number together, "All Day All Night Maryanne" in the key of F, with the following lyrics:

> *Welcome, welcome, to Cat Cay!*
> *President's weekend's gonna be,*
> *Time of great frivolity,*
> *Thanks to the Pres and the First Lady.*
> *Golfin', swimmin', fishin' too*
> *Whatever is your whim,*
> *Maybe if the sun's too hot,*
> *You'll take a little swim,*
> *Drink a Cat Cay cocktail or*
> *Whatever is your choice,*
> *It's president's weekend party now,*
> *Come join us with your voice,*
> *Everybody now!*
> *Welcome, welcome to Cat Cay!*

Dave and I have rehearsed this song with Doctor Love and the Bahama Cats. Last night, for two hours, we fiddled with the arrangement and sang it through with the band about fifty times. Now we're in position on our little stage next to the immigration desk. The first plane arrives, and Don gives me the cue to start.

"Okay, guys, let's go!" I say. I count off the tune.

"Hey lady, what we playing?" says Doctor Love.

Doctor Love and the Bahama Cats are stoned out of their minds.

"'Maryanne' in F," I say.

"Who's Maryanne?"

"The song! 'All Day All Night Maryanne!'"

"Oh, yeah, we know dat."

"So could we play it? Now? Please, Doctor Love."

The first pink-and-green-clad ladies are ushered past us. A waiter hands each of them a cocktail and they stand there, in the blazing sun, with expectant smiles on their smooth faces, waiting for us to do something.

I count off again.

You know, says Voice of Doom. *There is nothing worse than snapping your fingers and saying one, two, one, two, three, four, and having a band just stare at you. Look at them! They have NO CLUE what they're supposed to play. What kind of a musical director do you think you are?*

"What kind of intro you want, lady?"

"The one we rehearsed last night would be nice," I say. "Never mind, just play the song. In F."

"Sounds better in G."

"FINE. Just play it."

Doctor Love takes a big swig from his rum-filled Coke can and plays. The Cats play along. Dave and I, dressed in flowered shirts and silly straw hats, do our little song-and-dance routine, and everyone starts to feel the Island Spirit.

"So why do they call you Doctor Love?" I ask as we sit relaxing after our afternoon gig.

"Why you tink?" says Doctor Love.

"Because you're, uh, romantic?" I really sound like a twit sometimes.

"Oh, dat is true," he says. "But I am also de fahder of twenny-two children, each one wid a diff'rent woman."

I manage to resist Doctor Love's charms in spite of his good looks and gleaming, gold-toothed smile. His band performs on Cat Cay several times during the week. Doctor Love and the Cats make a living playing for rich white folks who want a touch of island flavor added to their parties. They're quite good—when they lay off the weed for a couple of hours.

～

We're invited to a big pool party. There are flowers and candles floating in the water, torches on the beach, and huge tables of food that everyone—except for us—pretty much ignores. At the far end of the pool is a large animal roasting on a spit. Dave and Danny and I balance oversized plates on our laps as we perch on the diving board with our feet dangling over the candlelit water.

"Long way from Pittsburgh," says Danny.

"Yeah," I say. "A long way from anywhere."

"Anywhere real," says Dave, licking his fingers.

"I saw one of those pig-on-a-spit things in Pittsburgh one time," says Danny. "At a Tamburitzan festival at the Civic Arena. I think they cook stuff like that in Poland or Yugoslavia or one of those countries."

"I think this one here is a goat."

"Goat, pig, doesn't matter. You cook something on a spit and dump enough sauce on it, it all tastes the same."

"Look at Don and Leslie." They're holding hands and walking down to the beach. Making an escape from the party, no doubt. There is a full moon low in the sky behind them.

We're quiet for a moment.

"I wonder how long it will be before someone falls in the pool." I look around at the men in their jewel-colored dinner jackets and the women in their designer evening wear. They foxtrot around the edges of the water while Doctor Love and the Bahama Cats serenade them.

"Oh, my God," says Dave. "Listen."

"What?" I say. "That's the same song these guys have been playing all week."

"No," says Dave. "Listen to the words."

Doctor Love's song is called "Sell That Pussy." And that's the tame part of the lyric. It's probably the raunchiest tune I've ever heard. But it's catchy.

"Hi, kids!" says the First Lady as she cavorts past the diving board. "Isn't island life just fabulous?"

All I can hear is Doctor Love singing *sell that pussy, sell that pussy, sell that pussy*.

"Fab-u-lous!" yell Dave and Danny in unison. They get up, stretch, and mambo back to the buffet.

The invited guests don't notice the lyric to the song. Or if they do, they ignore it. They frolic around the pool, a cotillion of madras jackets and Lily Pulitzer prints, swirling and swaying under the starlit sky as if they're the lucky ones. The band is on one side of me, the guests on the other. I'm perched on a diving board over the deep end of an azure pool, not quite sure where I belong. The song ends. I look over at the band. Doctor Love nods, smiles, and toasts me with his Coke can.

They Say the Neon Lights Are Bright

Back at the Marriott Marquis, Pigeon Man is determined to win the music-versus-food battle. Just when the breakfast-trough scenario has played itself out and I think I'm safe, I must contend with the Cake Buffet. I arrive at work one day and there it is, an elaborate three-tier cake table next to the piano, so close to my left hand that I can reach out and swipe a chocolate-covered strawberry without skipping a beat.

"What's this?" I ask Joy, like I don't know.

"Cake," she says. "You know how it is around here. Management thinks our customers can't go for ten minutes without eating. We started out as a cocktail lounge, but we're turning into a cafeteria. We're offering an English high tea in the afternoon."

"Oh, no," I say. "Is the cake self service? I hope not." I'm envisioning great gobs of cream-cheese frosting smeared all over the high-gloss surface of the piano.

"No, we have to serve it ourselves. You know, this hotel is not that kind of place," Joy says. "Theme park, yes. Elegant English hotel, no. I mean, why come here if you can go to the Algonquin?"

The cake buffet never takes off. Every day Patrick brings giant trays of fancy-schmancy cakes. Over the course of the next two years I will see, maybe, six people order cake. I wonder if they even bother to change the cakes. I'm sure they do, but still, I wonder. Maybe the cakes are plastic, like the ficus.

We've all read stories about the cockroaches living in New York City, how they're resistant to just about everything, how they'll survive a nuclear attack, how eventually they'll take over the world. Times Square plays host to a large colony of these creatures, but it's not evident inside the pristine walls of the Marriott Marquis. Maybe the roaches can't get past the Highly Trained Security Team on the ground level, maybe they're confused and think they're in the wrong city, maybe they're freaked out by the glass elevators; but for whatever reason, I never see a single cockroach at the Marriott, unusual for a Manhattan hotel. Until they put out the cake.

I'm playing my Jobim medley, and *plop*, a very large cockroach comes out of nowhere and lands on the D, two octaves below middle C. Very inconvenient, as I'm playing in D minor. What to do. There's a nice little crowd of people around the piano, and they're listening. I can't leap away from the piano and scream, like I would in the privacy of my own home. And I don't want to actually touch the thing. But the critter is screwing up my bass line, big time.

I take a big breath and—*poof*—I blow the little bastard right into the coconut creme layer cake that's next to the piano. He dives headfirst into the cake, boring his way through the top layer at lightning speed. Cockroach heaven. I spend the rest of my set watching the icing to see if it moves.

～

Harlan sticks to his promise about keeping me away from the spinning areas, but occasionally the Atrium Lounge closes for ficus maintenance or marble polishing and I'm sent back to play in the revolving Broadway Lounge. The piano, also a Yamaha conservatory grand (Yamaha has a very good sales team) stands in a part of the lounge that remains motionless. The guests sit guzzling their cocktails and munching on smoked almonds on a revolving platform that makes one revolution every thirty minutes. They whirl around the lounge, past the windows and the flamboyant spectacle of real life unfolding on the streets beneath them. It makes me crazy to play in this lounge. I focus on the horizon, like I've learned to do in boats and cars, but when a guest talks to me from the platform I'm forced to look directly into the whole gyrating mess. I drink ginger tea and wear seabands on my wrists to prevent motion sickness. When it gets really bad I take Dramamine.

Sometimes, in the middle of a song, an inebriated customer might yell from his table, "Hey, Miss, how about a tune from *Chorus Line?*" I honor his request after I finish the song I'm already playing, but by that time, the guy has revolved out of hearing range. On the next revolution, after the customer orders another round, he yells at me to play his song again. It's horrible. After a little practice, I learn to wait and play the request after the guest has made a three-quarter rotation and is spinning back towards the piano.

In the revolving lounge, I time my breaks to get away from obnoxious drunks. "Here comes Arnie the toy salesman with the squirting lapel flower," Joy says. "He's at four o'clock, he's comin' around the bend, and he's had two more martinis. Better take a break." Joy is the best kind of New York City waitress—bored, sarcastic, and hopeful about her future. Sometimes I overhear her telling groups of earnest-looking women from Nebraska that she's really Naomi Campbell and she's working as a waitress to get away from the stress of being a supermodel.

People flock to the Marriott. It seems like everyone in the world passes through the eighth-floor atrium lobby. Crazy people, rich people, third-grade classmates of mine from Whittier Elementary School, retired friends of friends of my great-aunt's second cousin, every boyfriend I've ever had, their wives, the occasional Saudi prince, his wives, truck drivers, sitcom stars, hairdressers, porno stars, my pediatrician, my college drama professor, the entire U.S. Marine Concert Band, $2,000-a-night hookers, FBI agents, nine-year-olds celebrating birthdays in the big city, traveling salespeople bored with the road, senior citizens seeking a refuge from their loneliness. They're all here. Not all at the same time, but in a random ebb-and-flow cycle. They drift in and out of the Marriott lobby in featherweight clusters, carried in on a breeze from the recesses of my fantasies and nightmares. The lobby is a fusion of glass and light, music and space, life and illusion.

Joy is right. The hotel is a theme park without a theme. The theme should be New York City—the city that lives and breathes outside the confines of the hotel's insulated walls. Sure, a guest can check out Times Square through the thick glass windows at the front of the hotel—but the sounds, the smells, the tastes of the city are missing. From those giant windows, Manhattan looks in on the hotel. Gaudy advertisements, flashing lights, and billboards featuring heroic celebrities in their underwear glare at us as we pretend to be somewhere we aren't. It's bizarre.

Virginia

―――――――――――

"*H*ey you, Piano Girl! Your spindly legs are not strong enough to support the weight and burden of your soul."

Virginia is a mentally ill woman who hangs out on the corner of Thirtieth Avenue and Twenty-ninth Street in Astoria, Queens, where she takes her position every morning in order to hurl philosophical insults at female pedestrians. She wears her long hair piled high on her head. With her old heavy coat and torn and laced-up boots, she reminds me of a rock star who has stayed out all night at an after-concert party. But the sheen of dirt and oil on her skin and the deep creases on her face tell a different story, a mystery that I'll never unravel. She shows up every morning on her corner and departs at six in the evening. Ranting is her job. Where she goes after working hours, I haven't a clue. I suppose I could ask, but I'm afraid to get too close.

"Hey you, Piano Girl! Your spindly legs cannot sustain the pressure of that so-called job of yours."

On my daily walk to the elevated N train in Astoria, the one that burrows under the East River and carries me to the Marriott Marquis at Times Square, I pass Virginia and listen to her verbal abuse as her eyes and words follow me up the avenue. She knows

I'm listening, for sure. Virginia knows lots of things. She knows I'm a piano player, but how?

"Hey you, Piano Girl! Your spindly legs will carry you right into a bottomless pit full of tarnished dreams."

That's a good one, I think, and make a mental note to write it down in the little journal I carry with me in my gig bag.

It's hard not to listen to this stuff. It's half Milan Kundera, half Danielle Steele. I admit, the *spindly legs* thing bugs me. My legs are on the thin side, but I wouldn't call them spindly, thank you very much.

One day I make the mistake of pointing this out to her. Our eyes lock.

"Virginia," I say. "My legs are not spindly."

"Pins!" she screams. "You're walking around on pins! No legs for you, Piano Girl. Just pins!!!"

"Oh, Virginia knows everything," one of my neighbors says with a shrug. "Sometimes she'll tell you things about yourself that you don't know yet. She knew about my ulcers before they were even diagnosed. And she knew that Mrs. Tantalo had a metal plate in her head."

I wonder if Virginia can tell me how to straighten out my personal life.

I have tons of work, a nice apartment, a therapist who analyzes my dreams, and boyfriends who escort me to wonderful places and buy me pretty baubles to apologize for their wives or girlfriends or boyfriends or busy careers.

I'm lonely. And I'm ashamed of my sadness.

I live with Lucky the cat and my grand piano and wait for my real life to start. I try not to drink too much, but I know I do. I'm not anorexic, but I often forget to eat. At five-feet, eight-inches tall, I now weigh 110 pounds, just enough to keep the East River wind from lifting me up and carrying me off to Oz.

Maybe I've seen too much, or maybe I haven't seen enough of what really counts. I know that *what counts* is out there, because I had it as a kid. I mean, you can get *what counts* back again, can't you?

"Hey you, Piano Girl! Your spindly legs are stomping all over the music you secretly want to hear. Tatters! Tatters! The tatters are tumbling around you."

I don't know what a tatter is, but I sure as hell don't want to be hit by one.

I finish work each night and grab a taxi at the hotel door. I have cab drivers who claim to have been assassins in their native countries, cab drivers who practiced medicine before moving to America, cab drivers who watch Spanish soap operas on TV while driving. Each night a new reckless driver ferries me across the Queensboro Bridge, over Twenty-first Street, and past Virginia's vacated corner, then deposits me on the doorstep of the two-family house where I live. The Politos live downstairs; they are a real family with two kids and a garden. The upstairs family is just me. And Lucky.

Each morning, Virginia returns to her station, tormenting me with half-truths, pitching thoughtful indignities, and chucking offensive tidbits of wisdom onto the cracked asphalt pavement where they bounce back and hit me in the face if I actually listen. It's Virginia's way of making music.

"Hey you, Piano Girl! Your spindly legs will only take you as far as the truth allows. Then they'll collapse and you'll lie in a smoldering heap of loneliness, listening to songs in minor keys as you look up at the polluted sky and wonder where you went wrong."

Don't listen to her, Voice of Reason says. *She's obviously crazy.*

I don't know, Voice of Doom replies. *I'd say she's got a point.*

Like an Angel

*I*t's after midnight. I come out of the ladies' room at the Marriott Marquis and see Robin Spielberg, a waitress, sitting at the piano. Robin waits on tables in the revolving Broadway Lounge—she's a struggling actor schlepping drinks to pay the rent on her over-priced apartment on Tenth Street in Greenwich Village. She's thin and exhausted, like most of the girls working in the lounge. The lounge is empty—the guests have left the vast lobby and returned to their $200-a-night rooms—and the only sound is the whir of the vacuum as it sucks away the debris left by the after-theater crowd. Robin has finished cleaning her tables. It has been a tumultuous night in the Atrium Lounge, and she looks wearier than usual. She starts to play, and I watch the tension in her shoulders dissipate as she journeys deeper into her song. The music sounds the way Robin looks: pretty, fragile, a little sad, but very hopeful. I sink down into one of the soft leather bar chairs and listen for twenty minutes. I think how odd it is that musicians often sound the way they look—in Robin's case, this is a good thing.

"Hey," I say, after she notices me sitting there. "You're crazy killing yourself waitressing when you could be playing the piano."

"Oh," she says. "I could never do what you do."

"What do you mean? You just did. I was listening. You sound wonderful."

"But I've never worked as a pianist. I mean, in a cocktail lounge."

"There's always a first time. I got my first job because a crazy old nightclub manager named Lino heard me practice and practically forced me to take a job. It was an accident. If it hadn't been for Lino, I'd be living off waitress tips and wearing a monkey hat, too."

"Okay. I mean, it would be a dream come true to just sit and play every day like you do. How do I get a job? It all seems so mysterious."

"No mystery, believe me. Can you play four or five hours of music without the notes in front of you? Memorized or improvised, it doesn't matter."

"I don't know. I've never tried."

"Okay, go work on that and then let me know when you've gotten it together and I'll call Harlan Ellis. He's the agent who books all of these gigs. He'll love you. And I know he's on the lookout for female musicians. We're in demand, you know. Believe me—really."

Three weeks later Robin tells me she's ready. I phone Harlan, and he comes to the Marriott and meets her. Two days later he subjects her to the piano audition from hell—featuring the requisite *Rhapsody in Blue* girl, a woman wearing combat fatigues who sings in four languages, and a lady from Prague who plays a Mozart piano concerto. Robin calls me from the audition, hysterical, sure that she won't be offered the job. I've been there, I know the feeling. I also know she'll get the gig.

Robin lands the daytime lunch job at the Grand Hyatt and will stay there for twelve years, developing her repertoire, fine-tuning her compositions, and launching a recording career that will take her all over the world as a concert artist. She'll also become my best friend.

It's all a little silly, really, that we have so much in common. We yap on the phone about cute guys, gossip about hotel work-

ers, and discuss where to buy the most absolutely, fabulously perfect black cocktail dress ever made. We compare notes about
whacko customers and potential stalkers, and we figure out you
can avoid playing Scott Joplin pieces if you hold up your left hand
like a claw, say you were born with a deformity, and you can't
possibly stretch a major tenth. We make fun of the male pianists
we know, mainly because we know they make fun of us. And we
trade piano shifts and help each other out all the time. Never
once does money change hands. If Robin plays five hours for me
at the Marriott, I'll play five hours for her at the Hyatt. We keep
little charts in our datebooks, and we always know exactly where
we stand. It's our girly-girl form of bookkeeping, and even
though it makes Harlan shudder, it works out just fine. We both
shop at Stall for the Handicapped and Betsey Johnson and even
have some of the same outfits. Roy, one of the regular Lobby
People, calls us Robin Senior and Robin Junior.

In years to come we will see each other through pregnancies,
serious illnesses, the deaths of loved ones, and the triumphs of
our children. But in 1986 we're too busy with our careers and
social lives to notice that we're practically joined at the hip.

"Who's playing tonight?"

"Robin."

"Oh. Which one?"

"Does it matter?"

"No."

Half the time Harlan doesn't know which Robin is where.
He knows if one of us is playing, the job is covered and everyone
stays happy. "Don't tell me the details, I won't be able to sleep,"
he says. It's not unusual for each of us to work three jobs in a day,
starting with a breakfast shift, then playing lunch and dinner. My
current piano marathon record is fifteen hours, spread out over
three hotels in one day. I wonder exactly how many notes a
pianist plays over fifteen hours. Better not to think about it.

Robin's innocence, optimism, and love for the piano are my
rewards for taking the time to listen to her play that first night.
I'm on the edge of my career, five years ahead of her, teetering

on the precipice between cynicism and disillusionment—the dangerous place you get to when you realize that what you have to offer, the very thing you're most proud of, isn't of much value to anyone but you. Without knowing it, she nudges me away from the brink of my disenchantment. "There are real people out there," she reminds me, "individual customers and workers—unique human beings with uncommon desires—each of whom deserves ten minutes of beautiful music.

"That's why we're musicians," she says. "You never know who is listening. It might be someone who really needs the music you play. Maybe the person who needs it most is you. But that counts, right?" I can't listen to Robin and stay cynical. Her enthusiasm gets under my skin, and, before I know it, I adopt her philosophy and claim it as my own. I don't know where she stops and I start.

She gives me a reason to keep playing.

The Almond Tree

L'essential est invisible pour les yeux.
(The essential is invisible to the eyes.)
                                    —Saint Exupery, *The Little Prince*

*N*ever ever, *never ever, never ever kiss the boss,* says Voice of Reason. But I don't listen.

I've been going to Haiti for many years. I play the piano and lull away the time eating fresh mango and roast *poulet* and lying in the sunshine. Yes, I kiss the boss, but not as much as I'd like. The man I love is a busy guy. In addition to running a large casino, hotel, restaurant, and nightclub in Haiti, he has a wife and grown children in the States. For six years, Owner-man has been telling me that he'll be leaving his wife *any day now.* His beautiful baritone voice resonates with promises he thinks he can keep, but I don't believe him any longer. He'll never leave his wife. Maybe for his next girlfriend, but not for me. I sit in the shade of a poolside umbrella and listen as the Yellow Bird trio sings.

> *Wish dat I were a yellow bird,*
> *I fly away wid you,*
> *But I am not a yellow bird,*
> *So here I sit,*
> *Nothin' else to do.*

These days when I'm not playing I whittle away the time in Haiti under a big almond tree with my friend Mona, a stunning Haitian woman who runs the restaurant and supervises the interior decorating of the hotel's rooms. We feed scrambled eggs to a three-legged iguana named Lefty who visits us every morning as we sit under our tree, and we plot the details of the trip we'll take someday to Provence.

Another friend, a red-haired Lebanese woman named Gladys, owns the island's Kentucky Fried Chicken franchise. Gladys is famous. When the Pope visited Haiti, she fried 3,000 buckets of chicken to feed him and his entourage. I'm sorry I missed that spectacle. I love the idea of the Pope eating a large bucket with all the fixins. Gladys teaches me to play golf and how to tee off from the first hole of the Petionville Country Club without injuring the goats grazing on the fairway. Mona teaches me how to crochet a bedspread. We are an unlikely trio—a Haitian, an Arab, and a WASP—and we think we have answers for everything. We talk politics and tell jokes and solve the world's problems. Easy to do, when you're sitting poolside in the shade of an ancient almond tree being served champagne by smiling waiters with ebony faces. You can forget who you are.

Inside the hotel I lose track of the poverty on the other side of the wall. I play the piano for the rich and educated elite, government dignitaries, and the Seventh Avenue garmentos who run factories and sweatshops in neighboring Port-au-Prince. But that gets boring, and before I know it, I break out of my golden cage and begin exploring the neighborhood around me.

The streets are full of life—music and art and optimism beyond belief. I can't understand all the cheerfulness in the face of so much destitution. Owner-man talks about the "privilege of poverty," like there is some kind of honor in growing up poor. He speaks with pride about his own childhood in a New York City slum—walking to school with playing cards under his socks to prevent the wet and cold from seeping through the tears in his shoes, taking manual-labor jobs as child to help his mother pay for groceries, playing soccer with a rolled-up newspaper in the streets of Brooklyn. "That's the kind of thing that gives a kid ambition," he says.

I don't think so, not at all.

I meet a teenaged boy named Rodley who has been left an orphan by the AIDS epidemic. He dusts my piano, serves drinks, and chatters about getting away from Haiti someday and going to college in America. Owner-man has given Rodley a job and paid for his schooling. For my birthday, Rodley gives me a flower pot that he has painted himself.

My favorite casino waiter is a middle-aged man named Pressoir. He's shy, wears big thick glasses, and is suffering from localized alopecia, a stress-related-disorder that has left one side of his head bald. Pressoir supports a family of eight on his waiter's salary, about a $100 a month. He carries pictures of his children and his brother's children in his wallet. *"Les gosses sont ce qu'il y a de plus cher dans ma vie,"* he says. They are everything to me.

> *Let her fly away,*
> *In de sky away,*
> *Picker coming soon,*
> *Pick from night to noon,*
> *Black and yellow you,*
> *Like banana too,*
> *He might pick you someday.*

Mona introduces me to local craftspeople who sell their brightly colored paintings and bed covers on the street outside the hotel grounds. Marie-Claude, a woman I've commissioned to make dresses for me, invites me for tea. Her home is a thatched-roof hut with no walls and a mud floor. Red and yellow fabric hangs from the roof and creates privacy for the family. The table is covered with red oilcloth. Her six children all sleep on one large straw mat on the floor. There is no electricity or running water. The hut is cheerful and colorful and full of art. No walls, but the paintings are everywhere, suspended from the ceiling and propped against the old wooden cupboard.

"My children paint," says Marie-Claude. She speaks slowly, in French, aware that I don't understand Creole.

"Where are the children now?" I ask. "Are they at school?"

"*Non. Les gosses ne vont pas à l'école.Ils y iront peut-être l'année prochaine, quand j'aurai du fric.*" The children don't go to school. Maybe next year, if there is money.

"The little ones are playing football and the others are in the mountains collecting wood for charcoal. My daughter has gone to the market with her father to help him sell the paintings. But these paintings here, I will never sell them. They are my favorites," she says. "*Regardez, ce tableau pourrait s'intituler l'espoir.*" This one is about hope.

Every single painting I've seen in Haiti is about hope.

On top of the cabinet I notice a small drum and a guitar.

"You see, we make music, too. Just like you. Every night, when the sun goes to sleep, we pray and give thanks for the good things. Like music. And the colors of the dawn. Some people aren't so lucky—they can't hear or see what is there for the taking. You know, I listen to your music over the wall of the hotel in the evening. I always try to get closer so I can swim in the sound of the piano."

"You should come in," I say.

"It is not my place to do that," she says with a little laugh. "*Je resterai dans mon petit coin et j'y serai très heureuse de vous écouter.*" I'll stay on my side of the wall and be happy to hear what I can. "My cousin is a waiter at the hotel. He tells me it's a dream come true to have such a job."

She pours the tea into spotless china cups that are chipped around the edges. With her graceful index finger she points to the faded floral design on the edge of the delicate saucer. "Aren't these flowers the most beautiful color?" she asks.

"Yes, they're beautiful. Your home is beautiful," I say. And I mean it.

"My life is beautiful," Marie-Claude says. "Where there is life, there is beauty. Where there is beauty, there is life."

> *Did your lady frien',*
> *Leave de nest again?*
> *Dat is very sad,*
> *Make me feel so bad,*

You can fly away,
In the sky away,
You're more lucky dan me.

This will be my last trip to Haiti. Owner-man pleads with me to return, but I've grown tired of feeling useless. I've seen too much and learned too little. I'm a piano player. The Haitians don't need more music. They don't need more art, or hope, or compassion, or nodding, spoiled young American women pretending to understand the unfairness of life. What they need is a break.

Little Scraps of Paper

*K*ids and drunks have a lot in common. They're brutally honest, totally unpredictable, and anxious to be noticed, even if it means jumping up and down on a red velvet seat and pouring the remains of a beverage down the collar of any guy who happens to be in fun's way. With this in mind, it's not such a stretch for me to go from lounge pianist to musical director of a touring *Sesame Street* show.

I've done kids' shows before, as an actor. I played Tanya Baum the Talking Christmas Tree at a "wake up Santa Claus" breakfast in Pittsburgh. And I've worn so many Easter Bunny costumes in department stores that it's hard for me to go through the revolving doors of Bloomingdale's without hopping. I once had a Valentine's Day job at the Pittsburgh branch of Saks Fifth Avenue dressed as Cupid—I wore a red leotard with wings and ran around the store shooting foam-rubber arrows at customers with kids.

In the late seventies I donned a full-body Winnie the Pooh suit and marched in a parade to greet Santa Claus as he parachuted into the parking lot of the South Hills Village shopping mall outside of Pittsburgh. As the official parade marshal, I was scheduled to ride in a big red fire truck in my Winnie the Pooh costume. Not surprisingly, there was a fire that day and the truck canceled.

"No problem," I said to the promoter. "I can walk the parade route." I didn't want to disappoint all those kids. So I marched in front of an eighty-piece high school marching band. I started off strong, but the parade route was long. Very long. Those big steel Pooh boots got heavier and heavier as we neared our destination. I could see—but just barely—through the honey pot on the head of my costume. I heard Santa's airplane circling around and around. It became increasingly difficult to put one foot in front of the other. I couldn't get enough air. I still remember the sensation of the trombone slides nudging me in my back, getting closer and closer as I dragged my legs and tried to wave at the throngs of kids lining the mall parking-lot parade route. My vision grew dark around the edges and my ears started to ring. Next thing I knew, my knees were buckling and I was sinking to the concrete. I had hyperventilated and passed out, causing a high school marching-band pile-up behind me. The drum major and two women from the marketing office carried me back into the mall before they took off my Pooh head.

"You really should have gotten her out of the suit immediately," said the doctor examining me. "It's very dangerous to be in one of these costumes for more than fifteen minutes."

"Well," said the promoter, who was nervously looking out of her office window. "We didn't want the kids to know that Winnie isn't *real*."

"What?" said the doctor. "Better they should think Winnie is dead?"

Didn't matter much. Santa missed his parachute target and got tangled in an oak tree at a gas station across the highway. It was a traumatic day for those kids.

꙳

When Emilio Delgado—Luis on *Sesame Street*—calls to ask if I'm interested in being the musical director of his show, the first thing I ask is, "Do I have to wear a Muppet suit?" After the Winnie episode I've sworn I'll never again wear another big furry costume with a twenty-pound head and lead boots. No way am I going to play the piano in a Cookie Monster outfit.

"No!" says Emilio. "You're thinking of the *Sesame Street Live* show. That's the Muppet show. My show only involves Roscoe Orman—the guy who plays Gordon—and me. And you on piano, if you want the gig."

"But you said musical director," I say. "Is there a band involved?"

"No," says Emilio. "You would just be directing yourself. And us."

"Oh," I say. "I think I could do that. What's the tour schedule? I'll have to take time off from my Marriott job."

"We'll go out maybe one weekend a month. Sometimes more, sometimes less. The money is good, and I'm sure we'll be treated very well. There's just one catch."

Here we go. There's always a catch. The last time someone told me there was a catch to a piano job, I'd ended up topless in a Boston dinner theater with policemen and attack dogs in the wings.

"We need you to warm up the audience before the show starts. You know, do a little stand-up comedy routine and then move over to the piano and get the kids singing."

"Oh," I say. "I can handle that." I envision us in school classrooms, with thirty attentive children sitting with their sweet little hands folded neatly on their tiny desks.

One month later I find myself in Frankenmuth, Michigan, at the Frankenmuth Bavarian Festival, wearing an orange baseball cap and hightops, standing backstage getting ready to run out and tell jokes to 1,500 screaming children. Gordon and Luis are big stars. Kids have come from all over Michigan to get a chance to see them in person.

I watch from the wings as three children leap onstage and play a game spitting ice cubes at each other. The first waves of doubt creep over me.

You'd be much better off in the bear suit, says Voice of Doom.
I run onstage and start the show.

◦⁓

As the daughter of a *Mister Rogers' Neighborhood* musician, it's ironic that I'm playing for a *Sesame Street* production. But though the two shows are completely opposite in their philosophies—one stimulating and aggressive, the other calming and gentle—they share a love of music and an awareness of the importance of music in a child's development.

Emilio Delgado and I attend the same acting class—two working professionals trying to better ourselves by studying the two-year course in the Sanford Meisner acting technique. We're friends and acting partners, spending long hours together rehearsing impossible scenes, and doing acting exercises that tap our emotional resources and usually result in either fits of laughter or trails of tears.

Emilio, with his beautiful wife, Carol, come to my Marriott gigs or anywhere else I'm playing. They're quite a pair, Emilio with his dashing Mexican good looks, and Carol, a lithe blond who can't decide if she wants to be Margaret Mead or Lovey Howell. I turn on the TV in the morning and watch Emilio sing (as Luis) about the number "5." I laugh out loud at his antics with Big Bird and his rendition of "La Bamba" with a herd of Muppet sheep singing *baaaa, baaaaa, baaaaaamba.*

But both Emilio and I want more from our careers. We want to be challenged, to be stimulated, to follow a more artistic path. So we torture ourselves in acting class trying to get out of our creative ruts. I don't want to be just a piano player—I want to do modern American drama. He wants to do film. We end up doing *Sesame Street Live with Gordon and Luis.*

Pasting together a live kids' show, especially for such large audiences, means scrapping our adult concepts of entertainment. We start from scratch, trying to remember what it's like to be five years old. Being quiet and gentle and singing hushed songs about love and family values? Those things function brilliantly in a small classroom or on a television set. But in a theater packed with 2,000 spirited children and their stressed parents—no way.

My job at the beginning of the show is to get the kids to guess where Gordon and Luis are hiding. After we exhaust all the usual possibilities—under the kids' seats, in their mothers' purses, in their neighbor's ear, I go into the audience with the microphone and ask for suggestions to get Gordon and Luis to come out of hiding. I have a notion that one of the kids will say "music!" But the kids have other things in mind.

"Gordon, if you don't come out, I'm gonna rip my sister's hair out."

"Luis, if I don't see you in one second I'm gonna slap Timmy in the face with a wet washrag."

"Gordon, if you don't show up, my Dad's gonna sue you."

"If you guys don't get out here soon, I'm gonna kick this microphone girl in the knees."

"How about music, kids?" I say.

"It smells like sweat socks in here."

"Gordon, I bet you're on the potty!"

"Luis, come out or I'm gonna tell Santa you're a jerk."

"How about music, kids?" I say once again as I leap over to the piano. I get them clapping in time, tear into the *Sesame Street* theme song, and Gordon and Luis charge from the wings as the kids cheer and sing along. Many children wonder how Gordon and Luis have gotten out of the television set.

In the beginning we try, we really do, to do a variety of music, alternating up-tempo audience participation sing-along and dance numbers with poignant ballads about love and sadness. The ballads are a disaster. Both Gordon and Luis have gorgeous voices, and there is a ton of great music from the television show that we would like to do. But the same thing happens every time Gordon or Luis try to sing something slow. Halfway through the song, members of the pint-sized audience get distracted. They crawl under their seats, hit their neighbors, and cry out of boredom. Every singer's worst nightmare.

At a beautiful concert hall in Calgary, when Roscoe goes downstage to sing a wonderful ballad called "Family" there's a huge ruckus in the first few rows. Roscoe sits on the edge of the stage for this number in his casual "get down on their level" pose. "There's more than only one way for a family to be," he sings in his deep baritone.

Not even four bars into the song, a bucket of popcorn flies up into the air. Three or four kids start bawling. A mother drags a couple of the offenders up the aisle. Another kid screams, "Sing the doggie song!" and everyone claps and laughs. I see a tennis shoe soar through the light from the spotlight and land a dozen rows back. A ten-year-old boy jumps up and throws the shoe back where it came from. Three or four kids begin chasing each other up and down the aisles, trying to retrieve the shoe.

Really, it's not all that different from the Atrium Lounge at the Marriott Marquis.

Through all the commotion, Roscoe maintains his concentration and continues singing, "You could have a brother, a sister, an aunt…"

One of the silver helium balloons attached to our set gets loose and floats up to the ceiling of the theater. While continuing to pound my way through the ballad, I look out at the audience. Not a single eye is on Gordon as he forges ahead to the big dramatic ending of the song, "Oh, oh, family, family, family…"

The audience has been hypnotized by the balloon, and they're still sitting there, heads back, mouths open, looking at the ceiling when Roscoe finishes the piece. Luis and I have to force the audience to clap for him. We move on to "The Doggie Song."

"Robin," says Gordon after the show. "No more ballads for me. Did you see what happened out there?"

"Yeah," I say. "Unbelievable. The chase thing with the shoe was terrible. And then they couldn't stop watching that stupid balloon."

"What balloon?" says Gordon.

"The one everyone was watching while you were trying to sing."

"Oh, I didn't even notice that. The whole time I was singing there was this little kid in the front row bugging me. He had scissors with him and he was cutting up little scraps of blue paper and putting them on my shoes. Then he started going after my shoelaces."

"Oh. That must have been, uh, annoying."

"Yeah. No more ballads. Enough is enough."

Everyone has their limits.

It takes a few months of trial and error, but eventually we've got a nice show. We adjust to the constant *buzz buzz buzz* that lives inside theaters filled with preschoolers. There's a lot of positive energy and power in these young audiences, and it's a blessing to be part of it. I travel all over North America with Gordon and Luis. We're quite a representative trio: the Mexican American, the African American, and the blond American. Gordon and Luis are swarmed at airports by starstruck stalker moms and their kids. They sign autographs and have their pictures taken with four-year-olds from Seattle to Atlanta. I stand off to the side and observe as the two men perform their public-television celebrity duties with grace and good humor. Then the three of us climb into an airplane and wing off to the next city, the next hall, the next zealous group of kids that will allow us, for sixty minutes, to share their fun.

It's an honest job, and I love every minute of it.

Crash Test

My dad always warned me that I'd eventually be fired from every job.

But I've been playing at the Marriott Marquis for six years, and I've developed a false sense of security. I've got a loyal set of fans. Okay, some of them are nuts, but at least they spend money in the lounge on a regular basis. And I have a good relationship with my co-workers. I'm reliable. For over six years I've covered every single shift, five hours a day, five days a week. That's 7,800 hours of music. I should be awarded a framed certificate and a Purple Heart. But the Marriotts have other rewards in mind.

It all starts with the cocktail nuts. When management changes the bar snacks, I don't need Voice of Doom to tell me that the end is near. Overnight, we go from expensive smoked almonds to pretzel nubs. Then the waitresses get new uniforms— also a bad sign, although the new uniform is a big improvement over the old hooker-in-Las Vegas model. They remove the vases of fresh flowers from the cocktail tables and replace them with Chia-pet centerpieces.

They're out to get you, says Voice of Doom. *You're a goner. Dead meat.*

Don't be silly, Voice of Reason argues back. *You've been playing here for six years and everybody loves you. Of course they'll be faithful to you!*

Pigeon Man has moved to the corporate office, which means he can make music-policy decisions without having to argue with me. Life is calm for a few months and then—*WHAM!*

"Look at ze new machine," says the room manager, an Austrian guy named Sebastian. He has cleats on his shoes. "You just flick zis little svitch und *voila!* The piano plays by itself."

I give you another two months on this gig, says VOD.

"Sebastian," I say, trying really hard to remain calm. "This sounds terrible." The piano is playing, all by itself, "In the Wee Small Hours of the Morning." The device, called the Pianocorder, is not connected to the sustain pedal, so the music sounds staccato, disconnected, almost march-like.

In - - - the - - - wee - - - small - - -hou - -rs - - -of - - - the - - - morn - - - ing.

"Ah, no," says Sebastian. "It's great! Now ve have ze musik all day long, even ven you're not here, even ven you take ze break! If you can't come to vork, no problem! Ve just turn on ze machine! Look, ze customers love it!"

There are two five-years-olds standing next to the piano, laughing and pointing. Everyone else is seated as far away from the piano as possible.

"Turn that thing off; it's giving me a fucking headache," says Joy.

I know about these machines. I saw a Pianocorder in California several years ago, but it seemed so, well, California-ish, that I never imagined that one would surface in the lobby of a five-star hotel in Manhattan the middle of the Broadway Theater District. I am stunned.

I run to the bank of pay phones. I call Harlan. I call Robin Spielberg. They both listen sympathetically as I rant about this being the beginning of the end.

"Hey, think about it," says Harlan. "This is Manhattan. A hotel like the Marriott would never replace live music with a player-piano machine."

"You'll see," says Robin Spielberg. "It'll be a novelty for a while, and then they'll get sick of the thing." I detect a note of doubt in her voice. "I mean, they can hear the difference between that thing and a real musician, can't they?"

I call a meeting of the other musicians. We decide that sabotage—dumping a glass of water into the machine or running magnets over the cassette tapes—might be our best strategy. But we chicken out for fear of being fired. Like they aren't planning to fire us anyway.

Everybody hates the machine: the customers—tourists and New Yorkers alike—and the staff who must deal with the customer complaints, change the cassette every thirty minutes, and mess around with the volume—or the dynamic sensitivity knob, as the Pianocorder salesman called it. I'm embarrassed to sit down at a piano that's already playing itself. Every so often when I start to play, someone asks me if I'm really playing; they think I'm a model who has been hired to sit there and pretend.

You watch, says VOD. *Your days are seriously numbered.*

The axe falls, of course. The four pianists playing in the Atrium Lounge are given six weeks notice, and then—*presto!*—without a word of thanks from management, an apology, or even a patronizing pat on the back, we vanish. That beautiful Yamaha, struggling to play Cole Porter songs at march tempos, retaliates like it has a bad case of the hiccups, spitting and regurgitating the automated music, longing for the touch of a human hand.

Usually I'm a good sport about being fired. I've been replaced by better musicians and worse musicians. I've been replaced by a table for four because management decided the piano is taking up too much room. I've been fired because the hotel or restaurant runs out of money, because new management wants to try something *different*, or because the general manager of the hotel has a girlfriend who sings a little. Fine. No problem. There's always another job. Usually a better one. But being replaced by a machine is a different. I can't get over it, hard as I try.

Two weeks after I leave, I get a call from one of my former Marriott fans.

"You've gotta see this," says Max. Max is a cute little guy who came into the hotel every week for six years. "They've got a dummy at the piano."

"What?" I say. "A dummy?"

"Yeah. You know. Like a big stuffed man in a tuxedo."

"You're kidding."

"No. You can't make this stuff up. You gotta go see it. If it weren't for the tuxedo and the moustache, he'd look like one of those dummies they use for crash testing."

I grab my camera and get to Midtown in twenty minutes. As the glass elevator doors open on the eighth floor of the hotel I think, *No, Max must be wrong. There's a person at the piano. I guess they hired someone new. Wonder who it is.*

From a distance it looks like Earl or Howard or…

But the person sitting at the piano isn't moving. I hear the uneven clatter of the Pianocorder as it extorts sound out of the abused instrument. There, sitting in my place on the piano bench, is a dummy.

This is a real slap in the face.

Wow, says VOD. *This is even worse than I predicted.*

Oh, shut up, says VOR. *At least it's not a girl dummy.*

I take a couple of pictures and a couple of deep breaths, say hello to the waitresses, and leave.

᠅

One week after the dummy sighting I take a trip to Hawaii, a tactic I would recommend to any unemployed woman who is trying to pretend that she is not unemployed. When I get back to the city my head is clear. So I do what I always do when I need to think. I write. I compose a long editorial for *Allegro*, the monthly newspaper published by Local 802 of the American Federation of Musicians. Six months after the dummy takes my place on the piano bench in the Atrium Lounge, Local 802 prints my article, along with a photo of the dummy. A writer from *Billboard* magazine sees my article and writes an editorial of his own, describing the dummy and the Pianocorder. He suggests that live-music trade shows and conventions take their business elsewhere, to a hotel that employs real musicians. *Billboard* receives a flurry of letters in support of live music, several in support of "modern technology," and one from the manufacturer of the dummy— claiming that I am out of touch with the wave of the future and that the Marriott Corporation is on the cutting edge of the dummy field by choosing to place a dummy in its Broadway Theater District flagship hotel.

Live music returns to the Marriott a month later. What prompts the decision—whether it's the bad press, complaints from customers, threats from trade-show organizers, or just declining revenues in the Atrium Lounge—I'll never know. But several new pianists are engaged, and the lobby once again reverberates with the glorious sound of live piano music. I move to another piano job in another hotel. Score one for the humans.

The dummy disappears from the lobby and never returns. Perhaps he has been kidnapped. Maybe the dummy has donned a bordeaux jacket and an earpiece and taken a job with the Highly Trained Security Team positioned by the bank of television monitors at the entrance to the hotel. Perhaps he has been given a position in the corporate Food and Beverage Department working as an assistant for Pigeon Man, or maybe he just rides in the passenger seat of Pigeon Man's car so they can travel to work in the commuter lane. Hopefully, the dummy has gone someplace where he's being appreciated for a job well done.

Playback 1990

It's 10:30 on a Friday night. I sit at the Steinway in Trumpet's at the Grand Hyatt. The room is three-quarters empty. The dinner crowd has gone to dinner, and the after-theater crowd is still at the theater. I play "Killing Me Softly" for Pam the bartender. Melissa the waitress sings along.

Oh, look, there's a man with no arms.

Melissa stops singing and goes to get her tray.

The man with no arms comes and sits down at the table to my right.

"Good evening," I say.

"Good evening," he replies. He is short, with nicely styled long hair and a trimmed beard. He's wearing an expensive cotton shirt, the sleeves of which are not detectable, and a cashmere sweater tossed casually around his shoulders.

"What can I get for you tonight, Sir?" says Melissa.

How about some arms, I think.

"Grand Marnier, in a snifter, please. And I'd like an ashtray."

I keep playing. This is getting interesting.

The man kicks off his Gucci loafers. He is barefoot. With his toes, he removes a cigarette from a golden case. With the other foot he lights it.

I look over my shoulder. In the window by the service bar, the entire restaurant and bar staff stares as the man with no arms smokes a cigarette with his feet.

I start playing "Embraceable You." Bad choice, I think. Shit.

Melissa brings the Grand Marnier to the table. Now the man with no arms has a brandy snifter in one foot and a cigarette in the other.

I keep playing, trying not to stare, but really, it's remarkable what he's doing.

I noodle around the piano trying to think of something appropriate to play. I want to be nonchalant, to accept his unique ability as the norm, a fact of life. I don't want to gawk or do any of the cliché things people do when confronted by a person who is different in a remarkable way. I want to be cool and ignore what's going on at the table next to me.

But I can't stand it any longer.

"Excuse me, Sir, but I have to say something. That's the most amazing thing I've ever seen, what you're doing. I can't just sit here and pretend not to notice. You're so, uh, dexterous with your feet. I've been playing in bars for a long time, and I've never seen anyone smoke and drink with his, um, toes. It's astounding. Anyway, I'm sorry to bother you, I just had to say that."

"Oh, that's okay. Most people pretend there's nothing unusual going on. But let's face it, it's weird. This is normal for me, but I know I create quite a ruckus in public places. You should have seen them at the reception desk when I arrived."

"Oh. You mean all the paperwork and signature procedures? How did you sign in?"

"Same way I do every thing else. With my feet."

"You can lift your leg up that high and sign a form with your toes while balancing on the other leg?"

"Of course. That's as easy for me as you doing it with your arms."

"Next thing you'll be telling me you can play the piano with your feet."

"Yes. I can. But you'll have to hold me up from behind, or get me a chair with a back on it."

"We've just seen *Phantom*! " says a woman in a Christmas-motif red-sequined sweater as she enters the lounge with her husband and another couple. She has helmet-head hair that looks like it might crack and shatter into a thousand pieces if anyone touches it, not that anyone would want to. She has apparently bathed in buckets of high-priced perfume, probably Giorgio. Behind her back, Melissa and Pam are holding their noses.

"What's your name?" I say to the man with no arms.

"Henry," he says.

"Henry, it's a pleasure to meet you. Would you like to play?"

"We've just seen *Phantom*!" says the helmet-head lady again.

"Sure, why not?" says Henry.

He slides over to the piano bench. I stand behind him and support his back. He plays "My Funny Valentine." With his feet.

The general manager of the hotel walks into the lounge and stops dead in his tracks when he sees what is going on. He can't figure out what else to do, so he gives us the thumbs-up sign. Henry gives him a big toe up in return. The general manager makes a little gurgling sound, halfway between a giggle and a hiccup, spins on his heels, and leaves.

Henry finishes his song with a loud arpeggio and a bang of the little toe on the high G. The restaurant employees and guests cheer.

He returns to his seat and picks up his brandy snifter, gives a little toast to the room, and lights another cigarette.

This is a tough act to follow, I think.

"We've just seen *Phantom*!" says Helmet Head.

"What does she want, a fuckin' award?" mutters Melissa.

"Great show, *Phantom*. Just great," says Henry, grabbing a couple of almonds with his left foot and popping them into his mouth.

"Henry," I say. "You play really well." I'm back on the piano bench. I vamp on a turnaround in B-flat while I continue chatting. "How did you learn to use your feet like that?"

"I was born this way, and my mother was determined I would learn to use my toes like fingers. All of us have this ability, you know. It's just a question of use. Most people have lazy toes because they rely on their fingers."

"Will you please play something from *Phantom*?" says Helmet Head.

"I'll be glad to," I say. "One moment please."

Helmet Head huffs and stomps off to her table. The back of her sweater has a reindeer on it with a nose that lights up.

"I can play the guitar, too," says Henry. "My mother was very, shall we say, insistent that I learn how to do these things. I know it's a little bit of a circus act to regular people looking on, but to me it's just music. I like to think when people cheer for me it's because of what they hear, but I know better. They're impressed cause I'm using my feet. That gets me down sometimes, but then I think, what the hell, you've gotta have a gimmick, and I've got a pretty good one. Playing 'Malaguena' with my toes might be considered grandstanding by some, but I figure if you've got it, flaunt it."

I can't even play "Malaguena" with my fingers.

"Can you please play *Phantom* music for the lady in the Rudolph sweater before she has a hissy fit?" says Melissa.

"I guess I'd better play the *Phantom* songs," I say to Henry. "Unless you want to do it."

"Sorry," he says. "I don't take requests."

"Good for you," I say.

Starry, Starry Night

════════

"Pardon me, Miss, what's the name of the piece you just finished?"

"It's called 'Twilight,'" I say. "I wrote it. It's about my favorite time of day. You know, when the light shifts and the sky turns beautiful shades of pink and orange?"

"Ah, yes," says the man. He has a lovely foreign accent. "I know that color. It resembles crushed rose petals on antique linen."

Wow. Who is this guy? Most of the men I know think there are only three colors in the world; brown, red, and blue.

He appears to be in his sixties and has thinning hair and dark intense eyes. He's a large man with an elegant carriage.

"Where are you from?" I ask. We have customers from all over the world coming into Trumpet's. He could be from any-where, anywhere at all.

"I come from Brazil," he says.

"Oh. How wonderful! The man I'm marrying next month is a jazz musician. He's a big fan of Brazilian music. We hope to visit your country someday."

"Does your fiancé play with as much passion as you do?"

"Oh, yes," I say. "Probably more. He plays the bass. The upright bass."

"Ah, that's also a splendid instrument. You'll have a long and happy marriage, I'm sure. I'm a pianist and composer. May I play one of my compositions for you?"

"Yes, of course," I say.

I sit at the bar where I can watch his fingers. He pauses for a moment and begins playing. The composition captivates me. It's not showy, or loud, or an exercise in technical prowess. It's a piece of music that sounds like a waterfall. It flows, bubbles, and traverses the range of the piano, moving peacefully, contentedly. The song ends, but in my mind it continues.

"That was lovely," I say. "Does it have a name?"

"'*Floresta Tropical*,'" he says. "'The Rain Forest.' Now please, continue. Play some more of your music. I've had a long day and your songs are soothing."

I usually intersperse original material with standards, pop tunes, and Broadway classics. But tonight I play an entire set of my compositions. I float along and improvise some sections. My Brazilian friend and his companion listen. The other twelve people in the bar pay attention as well. The atmosphere around me begins to change. I drift into dreamland—the perfectly balanced state where the act of making music and the music itself are one.

I play a piece I've written about my grandmothers, and I swear I feel them standing behind me with their seasoned, gentle hands on my arms. I feel the cool breeze coming through the screen door next to the piano I played as a child. I see my father waving goodbye to me, and hear the sound of my mother's voice telling me to be strong and fight for what belongs to me. I smell a garden of roses and lavender, and hear the cry of gulls as they soar over the waves banging away at the Nantucket shoreline. I see Michael's serene face, and sense the weight of a decade of loneliness lift from my troubled shoulders.

All of this, from music.

I'm somewhere else tonight, not in Donald Trump's smoke-filled den of luxury, but outside of it, listening to the echoes of my youth as they resonate, beautifully flawed, from my adult fingertips.

"Thank you for a lovely evening," says the Brazilian man. "If you will please fax this information to Miami in the morning, I will see to it that you and your fiancé fly to Brazil for your honeymoon." He hands me a cocktail napkin with a name and a telephone number scribbled across the top. "This is the fax number for my daughter. She will take care of the details."

His name is Omar Fontana. He's the owner of Trans Brazil Airlines.

"I don't know how to thank you," I say. "This is such a generous gift." I fold the napkin and place it carefully in my evening bag.

"All artists should be treated with generosity and respect," he says. "It's the duty of society to treat them well. This is the least I can do."

✧

"What do you mean, he gave you a trip to Brazil? I've been waiting on that guy for a week and I didn't get a trip to Brazil," says Nibor the waiter.

"Yeah, well, he likes artists," I say.

"Maybe I should get a blond wig and tap-dance when I serve the soup. Or I could spill the soup and make a painting with it on the tablecloth. Shit. I can't believe you got a trip to Brazil after playing the piano for twenty minutes. Maybe I should be a piano player."

"Go ahead, Nibor. It's never too late. It'll take you about one decade of practicing a couple of hours a day. After just a few years, you should be able to play a nice rendition of 'The Volga Boat Song.' Then, if you really apply yourself, in another couple of years you'll be able to bang out 'Turkey in the Straw.' After that, all it takes is another five years of patience and practice. Before you know it, you'll be ready to play your first set. Then you'll hear a Bill Evans record and realize that you can't play very well at all. On the other hand, you could use the time wisely and become a neurologist. That takes just about as long as learning to play the piano."

"What you do is easy."

"Is not."

"Is too."

"Is not."

"Tell you what, Nibor, let's trade jobs. I'll serve the dinner. You go play a set. But no singing. That's cheating."

"Okay, okay, I get your point," he says, scowling. "But still. A trip to Brazil?"

༈

"What do you mean, a trip to Brazil?" says John, my bass-player husband-to-be. "You're telling me that this cocktail napkin is going to get us a trip to Brazil?"

"Yeah, see, he listened to me play and I was playing really well and I played all my original material and I felt the presence of my grandmothers and everyone else from my past and the room smelled like roses and I could hear the ocean and I kept playing and then he said to fax the napkin to Miami and we could go to Brazil. Isn't it amazing?" I'm dancing around the living room in my underwear, waving the napkin like a flag.

"I have to say, Robin, this is the most ridiculous thing I've ever heard—the guy was obviously hitting on you. He'll probably come back tomorrow and give you a napkin with his room number on it. Why else would he do something like this?"

"Because he liked my music and he said that artists should be treated with respect."

"Obviously he's not a Republican."

"Well, he should be the president of something more than an airline."

"Okay," says John. "Let's fax the napkin in the morning and see what happens."

Faxing the napkin works. Mr. Fontana sends us two first-class tickets to Salvador, in Bahia. The day after our wedding, John and I leave for Brazil. The flight is endless, with connections in Miami and São Paulo, but we dine on pheasant under glass, drink champagne, and watch John Wayne movies dubbed into Portuguese. We're met at the airport in Salvador by a handsome young man named Sergio, a tour guide and musician whose mission it is, over the course of the next ten days, to show us the sights and sounds of Salvador.

After a long bumpy ride in Sergio's van, we arrive at our five-star hotel, dragging our travel-weary bodies along with our bags.

"Finally," I say to John. "We're here. Eighteen hours of flying, 6,000 miles. Can't get much farther away from America than that. Everything here seems so exotic, so different, so unusual."

In the distance I hear a piano. As we near the reception desk the music gets louder. There's no mistaking the piece of music being played by the hotel pianist. It's "New York, New York."

"Well," says John. "Small world."

"Yea," I say. "That's a little disappointing. It's like the time I went to see the changing of the guard at Buckingham Palace and the royal marching band played 'Tie a Yellow Ribbon Round the Old Oak Tree.'"

Next, the hotel pianist plays the Roger Williams arpeggio-extremo version of "Autumn Leaves."

"Tell you what," says John. "Let's dump the bags, drink a *caipirinha*, and hit the streets."

We're exhausted and we don't get far that evening. Holding hands, we take our first nervous steps together in a foreign land, listening for the clamor of the drums, the strumming of guitars, and the whisper of voices singing simple melodies with complex themes. What a way to start a marriage.

Married to the Bass

Okay, Ladies, listen up. Bass players make great husbands. There is no scientific data to support my claim. But having worked my way through the rhythm section, the technicians, and a handful of brass, reed, and string players, I'm a qualified judge.

First, consider this. A man who plays an upright bass is strong. He lugs the instrument around, carries it up steps, slides it in and out of cars, and maneuvers it through large crowds of people. If you marry a bass player you'll be getting a physically fit husband. Okay, there is the occasional back problem. This crops up two or three times a year—usually when you want him to move your grandmother's walnut armoire or need him to stand on a ladder and drill a hole in the ceiling. But you can cope with such minor inconveniences by calling a muscular clarinet player who is handy with a power drill. Good luck finding one. Here's the thing: When your bass player is pain-free, he's as strong as a bull. He has to be in order to make the gig. And he might even throw you over his shoulder and carry you over the threshold every so often, just because he can.

Next, ponder the shape of the upright bass. It's shaped like a woman. A bass player knows about bumps and curves—he even likes them. He has dedicated his life to coaxing beautiful music out of voluptuous contours. He'll do the same for you. Just don't marry a stick-bass player, unless you look like Kate Moss or intend to spend the rest of your life eating lettuce.

Examine the bass player's hands, especially when he's playing a particularly fast passage. Now imagine what those fingers can do to you. Enough said.

A great bassist is an ensemble player, a team member who executes, with confidence, a vital role in any band with the strength of his groove, the steadiness of his rhythm, and the imaginative logic of his harmonic lines. This doesn't just apply to the bassist's music. It also applies to his outlook on life. A bass-player husband will be loyal, true, and interesting, and will help you emerge from life's challenges looking and sounding better than you ever imagined. If you're in a bad mood, don't worry. He'll change keys. On the other hand, if you marry a pianist, he'll try and arrange everything and then tell you what your disposition should be. If you marry a guitarist, he'll try to get ahead of you by analyzing your temperament in double-time. If you marry a drummer, it won't matter what kind of mood you're in because he'll just forge ahead with his own thing. A bass player follows along, supports you, and makes you think that everything is okay, even when the world is crashing down around you.

There are some minor drawbacks. You need to have a house with empty corners, especially if your husband owns more than one upright bass. I know, you have that newly reupholstered Louis XV chair that would look fabulous in the corner by the window. Forget it—that's where the bass has to go. You can come to terms with these trivial decorating disappointments by reflecting on the sculpture-like quality of the instrument. Even when it's silent, it's a work of art.

If you have children—and you will because bass players make great fathers—your most frequently uttered phrase will be "WATCH THE BASS!" You will learn how to interject this phrase into every conversation you have with your children. For instance: "Hello, sweetie, watch the bass, did you have a nice day at kindergarten? We're having rice and broccoli for lunch, watch the bass, do you want milk or water to drink?"

You will be doomed to a life of station wagons, minivans, and SUVs. You might harbor a secret fantasy of zooming around town in a Mazda MX5 convertible, but this will never happen unless you go through a big messy divorce, give your bass-player husband custody of the children, and marry a violinist, which would be no fun at all. Better to accept the hatchback as an integral part of your existence and get on with it.

Any trip you make with your family and the bass will be a pageant that requires detailed organization and nerves of steel. In addition to your two children (one of whom probably wants to be a drummer—heaven help you), you will commence your journey with suitcases, bass, bass trunk, backpacks, amp, car seats, strollers, and diaper bag. Your husband, weighted down with an enormous backpack and a bass trunk the size of a Sub-Zero refrigerator, will leave you to deal with everything else. As you try to walk inconspicuously through the airport terminal, people will point and stare.

First Spectator: "They look the Slovenian Traveling Circus!"

Second Spectator: "Hey buddy, you should have played the flute!"

Things like that.

You will learn how to say *ha, ha, ha*, stick your nose in the air, and pretend that you are traveling with a big star, which of course he is, to you.

Your bass-player husband will know the hip chord changes to just about every song ever written in the history of music. This is a good thing. Just don't ask him to sing the melody. He might be able to play the melody, but he won't sing it—he'll sing the bass line. And, if you happen to play the piano, as I do, don't expect him to just sit there silently and appreciate what you are playing without making *a few suggestions* for better changes and voicings. He'll never give up on trying to improve your playing. But that's why you married him in the first place. He accepts what you do, but he pushes you to do it better.

If you marry the bass player, you marry the bass. Buy one, get one free. Your husband will be passionate about his music, which will grant you the freedom to be passionate about the things you do. You might not worship the bass as much as he does, but you'll love the bass player more every day.

Walkin' My Baby Back Home

*L*ike most pregnant women in the United States, I don't have the luxury of staying home during my pregnancy. Nor do I want to. Aside from the secondhand-smoke problem, playing the piano in a cocktail lounge is a perfect job for a pregnant woman. Most of the time it's safe, the money is good, and there's a lot of free food.

Through my pregnancy I hold down two jobs: an early cocktail hour at the Sheraton Center and a late-night gig in Trumpet's at the Grand Hyatt. I play a total of six hours a night, five nights a week. My husband, John, plays in the jazz trio at the Hyatt, so we see each other on our breaks. We meet back behind the bar on our twenty-minute intermissions, and he rests his hand on my expanding belly and feels the baby kick.

The early months are dicey because of the morning sickness, which affects me in the evening. The odor of food is nauseating, especially at the Hyatt, where a gourmet restaurant is connected to the cocktail lounge. The kitchen is thirty yards from the piano, but my heightened sense of smell detects every sauce, spice, meat, and fish that sizzles on the oversized grills back behind the big metal double doors leading into the hotel kitchen. I sit down to play the piano, and the odor of red snapper in a garlic-basil sauce wafts through the lounge and just about kills me. I've got the same problem in our apartment. My Baldwin is in the front of the building, and even when the windows are sealed tight I can smell the kitchens of every restaurant on the block: Chinese, Mexican, Italian, Greek. I think the Thai place is the most offensive. My sense of smell is so impressive, John says I could get a job at the airport helping the dogs sniff out drugs and illegal shipments of fruit.

I love being a pregnant pianist. Going to work is my favorite activity, along with perusing the Baby Gap displays and running my fingers over the tiny folds of pale blue overalls and onesies printed with snowflakes and bunnies. My own wardrobe is very black. I don't own a thing that fits, so I buy a huge black silk chiffon shirt and a black skirt with a drawstring waist. Coincidentally, one of the other pianists in Trumpet's, also a tall blond, is pregnant at the same time. We joke about the piano bench and call it the Steinway fertility stool. She's been having a secret affair with the general manager of the hotel, one thing led to another, and now it's not a secret anymore. The usual employee gossip ensues, and before we know it there are dozens of workers from all over the hotel poking their heads into the lounge to see the piano girl who "got knocked up by the boss." I think this is a riot until I realize everyone thinks *I'm* the one. I've been knocked up by the bass player, not the general manager, thank you very much. I don't want any confusion about this. I learned my lesson long ago. Never ever kiss the boss.

I treasure my time at the piano, fantasizing that my unborn son hears every note I play. Each song becomes a personal communication from me to him. I imagine my baby floating in his amniotic sea, humming along and tapping his tiny foot to the music. I play music I love. My baby responds by settling down and sleeping during my sets. At night, when it's quiet and I try to sleep, he retaliates by practicing time-steps against my ribs. "More music," he says. "Whatever you do, don't stop playing."

My pregnancy becomes very noticeable in my seventh month. I can't stop eating big buckets of Japanese soba noodle soup. I drink quarts of orange juice every day. I'm astonished by my changing body—I look like I have a basketball under my dress, along with the team. When I get to my third trimester, I'm ready to stop playing—I'm tired of waddling the three blocks from the subway to the gig. But we need the money.

I settle that by falling and breaking my arm two days after my due date. On my way to the Hyatt I slip on a wet sidewalk and land, belly up, right next to a bin of potatoes in the outdoor produce section of the Tradefair Supermarket. I'm instantly surrounded by a committee of concerned old Greek ladies, talking about me like I'm unconscious.

"Oh, my God. Look at her. She's pregnant. Quick, call the ambulance!"

"Oh, my God, this is how Ariadne lost little Niko. Quick, call the ambulance!"

"Oh, my God, look at the water! Look at the puddle. Quick, call the ambulance!"

"Oh, my god, her water broke."

"Her water broke."

"Her water broke."

"Did someone call the ambulance? Someone give her onions to smell. That will stop the labor!"

What labor? A woman shoves a raw onion in front of my nose.

"She's in labor!"

"She's in labor!"

"She's in labor!"

"My water hasn't broken," I shout. "There's a puddle on the street because it's raining, and I'm fine, really I am, except for your damn onion. Please just help me get up so I can go home."

"But you're in labor!"

"No I'm not. I think I would know if I was in labor," I say.

"It's coming!"

"The baby?"

"No! The ambulance!"

"The ambulance is coming!"

I hear sirens blaring in the background. Now there's an even bigger crowd around me. I look up and dozens of white faces stare down at me like they're peering into a wishing well to see where their pennies have landed. I yell at them to let me up, but they won't hear me. It's cold on the sidewalk. I try again to get up, but wrinkled hands hold me down.

"Don't move!" shouts one of them. "Remember little Niko!"

I lie there a long time, long enough that I begin to feel injured. What if I've hurt my baby? What if he really does end up like little Niko? I feel my baby kick, and I know he's okay. I know I'm okay. But the ladies still won't let me get off the sidewalk. The ambulance arrives. Two guys who look like Cheech and Chong hoist me onto a stretcher. One of them makes a joke about needing a crane, which I certainly do not appreciate, not one bit.

"It's Elmhurst for you, little lady. That's the closest hospital with a maternity ward."

"The baby's fine," I say.

"These ladies say you're in labor."

"No I'm not," I say.

"Not for you to decide."

I sigh and turn my head away from the crowd.

"Give her oxygen!" shouts an excited Greek woman.

The baby is fine. I have a hairline fracture of my left elbow. I call John at the Hyatt, where he's in the middle of his second set. He arrives at Elmhurst Hospital thirty minutes later, wearing a tuxedo, and cringes as the resident puts a cast on my arm. If the Borough of Queens holds a contest tonight for its most pathetic-looking resident, I will surely win. I'm soaking wet in a black chiffon caftan, ten months pregnant, with my arm in a cast.

Baby Curtis arrives two weeks later by caesarean section. He weighs a whopping eleven pounds, two ounces and breaks a six-year biggest-baby record at NYU Medical Center. He's enormous. He's beautiful. I fall in love with him.

When I return to work six weeks later, I'm sad. For the first time ever, I dread going to work every night. I still enjoy the piano, but I hate taking Curtis to the babysitter and leaving him there for hours so I can go play tunes for a bunch of traveling salesmen. I hate running off to the ladies' room every forty minutes to siphon milk from my breasts with a medieval torture device. I hate being across town from my child. And I hate playing songs that he can't hear.

Then again, there is so much to love about my life. I love my healthy baby boy, who laughs and bounces around in his jolly jumper swing every time his dad plays "Blue Skies" or "Lulu's Back in Town." I love my brand-new English stroller with its Pope-mobile plastic cover. I love wheeling my son all over Manhattan in every kind of weather. I love my friends, my health club, my grand piano, and my bass-player husband, who keeps me laughing by bringing me goofy souvenirs from his concert tours to faraway lands.

Most of all, I love the long hours in the afternoon when I can play the piano at home while my son sleeps, curled up and content under his pale yellow blanket, dreaming, I like to think, of bears and butterflies, dancing shadows, and music that never stops.

Part III

1994–2004

Music of Good-bye

"*I* can't believe you're leaving New York," says Robin Spielberg. "It doesn't seem real."

We stand, holding hands, by the turnstiles leading to the N train at Fifty-seventh Street.

My family will be moving to Europe next week. Robin and I have just recorded my first solo piano CD, *Somewhere in Time*. She pitched the idea to a small record company in New England, and they hired her to produce the recording. I've never pursued a recording career, so I'm blown away by the very idea of the project. Hard as I try, I can't imagine that anyone will buy one of my CDs in a record store unless they want to recreate that hotel-cocktail-lounge environment in the privacy of their own homes. Why not throw in a package of salted nuts, an overworked waitress, and a crowd of noisy chiropractors. But Robin Spielberg has more faith in my music than I do.

After a pleasantly intense six hours at Nola Recording Studios in Midtown Manhattan, we've got the makings of a nice CD. Ten years of rehearsing in Manhattan hotel lobbies gave me time to prepare.

꒰

The timing of the record contract is ironic. After a decade of playing in Manhattan piano bars, my time in New York City has come to a close. John has accepted the jazz bass chair with the Westdeutscher Rundfunk (WDR) Big Band, a jazz group sponsored by a large public television and radio conglomerate in Europe. I'd like to say that we've struggled with the decision for months and that we've lost sleep wondering whether we should leave New York. But we haven't. We're ready for a change. Both of us are working round the clock, our son spends way too much time with the babysitter, and the cost of private schooling in New York City looms like a five-headed monster. The job in Germany will mean a better education for our son, a chance for him to be bilingual, a great salary and benefits for my husband, and time for us to be a family. More than anything, we want time together, a luxury that too few American families these days can afford.

We've hired a *very serious* German teacher named Brunhilde, given notice on our apartment and various jobs, and called the German moving men. In five days they will pack all of our belongings, large and small, into organized boxes, stack them in a container, and ship them across the water to our new home.

჻

I've never been good at farewells. Saying good-bye to my friends isn't easy. I know that the promises we make to stay in touch, as well-intended as they may be, will be eaten alive by distance and time. In the end I'll be left with an overstuffed photo album, scraps of conversations that cling to my memory, and the echoes of songs that remind me of a place I once loved. I know how much kindness I'll be leaving behind. All I can do is trust that, no matter what, the memory of these friendships will sustain, nurture, and guide me. It won't be enough, but that's the price I'll have to pay for moving on.

Robin and I embrace one last time before going to our separate subway platforms. She gave me a blue crystal globe at the recording session this morning, and I feel the weight of it in my pocket as I wave to her on the opposite side of the station. This phase of my life—the New York phase—is coming to an end. Trains roar and squeal in the station, but in my mind I hear Robin's laughter, her words of encouragement, her gentle reminders that my music has a place in the world. She has been my cheerleader, my sounding board, my fellow musician, my friend. I'll never replace her. I start to cry. A train pulls up to the platform between us. When it departs, she is gone.

ॐ

The last hotel piano job I play in New York City is right where I started—in the Grand Hyatt. It's a warm June afternoon, a perfect New York day. The lobby swarms with tourists eager to eat and drink and get outside to experience the city I'm preparing to leave. It's an odd feeling, playing my last job in Manhattan. I want something meaningful to happen, but it doesn't. I'm disappointed but not surprised. Last jobs in the lounge-music field are just like first jobs. The interesting part is what happens in between.

Today at the Hyatt, I play all of my favorite songs and end my last set with Carole King's "Far Away." Some of the regular Lobby People pass the piano, but not one of them even bothers to say hello. The sunlight filters through the skylights and reflects off the shiny surfaces in the marble lobby. I notice the mottled patterns of shadow and light on my hands. I long for fresh air. It seems a perfect time to leave.

ॐ

"Hey you, Piano Girl!" yells Virginia the street lady as I pass by her corner. I've just been to the babysitter to retrieve my son, and we're going for a last walk around the neighborhood.

"Where the hell do you think you're going?" she shouts.

It's almost 100 degrees today, but Virginia is wearing a heavy winter coat. I try to ignore her, like always, and hurry past with my head down. Curtis waves at her. He waves at everyone.

"You think you're going somewhere better, but you're not, you know. Anywhere you end up is good enough for the likes of you."

Well, that's sort of a compliment. Or maybe not. Virginia confuses me. How does she even know I'm leaving the city?

"You're not the mother of that baby," she says. That stops me dead in my tracks.

"That baby belongs to everyone else. Not you."

Oh, brother.

"Goodbye Virginia," I say. "Good luck to you."

"But you're not going anywhere. Not really. Your spindly legs won't carry you far. You've ascended to your level of incompetence. The rest is futile. Everyone leaves. No one stays. Not even babies. Not even music. Time moves past you before you have a chance to grab on and go for a ride."

I push the stroller up the avenue and hope she's not right.

༜

We call two cabs on the morning of our departure: a van for John and the bass in its big white fiberglass flight case, and a station wagon for Curtis and me, all of our suitcases, and the baby paraphernalia necessary to travel anywhere with a toddler. As John and the drivers load the cars, I walk around the apartment one last time, with Curtis in my arms. He is eighteen months old.

"Here's where you took your first steps," I say. "And here's where you said your first word. Hot. Your first word was 'hot.'"

"Hop," he says.

"Here's where you liked to sit and swing while Daddy played the bass. And here's where Mommy's piano once stood."

"Panno," says Curtis. "Mommy panno."

"Yes," I say. "Mommy's piano. Where Mommy hung out and wrote songs about someday meeting a man like your daddy and having a baby boy like you."

"Mommy music."

"This is your first home, Curtis, the place where I dreamed about you before you were even you." I whisper. "Your first home. I hope you'll always remember it."

"'Member," he says. "Curty 'member."

I take him downstairs and strap him into his car seat. It's sweltering outside. John peers into the open window of our cab.

"You okay?" he asks. He knows I'm not.

"Yeah," I say. "I'm okay. Let's get this show on the road."

Across the water you stare,
You've saved enough for the fare,
Waiting your turn, you dare yourself to leave,
Across the water you'll sail,
You can always come home again.
Across the water you gaze,
Into a tunnel of haze,
Standing on shore, and trying not to cry,
Across the water you'll sail,
You can always come home again.
Sailing away,
Sailing away...
Across the water you row,
Into the sunrise you go,
Picking up speed, the wake grows ever strong,
Across the water you sail,
But you'll never come home again.
Sailing away,
Sailing away...

Intermission

My Baldwin grand survives the move to Germany with grace, in spite of three hulking furniture movers named Hans, Hans, and Franz. They wear bright red overalls that are too tight in the crotch and take long breaks during which they sit on my living-room floor and consume man-sized portions of *Schnitzel und Pommes*. Hans, Hans, and Franz, who normally move sofas, boxes of books, and large oak closets, are baffled by the grand piano, which has come off the container truck with our more-pedestrian belongings. After much consultation, head scratching, and a phone call to an expert at the *Zentrale*, Hans, Hans, and Franz hoist the piano off of the floor and onto its three legs by using a tiny block of wood, a string of German expletives, and brute strength. I cover my eyes during this procedure. They succeed, but I'm not sure if it's dumb luck or absolute brilliance that guides them. I have my piano back, and it looks very much at home in front of the big bay window that faces the garden.

No one offers me a job in Germany, and I'm not out looking for one. I've got a new language to learn and a toddler son who needs constant supervision. His favorite activities include turning CDs into Frisbees and unwinding cassette tapes from their spools to make "spaghetti." On his good days Curtis is a little prince. On his bad days he turns into the Robert DeNiro character in *Cape Fear*.

We live in a spacious apartment in a little village outside of Cologne, Germany, where it's difficult to find people willing to speak English. German is a demanding language, and although my son takes to it without hesitation, my thirty-seven-year-old brain has difficulty processing the new words and sounds.

"Mommy, snort more," my son says. "Snort and spit."

Unless you're a devotee of Wagner operas, German is not a musical language. It's rough, guttural, and fragmented-sounding, and it doesn't roll elegantly off the tongue like French, Italian, or Portuguese. My work is cut out for me. John, playing and recording in Cologne with the jazz band, has daily contact with English-speaking musicians. I'm at home, trying to have English conversations with my two-year-old and German play dates with other kids and their mothers. I serve cake and coffee and try to make small talk. I sound like the *Hausfrau* version of Colonel Klink.

ॐ

What a pleasure it is to play every day for my own amusement. I discover the gratifications of a hobby musician. On the job, I'd played what I had to play and tried to make it agreeable to my ears. At home I play what I want to play and don't care if it sounds awful. I start writing music during Curtis's nap times, thinking about projects I will complete when my family is more mature, and experimenting with melodies and themes that develop into the compositions I will one day record.

Curtis, before he was born, had listened to me play my perfect little hotel-lobby arrangements every night on the job. I'd hardly ever practiced while pregnant with Curtis—I was too busy playing five-hour gigs. While pregnant with our second child, Julia, my approach to the piano is very different. Her prenatal music-appreciation classes are my practice sessions, full of mistakes and false starts as I struggle to find the harmonic structure of the pieces I compose during my pregnancy. Later, when my children are older and have developed their own musical personalities, I will wonder how much influence my music had on them while they were still inside me.

The birth of my daughter is stress-free. Julia, right from the start, is an easy baby, if there is such a thing. She has piercing blue eyes, inherited from her grandmother Eloise, and white blond hair that stands on end when it starts to grow. She has my sister's slapstick sense of humor, her father's creative intelligence, and the laugh of an old German lady who has had too much *Schnapps*. Her brother teaches her how to play the drums with two spoons and forces her to listen to Prince tapes (the ones he hasn't unwound) on his Old Mcdonald's Farm cassette recorder.

I battle with the language and finally get to the point where I'm understood by my patient neighbors. I fight with my music as I experiment with the new sounds coming out of my middle-aged fingers. I confront the stress of motherhood by composing peaceful melodies that soothe my weary brain. I beat back the loneliness of living without my New York pals by forcing myself to make new friends. Everything is novel to me. Each day is an exercise in finding out how much I don't know—about raising children, about the German language, about making music. I feel like a giant kid who has been sent back to the first grade. I have a child's eyes and ears in an adult body—an enlightening sensation for a woman pushing forty.

I start working again. One gray February morning, as I'm packing Julia into the Pope-mobile stroller, an agent calls with a job.

The Voice of Doom, who has been on vacation for over three years, says *no, no, no, you're not ready to go back*. But then the Voice of Reason grabs me by the back of the neck and tells me to wake up and get back to a place where I can share the company of other adults and make some money. My first gig in Germany is a private party in a stylish restaurant that used to be the waiting room of the Cologne train station. After a three-year hiatus, whipping myself into shape to play a five-hour piano job is a test. I've always played without fake books or sheet music in front of me, on principle. My challenge, this time around, is to remember what I know. I write lists of songs. I practice for weeks, trying to kick-start my muscle memory. It seems a little foolish, really, practicing for a cocktail piano gig, but three years is a long time to be away from the scene.

As I approach the Bechstein grand on that first night back, a dense fog of European cigarette smoke obscures the sea of German faces surrounding me. The rich din of casual chatting fills my ears with a familiar resonance. The waiters bustle back and forth with overflowing trays, stepping around the piano, through conversations, and back to the safety of the service bar.

I begin to play. I feel fragile and cautious, unsure of my music as it floats over the crowd. Moments later I am myself again, relaxed, happy, and savoring the evening as it welcomes me back. I might be in a foreign country. But sitting at the piano, I am home.

Playback 1998

"*Bitte*, Frau Goldsby, if you'll simply take your place at the piano, we'll begin lighting the remaining candles."

The piano, a white Bösendorfer grand, perches on a small platform in the middle of a huge ballroom in the five-star Quellenhof Hotel in Aachen, Germany. Surrounding the piano are 1,000 tall white tapered candles. Exactly 1,000, I've been told by the manager. I'm to sit in the middle of the circle of candles and play as 250 guests are escorted into the ballroom. All of the candles have been lit except for fifty or so at one end of the circle of fire. Management has thoughtfully left this group of candles unlit so that I can get to the piano without my ball gown catching on fire.

"*Uh, es sieht mir ein bisschen gefährlich aus,*" I say. "It looks a little dangerous to me. Once I get in there will I be able to get out?"

"*Natürlich!*" says Herr Lipp, the banquet manager. "Just signal me or the waiter and we'll escort you through the flames. Please, we must hurry, the men will be arriving."

"The men?" I say.

"Yes, our guests this evening are all men. From Italy."

"Oh! *Wunderschön!*" I say.

Shit, I think. The last time I played for a group of Italian guys, six of them ended up sitting on top of the piano singing "Volare."

"I will give the signal when to play," says Herr Lipp. "There will be a trumpet fanfare, then the lights will go out and the candle effect will become evident. Then you will play. *Alles klar?*"

"*Alles klar*, Herr Lipp," I say. This guy needs a new name.

I make my way to the piano. A flurry of activity commences behind me as tuxedo-clad waiters hurry to light the remaining candles, closing the circle behind me. I'm trapped. I look around. Over the tops of the candles I see the flowers lining the entrance to the ballroom—white amaryllis, perhaps 500 of them, each stem in a tall crystal vase. I play a few notes on the piano to check out the action. The piano is out of tune and the action is horrible.

Scheisse. They've paid a zillion deutsche marks for flowers and candles, but no one has thought to call the piano tuner. For a split second I think I'm back in Waterbury.

Perhaps management thinks the guests won't notice an out-of-tune piano. But the guests will notice something, that's for sure. People hear a crappy piano and they think the pianist is bad. I've been fighting this battle for too many years. Obviously, it's an international problem.

"*Bitte*, Frau Goldsby, we need to do a sound check," says the sound man hired for the evening. The Bösendorfer is miked to provide an even sound throughout the enormous room, which has been lined with speakers. A nice touch, if only they'd tuned the damn piano.

I play through a chord progression, trying to determine the safe areas of the instrument.

"*Danke*, Frau Goldsby," says the sound man over the PA.

"*Bitte*," I reply. Now we must wait for the Italians to show up, which could take forever. If only I'd brought a magazine. It's lonely in here.

And warm. It's getting very warm. One-thousand candles generate a lot of heat. It's winter and I'm wearing a pink silk taffeta full-length skirt with a matching cashmere sweater. The flames dance around me. It's a charming effect, really. But jeez, it's hot. I'm starting to *schwitz* like a fat girl. My make-up is melting and there are drops of sweat beading on my forehead. I wish the Italian guys would get here so we could get this over with. But they're Italian. They'll be late, of course.

All of the sudden, machines begin to blow clouds of fog around the piano. No one has warned me about this. Or maybe Herr Lipp told me, in German, and I didn't understand him. How do you say "dry ice" in German, anyway? Now I not only have flames, I have smoke. I thought all I would have to do tonight is show up, sit in the corner, and play "Misty." Now look at me. I don't look like a kitten up a tree. I look like friggin' Saint Joan. Still no Italians. I can't see much of anything, but suddenly I hear the blare of trumpets playing the theme from *Rocky*. The house lights go off, and the only light remaining comes from the army of candles surrounding me. I feel like I'm in a rocket ship about to blast off. I can't see Herr Lipp, but I assume this is the time to play. I have no idea what to play, so I bash out a big, loud arrangement of a processional piece I wrote. If it wasn't for the candlelight I wouldn't be able to see the keys.

I hate fog machines. They always make me cough.

I imagine the Italians drinking their prosecco and eating little pieces of prosciutto wrapped around melon balls. I wonder how long this *Aperitif Stunde*, or cocktail hour, will last. I feel like a *Schwein* on a spit. Please, please, please let them go in to dinner soon.

"*Danke*, Frau Goldsby," booms the sound man's voice. "Everything is in order and now we are prepared to start when the guests arrive."

Good Lord. That was only the dress rehearsal.

No wonder the piano is out of tune. It's about 400 degrees in this room.

"*Wasser, bitte!*" I say, to no one in particular. "*Ich brauche Wasser!* I'm so thirsty. Please, get Herr Lipp. I need water."

The lights come back on, and the waiters scuttle about replacing burned-down candles with new ones. I stand on the platform and wave my arms. The smoke has cleared enough that I can be seen. A waiter brings a bottle of water and rolls it toward me under one of the tables holding the candles.

That's good. There's space under the tables. If things get too bad I can always crawl out. As I open my water bottle, Herr Lipp runs into the ballroom, waving his arms like a madman. I guess this is the sign.

"Stand by," says the sound man.

For better or worse, the Germans are experts at making big productions out of simple things. I guess what we're doing tonight is artsy in a bizarre way, and I suppose, from the other side of the flames, my dramatic presence at the white grand piano inside the circle of fire will be appreciated by the throng of Versace-suited gentlemen eating and drinking in air-conditioned comfort. But this is one weird job. The smoke billows around me. I take a quick slug of water, wipe the sweat from my head, and prepare to play.

Some Enchanted Evening

On a crisp New Year's Day in 1999, I walk through the heavy iron gate leading to the front door of Schlosshotel Lerbach. History seeps out of the stone walls as I touch them with my fingertips. I step inside the main hall of the building. It is intimate and noble, fancy and relaxed, all at once. I feel like Cinderella at an informal ball.

Tonight I'm attending my husband's concert at the castle. Schloss Lerbach intrigues me—it's a grand country residence plopped in the rolling green hills of Bergisch Gladbach, Germany. The castle property itself dates back to 1384, with various restorations taking place over the centuries. In 1893 the castle was dismantled because of dampness and then rebuilt in another location on the same property. Centuries of precipitation have weathered the structure, but also given it a regal and noble complexion.

The Schloss perches on a small hill overlooking a park with grown-up trees and a fairytale lake inhabited by swans and ducks. The property, owned by the Siemens family, is currently operated by hotelier Thomas Althoff, a German businessman with a knack for finding landmark castles and buildings and turning them into five-star monuments of luxury, history, and style.

John's concert is wonderful. Sixty guests sit in a circle around the musicians. Tonight I'm listening to elegantly played jazz, but the intimate atmosphere and exquisite decor of the concert room inspire images of parlor concerts and soirees of centuries past. There are friendly ghosts in the room, I'm sure of it.

As John and I drink perfectly chilled French champagne with the guests at the post-concert reception, I study the oil-painted portraits of previous owners. I take in the polished black-and-white marble floor, the overstuffed furniture surrounding the crackling fire in the centuries-old fireplace, the winding oak staircase, the towering ceiling, the soft golden glow of the silk-covered walls, the shimmering candles burning in giant iron candelabras on each side of the grand piano in the center of the main hall. It's a hotel that feels like the best kind of home. I'm hooked.

But what about that piano in the main hall? Why isn't anyone playing atmosphere music? It's the only thing that's missing.

I haven't thought about taking a steady piano job again until now. I've been playing private parties here and there, but, because of the children, I haven't wanted to commit myself to a regular schedule. But Julia is in kindergarten now and Curtis has started elementary school, and maybe working a few hours a week would be good for all of us. Especially here. I know the style of music I've been working on would be a perfect match for the castle. I look at John. He guesses what I'm thinking.

"You know," says John to the director of the hotel. "You should hire my wife to play that nice piano of yours. She'd be perfect for this place."

Nothing moves quickly in Germany. It's a land of paperwork and red tape, even when it comes to piano players. I put my CD and a press kit—which I've patched together from scraps of my New York City life—into an overpriced and understated cream-colored envelope, and send the whole mess off to the Schloss. John, confident that it's just a question of time before I get the job, buys me a Laura Ashley rose-printed ball skirt lined with several layers of tulle and silk—cocktail-piano castle wear.

"This way," he says, "you'll be prepared."

Indeed I am. Three months after sending my press kit, the phone rings. There's a piano emergency at the castle. The band hired for the night is stuck in a twenty-kilometer traffic jam on the Autobahn. The hotel director wants to know if I can get to the castle immediately and play until the band arrives. "Sure," I say. "No problem." I've just gotten home from a swim session with the kids. I'm bedraggled and wearing gray sweatpants and my husband's T-shirt. I call the babysitter, throw on the Laura Ashley ball skirt and some makeup, and drive to the castle as quickly as I can.

I pull up to the front of the Schloss, and people in uniforms start taking things from me. The doorman takes my car, an assistant manager takes my coat, a man in a tuxedo takes my purse. I'm in a tizzy from all the rushing, but I take a couple of deep breaths and put on my *everything is under control and I'm perfectly calm* mask.

"Thank goodness you're here," says the hotel director. "May I introduce you to our client this evening? This is Frau Himpelhof. Frau Himpelhof, our pianist, Frau Goldsby."

"Oh, thank you for coming!" says Frau Himpelhof. She carries a clipboard and is wearing a perfect conservatively cut black dinner suit, black pumps, and the kind of bizarre eyeglasses you only see on Germans. They are silver with branches of cobalt blue that poke up over her eyebrows in abstract shapes that end in curlicues over her temples. It's difficult to look at her without thinking of a Japanese comic-book figure or a pinball machine. I want to pull the lever on the top of her glasses to see what happens.

"Who knows when the band will get here!" says Frau Himpelhof. "They're stuck somewhere in Essen! Now, listen! The first helicopters are arriving."

"The helicopters?"

"Yes, the guests are flying in from Köln."

Köln is only a twenty-minute drive from where we're standing.

"You should start playing immediately. Let me introduce you to your dancers."

"My dancers?"

"Yes, your dancers. Oh, where are they? These dancers are always sneaking off somewhere!" I hear the growl of the helicopters as they land on the long green lawn down by the lake.

"Someone get Jasmine and Heike!" yells Frau Himpelhof. "We must begin!"

Two very tall models wearing silver bodysuits scramble down the staircase and pose on each side of the piano. Their hair, teased and lacquered into an Afro style, has been sprayed silver. Each one of them looks seven feet tall—Amazon women dipped into silver paint.

"Whatever you do, don't play anything with a tempo," says Heike.

"Ja, ve vant zee free-form Musik!" says Jasmine. "Ve are zee interpretive dancers."

"Ah, yes. Interpretive dancing! How lovely. Okay, Free-form music, no problem," I say, and then play the way I always play. The guests stream through the door. They're greeted with glasses of champagne and trays of thinly sliced smoked salmon on tiny disks of toast. Overflowing pots of Stargazer Lilies line the main hall and scent the air with their hopeful fragrance. I glance at the silver dancers as they do jerky, mime-like movements on either side of me. Pretty wacky. But hey, it's show business, and it's Germany.

I continue to play. Jasmine and Heike look satisfied. Actually, they look orgasmic as they stop jerking and begin writhing and slithering around the piano and each other. One thing's for sure—our outfits are out of sync. My floral ball skirt doesn't match the high-tech silver bodysuits. But at least I match the room. There are pink rose petals on the piano.

The guests look like a contemporary acrylic painting of stylish Europeans. Clustered in the corner is a group of Spanish women dressed in eight different shades of green. The Dutch men standing to my left have fluffy hair, zany-looking ties, and cute leather shoes with elfin toes and silver buckles. I assume the two chain-smoking and bored-looking women lounging by the staircase are French—only French women drape their Hermes scarves so perfectly around their shoulders.

The silver dancers dance. I play. Everyone is happy, even though they're too sophisticated to smile. An hour ago I was careening down a giant slide with my kids into the bright blue water of the Oktopus Schwimbad. What a surprise this day has turned out to be. I absorb the unanticipated opulence around me.

Contrast in life is a good thing.

I participate in many wonderfully strange evenings at Schloss Lerbach. For a year I play private parties there, showing up to make music for state dinners, European soccer teams, golden anniversary parties, birthdays, and weddings. I play for parties of 400 and parties of eight. Usually the staff gets everything just right, in spite of hysterical clients, overworked banquet managers, and the occasional failed delivery. Management even remembers to tune the piano occasionally.

When I'm offered a steady job at the Schloss, playing Friday and Saturday evenings and Sunday afternoons, I'm delighted to accept. If I'd grown up in Europe, where there seems to be a castle on every corner, having a piano job in a such a place wouldn't be a big deal. But we didn't have castles in Pittsburgh. And there certainly weren't any in New York City, in spite of what Leona Helmsley told us.

Germany takes much better care of its artists than we Americans do. I observe this in my husband's career, but I also witness it first-hand on my cocktail piano engagements at the castle.

Maybe this is because the men and women working at Schloss Lerbach—in the kitchen, at the front desk, in the restaurants, in the bar—are artists as well. Many of them, enchanted by the castle and the secrets hidden in its ancient walls, are willing to work long hours to make magic for the guests who trust the special occasions of their lives to them. The hotel employees of Lerbach are masters of illusion, well trained in the craft of unassuming splendor. I work with grown men who can take six votive candles, two roses, and a piece of pomegranate and turn them into a breathtaking still-life arrangement on an old wooden table. I work with women who can make a guest feel at home in four or five languages. I work with an Italian bartender who never forgets to tell any woman who walks into the room how beautiful she looks.

Dieter and Birgit Müller operate the castle's Michelin three-star restaurant. Dieter, an elf-like sorcerer in the kitchen, turns out visually beautiful and gastronomically astonishing creations, while Birgit, a social virtuoso, welcomes guests as though they're old friends and chases the stuffiness out of gourmet dining. The Müllers and their staff are masters at making people happy. Yes, it's all smoke and mirrors. But the intent, and the desire to please, is genuine. In a world that has grown ordinary with indifference and disbelief, I embrace their enthusiasm. It's a joy to be part of it all.

In *The World According to Mister Rogers* (Hyperion) Fred Rogers said, "The thing I remember best about successful people I've met all through the years is their obvious delight in what they're doing.... It seems to have very little to do with worldly success. They just love what they're doing, and they love it in front of others."

Schloss Lerbach isn't perfect—there isn't a hotel in the world that runs smoothly for more than an hour at a time—but it's about as close as it gets.

Playback 2002

*I*t's Sunday afternoon. I sit at the century-old Bechstein grand in the lobby lounge of Schloss Bensberg, a sister castle of Schloss Lerbach. Guests arriving for cake and coffee hover around the elaborate dessert display at the entrance to the lounge, waiting for a free table. There are an *Apfelkuchen*, a strawberry cake, a cream cake with slivers of almonds on top, and a cheesecake dusted with cocoa powder. These will be served with enormous mounds of *Schlagsahne* and great steaming bowls of *Milch Kaffee* or delicate cups of espresso.

Maybe I'll get a piece of that *Apfelkuchen* on my first break.

The lounge is full. I start my set with "Somewhere Over the Rainbow," and four little girls dressed in fairy costumes get off the elevator and dance through the lobby. Where did they come from? They wear pink and yellow chiffon dresses, angel wings, and wreaths of flowers around their plaited blond hair. Shards of late afternoon light pierce the magnificent panes of glass at the front of the castle, and the little girls dance through the rays. They twirl in time to the music, flinging their magic wands to cast spells on the adults ambling through the ornate, cavernous lobby.

Over here! Point your wand this way! Cast a spell on me!

The grown-up guests in the hotel are staunch and serious. Their backs are straight, every hair on every head is in place, and they're dressed in their finest Sunday clothes.

I want to get up from the piano, put on a gossamer dress and wings, and join the little girls as they tumble and flit around the feet of the customers. But I'm too old for a fairy costume. The girls get some condescending smiles and a couple of disapproving looks. But they don't care, they keep dancing. I play for them, hoping to orchestrate their lovely choreography with appropriate fairy music.

I play "In My Own Little Corner" from *Cinderella*.

They dance.

I play a song from a musical I wrote about a giant rabbit and a group of fairies that live in the forest.

They dance.

"*Entschuldigung*, Frau Goldsby," says the pretty waitress, who has burns on her thumbs from steaming so much milk. "The woman at table eight wants to hear Andrew Lloyd Weber music. She has sent this champagne to you."

"Okay," I say, and I nod and smile at the woman. I was on television last month talking about my job, and I mentioned how nice it was to have a glass of champagne on the piano while working. I meant it to be funny, really. Now people keep sending champagne to the piano. There are worse fates.

I play the opening bars of "Memory" from *Cats*, and as I lead into the melody, I realize, too late, that Hans the International Tenor is sitting at the bar. Hans is a rich guy who is out of his mind. He believes himself to be an excellent opera singer and never misses an opportunity to break into song. I always know when he's about to let it rip—he sits up very straight, and his nostrils flare.

I've been told by management not to let him sing, ever. With all that marble in the lobby and the high ceilings, his voice—which is excruciatingly loud and out of tune—qualifies as an instrument of torture.

"All alone in zee moonlight," he sings. "Has zee moooooooon lost its memory? I am standink alone."

Now what? People are holding their ears. The fairy girls flick their wands in Hans's direction, trying to get him to stop. I have a smile frozen on my face as I try to figure out how to end the song quickly. I don't want to hurt Hans's feelings, but I also can't subject fifty paying guests to his braying.

Hans the International Tenor stands and gesticulates with wild abandon. We're coming up to the big key-change. I'm playing faster and faster, trying to get to the end of the song.

"Und zoon it vill be mornink!"

I'm at my wit's end. But look! I'm rescued. Here is the Gay Baron, Herr Karl Ditters von Dittersdorf, an aging queen of a man who dresses in head-to-toe sable. Sable boots, green sable coat, and a matching sable hat. He has diamond cuffs wrapped around each wrist and large emerald rings adorning each of his manicured fingers. His hair and eyebrows are tinted a curious shade of dark red, and he wears thick makeup. The Gay Baron's hat is a wool felt creation with a plume of ostrich feathers on one side and little sable pom-poms dangling from the wide brim. He struts into the lounge like he owns the place—for all I know he does—and completely upstages Hans the International Tenor. The guests stare, fascinated, as the Gay Baron strolls around searching for an empty table. He flashes his wrists as he passes each table, making sure that everyone sees his flamboyant jewelry. I love this guy. Accompanying the Gay Baron is a white French poodle named Mitzi on a jewel-studded leash. She wears a diamond collar and a little sable coat of her own.

A tastefully dressed couple gets up to leave a table close to the piano. The Gay Baron, ignoring the queue of people waiting for seats, slides into the vacated spot. No one argues with him. You can't argue with a man who has pom-poms on his hat.

Hans the International Tenor is coming to his big finish. "Touch me, it's so eazzzzy to leaf me…" He throws an arm out to the side in a final dramatic gesture, knocking over a sugar bowl, a candle holder, and a crystal vase of roses.

Giuseppe walks through the door. Guiseppe is very Italian, and he happens to be a midget.

This feels like a Mel Brooks film.

Giuseppe stands, with a hopeful look in his eyes, off to the side of the lounge. Any second now he will be asking me if he can sing "Ave Maria." Giuseppe is a good singer, but I have to bring the talent-contest portion of the afternoon to an end before I get fired.

Giuseppe sits down at the Gay Baron's table and orders a Coke. The waitress serves water in a silver bowl to Mitzi. The Gay Baron interrogates the waitress about every single ingredient in every single piece of cake on the cart.

"I have to watch my figure," he says.

There is a smattering of embarrassed applause for Hans the International Tenor.

The Gay Baron sends me a glass of champagne. Now I have one on each side of the Bechstein.

I play an original song called "Winter Lullaby." There, that's better. Hans the International Tenor can't sing along if he doesn't know the words. I pray he doesn't know how to scat.

"Excusa me, Missa Robin," says Giuseppe. "Could you playa fo' me 'Ave Maria'?"

I look out into the lobby. The little girl fairies are gone. I hope they didn't go somewhere and grow up.

Here Comes That Bride

"So. You'll play for us on the seventh of August, from seven to ten in the evening?" says Frau Braun.

"It's on my calendar," I say. "I'll be there thirty minutes early to make sure everything is in order."

"I just want some background music to be played during dinner, nothing too loud."

"No problem. That's my specialty. You have my CD. What I play on the CD is exactly the type of thing I'll play for your party."

"Perfect. I love that CD. You know what? Please send twenty of them to the banquet department. I'd love to use them as bridal-party gifts."

"What a nice idea. I'll give you a good price on them." I'm mentally calculating how much additional income this will generate. "So I'll see you on the seventh."

"Oh, wait, one thing," she says.

I should have known. Brides always start thinking of stuff if you don't get off the phone quickly.

"When the guests are coming into the room, will you play something from *Carmen*, or something that sounds like bullfight music?"

"You want bullfight music for a wedding?"

"Well, yes, I met my fiancé in Spain."

"Okay. Bullfight music." I make a note on my calendar to figure something out. "So I'll see you on the seventh."

"Wait! Another thing. Between the soup and the salad course, I'd like you to play 'Lady' by Lionel Richie. Heinrich says it reminds him of me. After the salad, before the soup, but not until all the plates have been cleared and Uncle Wilhelm has made his speech about his memories of me."

"'Lady.' Lovely song." I make another note. "Okay. Bullfight music for the entrance, 'Lady' between the soup and salad, plates cleared, Uncle Willi's speech—"

"WILHELM. UNCLE WILHELM."

"Right. Uncle Wilhelm. I'll have the banquet manager keep me posted about the timing of the courses. So that's it, then."

"Wait! I'm thinking, I'm thinking, I'm thinking! Oh! I know! I'd like to have you play a little song for Heinrich, you know, one dedicated to him from me. Something to let everyone know how I feel about him."

"Do you have anything in mind?"

"'My Way.' I think that's the name of it. You know, that Frank Sinatra song."

In Germany, when somebody asks you for "that Frank Sinatra song," they always mean "My Way." I hum a few bars of it for her, just to make sure.

"Yes, that's the one. Will you play that before the dessert is served? Uncle Wilhelm will do the second part of his speech about his memories of me, then you can play the song."

"Fine. No problem. Great choice!" I hate that song, but it's her wedding. If she wants to dedicate a song whose opening lyric is "And now the end is near, and so I face the final curtain…" to her brand-new husband, then that's her choice. No one will be singing, they'll be drinking, and they all speak a different language anyway.

"Anything after the dessert?" My page of notes is getting full. I figure if Uncle Wilhelm is going to do part three of his speech, after dessert would be the perfect time. Speeches give me a chance to take a break.

"No, that will be it. I've hired a magician and a belly dancer to perform after dinner. Then the dance band starts."

"Sounds like the perfect wedding, Frau Braun. I'll see you on the seventh. I really must go. I'm playing for a luncheon this afternoon." Not true, but I want to get off the phone before she requests anything else. We say goodbye and I hang up.

This is going to be one swinging party. Especially if the guests survive Uncle Wilhelm.

I love weddings. I love going to them, I love being in them, I love playing for them. I adore the *Gone with the Wind* white dresses, the pomp and circumstance, the father giving away the bride, the drunken weepy speeches, the little girls in their patent-leather shoes, and the little boys throwing rice. There's something about a wedding that gives me faith in humanity. The very idea that the love between two people can make the world a better place for each of them is, to me, a reason to celebrate.

At Schlosshotel Lerbach, it's not unusual for the bride and groom to arrive in a gilded carriage pulled by white horses. I play for big weddings and small weddings, for ceremonies and receptions, for wedding lunches, wedding dinners, and wedding cocktail hours. I play in the rose garden in the blazing sun of July or in the golden entrance hall with tremendous gusts of winter wind sweeping through the iron gates of the castle as the ermine-clad bride makes her first appearance. I play on the balcony, in the bar, and out on the old stone terrace surrounded by huge pots of fragrant herbs. Whenever the client has requested quiet background music, I'm the girl who gets the call. I've made a niche for myself playing music that doesn't interfere. Less is more. It's hard to find musicians who understand this, and even harder to find good musicians who are willing to put up with being ignored. But I love it. An elegant man once came to the piano while I was playing, took my business card, and said, "Your music is so perfect. I can hardly hear it." He called me a week later and booked me to play for his wedding.

Playing the piano for four or five hours straight is hard work. There's a meditative state that I sink into when I'm doing one of these marathon jobs. I call it the Piano Zone, and when I'm there I'm happy. I play for myself, I compose on the job, I improvise, I let my fantasies take me far away. I've always figured that my job is to tame the chaos beast, so that the people around me can feel as peaceful as I do. Married life is chaotic enough. You might as well get off to a nice quiet start.

I'm just packing the last of the CDs to send to Frau Braun when the phone rings again.

"Braun here. I have one more small request."

"It's your wedding, Frau Braun—anything I can do to make it special for you would be my pleasure," I say.

"Oh, thank you. You see, my best friend is a classical concert violinist."

Oh, no. Here it comes. The dreaded classical music request.

"I'd love to have him play a piece or two with you accompanying him. Beethoven. Shall I send you the music?"

"Uh…Okay," I say. "That will be fine."

Stupid stupid stupid. Classical music isn't easy. You have to actually play what's on the page. And here in Europe, where many people have studied classical music, there's no faking it. I break into a cold sweat. The last time I played Beethoven in front of an audience, I was in the eleventh grade. I'm about twenty-five years out of practice.

The music arrives two days later, exactly one week before the wedding. It's the Beethoven *Romanze*. After two hours of creeping through it at *tempo di-learn-o*, I have an idea of what it's supposed to sound like. There's so much work to do. I'm playing a reduced orchestral score. The violin part seems just about impossible to play, thirty-second- and sixty-fourth notes making the page look like one solid line of black. My husband, without seeing the music, volunteers to play the violin part on his bass. That's impossible, so he plays it on the upper register of the piano. He's a pretty good piano player, but at one point in a practice session I realize that he's playing sixty-fourth-note bebop lines, in tempo.

It's summer vacation, and the kids, ages seven and ten, are home. I practice about five hours a day, driving them both crazy. On day four of the marathon practice session, they have the piece memorized and can sing the entire thing.

"Look out, Mom, here comes the tricky part. Whoops, you screwed up again!"

"That sounds terrible, Mom. What if you make that mistake at the wedding? You'll ruin the bride's entire life."

"B-FLAT, Mom. How many times are you gonna hit that clunker?"

During the dramatic sections they march around the dining-room table clapping on two and four. Beethoven with a backbeat.

"Don't get nervous, Mom. You speed up when you get nervous. You'd better use that metronome."

But I'm very nervous. I'm a background-music piano player. I don't do concerts, I don't play classical music, and here I am volunteering to do both. I don't want a bunch of people sitting quietly and listening to me play something that's out of my league. I consider calling a kid I know named Benjamin Nuss. He's thirteen and a wizard classical player. Benny could sight-read the piece and play it without even thinking about it. Maybe I should pay him 100 euros and get myself off the hook. But I've got too many hours invested to give up now.

By day six, I'm up to speed—*tempo tantrum*—and I play through the piece every other time without a major flub.

"You've got it, Mom. Go, Mom, go!"

"Now that bride will have a happy life and you won't have to put a bag over your head."

My practice time seriously reduces my hourly wage for the gig. The night of the performance, I walk into the castle, a little shaken, but confident that I will get through the evening.

The violinist is waiting for me at the door. His name is Herr Winkel. He's about my age and dressed in tails. He looks very serious.

Confidence, Robin. Be Confident. Don't let him vibe you, says the Voice of Reason.

You never know, says Voice of Doom. *He could be a distant relative of Isaac Stern.*

"Well," Herr Winkel says, after we'd been introduced. "I hope they're paying you a lot of money to do this because I'm really terrible."

I burst out laughing. We talk our way through the piece and agree that no matter what happens, I will keep playing and Herr Winkel will follow me, because, he says, he knows the piece "really well," even though he can't really play it anymore. He had played *Romanze* twenty-five years earlier as a senior recital piece. The bride, a good friend from his college days, remembered his brilliant performance from 1978.

Herr Winkel paces back in forth in the lobby. "I'm afraid she's going to be very disappointed tonight, but what can I do, she begged me to play!"

Odd, but his nervousness calms me down. "Look, go and enjoy your dinner," I say. "Just stay away from the champagne. It's time for me to play bullfight music. I'll see you later. We're on between the dessert and the espresso."

The bride makes quite an entrance to her bullfight music. She's in her forties and she's beautiful, wearing a splendidly cut strapless white satin sheath. Aside from the tattoo on her shoulder, I think she looks about as perfect as a bride can look. The room dances with candlelight. Several of my CDs are on each table. But the bride has taken each CD and replaced my cover photo with a picture of herself. The diva in me starts to rear its ugly head, but I recover in time to smile politely and say, *What a wonderful idea.*

I play "Lady" as requested, and nobody notices, not even the bride. Uncle Wilhelm, who is in his eighties, makes a speech that starts, "It all began in 1956 in a little town close to Schwein-furt..." By the time we get to part two of his speech about his memories of the bride, he's still talking about her high school years. I escape to the lobby and call my kids. Uncle Wilhelm drones on for so long I feel like I could drive home and read them Volume Four of Harry Potter.

When he finishes, I return to the dining room and begin playing "My Way." The bride makes her way to the front of the room, places an outstretched hand on the curve of the piano, and poses there, dramatically. What's she doing? Maybe she's going to sing. I continue playing, not sure what to expect. I look over at her, and her eyes, which are focused on the ceiling, begin to overflow with tears. She puts the back of her other hand on her forehead.

Meanwhile, the lyrics to the song run through my head.

…And through it all, when there was doubt, I chewed it up and spit it out…

I finish the song very dramatically—with the world's most obnoxious arpeggio—and get a big round of applause. I turn to acknowledge the audience just as the bride takes a deep Onstage at the Metropolitan bow. I join the audience in the ovation and help her back to her throne.

The waiters serve the dessert, which is called A Study of Apricots. I'm pretty hungry, and I watch with envy as the guests eat. The moment of truth arrives. It's time for the Beethoven. I turn up the lights. The piece is difficult enough; I'm not about to try playing it in the dark. I spread my eight pages of music across the piano. The violinist makes a speech. I think he's stalling. He introduces me. Everyone claps. I take a bow. This is exactly what I fear. I've been completely ignored all night while doing what it is that I do well. Now, just as I'm about to demonstrate my musical weaknesses, everyone puts their drinks down, their cigarettes out. They fold their hands and stare at me. A nightmare.

Hey, hey, hey, says Voice of Doom. *It's a perfect night for a train wreck!*

Oh shut up, says Voice of Reason. *For once and for all, shut up. We're sick of you.*

Odd, I'm not nervous. My back is to the audience. I take a deep breath. The violinist counts off. Then he plays the most horrible note I've ever heard in my life. It isn't even a note. Perhaps it's one of those quarter-tones that might be identified in an East Indian musical system, but to the Western ear it's excruciating. I grimace. We're off and running.

The violinist tears through the piece, making all the correct entrances, playing the correct rhythms and keeping everything in time, but he doesn't play a single note in tune. Not one. The piece ends on an impossibly high, glass-shattering note. There's complete silence when we finish. I'm afraid to turn around for fear of seeing the entire wedding party dead on the floor with their hands over their ears.

Everyone jumps to their feet and cheers with wild abandon.

Go figure. The violinist winks at me. I wave goodbye to the people I'll never see again and go to the lobby where the manager has set up a little table for me. On it is a white rose, an autographed picture of the bride, and my very own Study of Apricots. It's almost too pretty to eat.

Playback 2004

"*Bitte*, Frau Goldsby," says Herr Klingball. "I want you to play the theme from *Titanic* as I give my speech about the birthday girl's life."

The birthday girl, Frau Pötzsch, is eighty years old today. This will be a long speech. She'll arrive in a few minutes with twenty-five of her old friends. I just hope I don't have to say her name. *Pötzsch*. I've been in this country for nine years, and I still can't get the hang of the "ö." And what's with the five consonants at the end of her name? I thought that was a Welsh thing.

"Are you sure you want music during your speech?" I say. Perhaps silence would be better. I have an ulterior motive for suggesting this. I'll be able to sneak out of the room and drink a glass of orange juice.

"*Nein! Wir wollen eine künstlerische Untermalung haben.*" An artistic musical backdrop to the speech. "*Verstehen Sie?*" Herr Klingball is speaking very loudly. Some might call it shouting.

"*Jawohl*, Herr Klingball," I say.

I'm not gonna argue with Herr Klingball. He's sort of scary.

Where were you in forty-two?

"Can you do that?" says Herr Klingball. Play *Titanic* underneath the speech?

"That's my specialty. *Künstlerische Untermalung*. No problem, Herr Klingball. When will this occur? The speech, I mean. Right before you go into dinner?"

"*Nein!*" says Herr Klingball. "During the aperitif. As soon as the guests arrive."

I see the headlights of a luxury bus pulling into the circular driveway.

"Frau Pötzsch is here! Begin playing at once! *Titanic! Jetzt!*"

Man your battle stations.

It seems a bit premature to play. A bus full of eighty-year-old Germans will take a while to unload. But I play the theme to *Titanic*. By the fourth time through the chorus, the staff looks at me like I'm crazy. I'm out in the lobby where there are other guests, but Herr Klingball is paying my salary this evening, so he's calling the shots.

Frau Pötzsch and two dozen of her contemporaries, most of them women, stroll into the hall. They look amazing—lifted, coiffed, and powdered to the max, dressed in silks and chiffons and taffetas that float like clouds around their dainty little feet.

I change to a different song, just to have some varied entrance music for the party, but Herr Klingball yells across the room, "*Titanic!*"

I'm tempted to click my heels, but I don't.

Okay, back to the *Titanic*.

"...And when I came out of the anesthesia, they were giving me my prosthesis," I hear a woman next to the piano say. She is wearing a Chanel suit.

I immediately try to figure out which part of her is *ersatz*.

"...But they gave me the prosthesis in the wrong color!"

"Hey Robin, what's with the song? It's making me nuts!" says Thomas the banquet waiter.

"...Stress, stress, so much stress," says the Chanel lady. "I couldn't even look in the mirror."

I'm looking at this lady now, and she looks perfect. Eighty, but perfect.

"A toast, *meine Damen und Herren*, to Frau Pötzsch," says Herr Klingball.

My instincts tell me to stop playing.

"*TITANIC!*" he roars from across the room.

Herr Klingball looks like the kind of guy who might have a stun gun in his tuxedo pocket, so I immediately resume *Titanic*. In a different key. By now the waiters realize what's going on. They smile each time they walk past the piano. I look over my shoulder and see the bartender, hidden from the guests' view, standing on a stool like he's at the bow of an ocean liner, his arms spread wide. All that's missing is Kate Winslet. A couple of lifeboats would be good, too.

Herr Klingball pulls out pages and pages of notebook paper. He balances on the staircase, looking down on his guests.

"*Guten Abend*, Frau Goldsby!" A lovely woman wearing a fuchsia sheath with a matching cape extends her hand over the keyboard. "*Mein Name ist Pötzsch*," she says demurely. It's the birthday girl.

I stop playing to take her hand. Herr Klingball bellows, "*TITANIC!*"

I sit back down, horrified, and resume playing.

"Oh, don't mind him," says Frau Pötzsch. "He means well. It was his idea to have the party this evening. We're all very old friends. We've been through a lot together. Herr Klingball really has a good heart." She leans in closer and whispers in my ear. "Just don't mention the war. It, uh, upsets him."

Well, that makes two of us. I smile and nod.

"Very nice to meet you, Frau Puuusch," I say.

"It's Pötzsch, dear."

"Oh, sorry. Pootzsch."

"Pötzsch."

"Pozzt."

"Pötzsch. It's okay, dear. I find your accent charming."

"And now, a fanfare, Frau Goldsby!" commands Herr Klingball from his perch on the first landing of the dark wooden staircase.

I play a fanfare. The guests turn to Herr Klingball.

"*TITANIC!*" he shouts at me.

I've now been playing *Titanic* for fifteen minutes, and the speech is just beginning.

"It all began in Hannover in 1923…"

Oh, my God.

The waiters serve more champagne.

I play and play and play. Finally when I can't stand it anymore, I switch to "As Time Goes By."

Herr Klingball, half of the guests and several of the waiters turn to me and roar, "*TITANIC!*"

This reminds me of the time my dad's trio had to play at a children's hospital and the kids wanted to hear the theme from *Batman* a million times. Every time the band tried to play something else, the kids threw crushed ice and popsicle sticks at them.

This crowd is a little more sedate. But I get the feeling they could turn on me at any second. They're eating little cups of pigeon mousse, and Lord knows I don't want to get clobbered by any of that. So I keep playing.

Herr Klingball skips the years between 1938 to 1948, and the eyes of the listeners sparkle with relief. He refers once to the "hard times behind us," a phrase I've often heard from Germans who feel compelled to mention the war but are either too ashamed to talk about their complicity or too proud to reference their suffering.

I wonder what vileness, or sadness, or despair, visited the young households of the old women with the youthful faces who teeter around the piano this evening. They smile and laugh and brush embarrassed tears from their rouged cheeks as they try to remember and hope to forget.

Herr Klingball addresses the small crowd of women with confidence and pleasure. Champagne flows. The *Titanic* music continues. Not once does his voice crack.

I will be here forever tonight, playing one song over and over and over again.

Julia's Playback

It seems the songs of our children may be in keys we've never tried.
The melody of each generation emerges from all that's gone before.
Each one of us contributes in some unique way to the
composition of life.

—Fred Rogers, *The World*
According to Mister Rogers

The fishbone pattern of the parquet floor of the Hoffnungsthal Burgerhaus reminds me of a game I used to play as a child: *Step on a crack, break your mother's back.* I'm attending my daughter's piano recital this afternoon. She is eighth on the program, and she's slated to play four pieces, including an original composition of hers entitled "In Egypt." Julia is seven years old.

The recital hall is on the second floor of the town hall building. It's an overcast day, but every so often the sun breaks through the clouds, and shafts of light gleam on the Bösendorfer grand piano that stands next to the tall open windows. A sudden breeze drifts through the hall, and a piece of music floats from the side of the piano and lands, delicately, at the feet of Herr Lehn, the teacher presenting this afternoon's program.

Julia, who has been practicing all month for today's performance, sits next to me in the front row. As Herr Lehn makes his introductory remarks, I realize that Julia and I are sitting in identical positions—legs crossed, arms folded, heads tilted to one side.

I'm nervous.

Earlier in the day I asked Julia what she intended to wear.

"Mom," she said. "It's not about fashion. It's about music."

Still, she has dressed with care, in a blue plaid skirt and an ivory cardigan sweater. She has tied her shiny blond hair back with a black velvet ribbon. She grabs my hand.

"Are you nervous?" I ask her.

"No," she says. She pauses, and gives me a serious look. "Mom, I thought this was going to be a *real* concert."

"Jul, this is a real concert."

"No it's not," she says, glancing over her shoulder. "There's hardly anyone here."

"There are almost eighty people here, Jul. That's a lot of people."

"But it's not like Daddy's concerts," she says. John plays at the Kölner Philharmonie, which seats 2,400 people. "I thought I was going to play a concert like Daddy."

No wonder she has been practicing so much.

"Julia, this concert is just as important as Daddy's concerts. Really, it is! All these people are here to listen to you and…"

"Calm down, Mom, you're way too nervous. I'm the one who is playing."

I almost forgot.

John and Curtis sit on the opposite side of Julia, fussing with camera and sound equipment.

The recital begins. A brave little boy marches to the Bösendorfer and bangs out a piece called "Charlie Chaplain geht spazieren." A beautiful fifteen-year-old girl named Ines plays a Bach prelude. She is followed by a nine-year-old boy whose fingers tangle into knots. He panics, starts to cry, bangs his head on the keyboard, and runs out of the hall. We clap for him, but he doesn't come back. Next up are twin girls, Lena and Lina, who play a four-hand version of a Robbie Williams pop tune called "Feel." They get lost when Lena takes the repeat and Lina forges ahead to the chorus. Now what? They glare at each other and point at the music, making quick one-handed jabs, each one of them trying to force the other back on track. Just as the performance threatens to spin out of control into a pile-up of frustration and anger, they compromise and finish the piece together. Amazing. Lena and Lina bicker as they return to their seats. I'm glad I'm not their mother. Those two will be fighting all weekend.

It's Julia's turn to play. She looks so little. Most of the time I think she looks so big. She's a sturdy girl, fit from horseback riding and playing in the woods. But right now, as she approaches the huge ebony piano, she looks tiny, almost fragile. I catch a glimpse of the determination in her eyes. Nothing will get in her way. Not today.

As she adjusts the height of the piano bench, my stomach flips over. Has it really been almost forty years since I first did this myself?

She plays a gentle waltz called the "Hupkonzert."

She plays the second piece, a dirge in C minor called "Hejo."

From the piano she smiles at me. There is a smattering of polite applause and she gives me a thumbs-up.

She plays "In Egypt," a song she has written that sounds just like something she might hear in Cairo while riding on a camel. Her dad likes this piece because she has discovered a jazz chord—D7♭9—to accompany her Egyptian-sounding motif.

She tears into her big finale, "When the Saints Go Marchin' In."

I try to hold back the tears.

I wonder if her passion for music will be a lifelong companion. I wonder if this recital is the start of a life guided and protected by the joys of playing the piano. I wonder if she'll find comfort in the challenges of intricate harmonies, or take her pleasure in the company of the simple melodies she sings as she climbs the paths leading away from our home.

For the second verse of "Saints," she plays a slow minor-key version of the song.

Julia's music will be different from mine. We look alike, and we may sit the same way, but she will hear her own songs.

She goes into the last chorus of "Saints" playing as fast as she can. Before my eyes she changes, becoming more and more immersed in the music as she approaches the final chord.

She stands, smiles, lets the praise of the audience wash over her like a shower of stars, and rushes back to her seat.

"How do you feel?" I ask as I hug her.

"Great!" she says, beaming. "I wanna do it again. Everyone was listening."

Acknowledgments

Many heartfelt thanks to the staff of Backbeat Books—and especially to Richard Johnston—for breathing life into this project. Richard's sense of humor and technical expertise are a magical combination. Publisher Matt Kelsey gave the ultimate go-ahead for *Piano Girl*. Thank you, Matt. Thank you to Kevin Becketti, Nina Lesowitz, and Steve Moore for their efforts in the sales and marketing departments, and to cover editor Kate Henderson and the fabulous Rich Leeds for getting the cover right. A tip of the hat to photographer John Popplewell, the restaurant and bar Martuni's in San Francisco, and cover model/piano girl Maddaline Goepel for creating the perfect piano-bar photograph. Maddaline, call me if you ever need a sub. Thank you to Amy Miller and Carole Quandt, and special thanks to Managing Editor Nancy Tabor for pulling it all together.

I offer my thanks to journalist Conny Frühauf and to girl-about-town Mariana Moreno Cederberg for their help with the French and Portuguese segments of *Piano Girl*.

Grateful acknowledgment is extended to my Joint Chiefs of Staff—Robin Spielberg, Leslie Brockett Wohlfarth, and Daralene Dobbins—for their love, support, and laughter. Without these three wonderful women, there is no Voice of Reason.

Thank you to the staff of Schlosshotel Lerbach for their enthusiasm and encouragement. Big hugs to Andrea Götze, who always listens, no matter what.

To the Choir Invisible, featuring Fred Rogers, Don Brockett, John Costa, Laura Curtis, Della Rawsthorne, Bill Ewing, Michael, Mona, and—the newest members—Libby Chrystal and Conny Traupe, I ask only that you keep singing. I hear you every single day. All of you.

Most of all, much gratitude to my family. My father taught me the honor of being a musician. My mother taught me the honor of being a musician's wife. I play both of these roles with great zeal because of them.

Finally, I thank my husband, John, and my two spirited children, Curtis and Julia. A family blessed by both music and love is a lucky family indeed.

About the Author

A cocktail-lounge pianist for 30 years, Robin Meloy Goldsby worked her way through Chatham College, an elite women's school in Pittsburgh, Pennsylvania, by playing piano in local motel lounges and roadhouse bars. After moving to New York City she played piano in many of Manhattan's leading hotels, including long-running jobs at the Grand Hyatt, the Sheraton Center, and the Plaza Hotel. In the mid-'80s Goldsby played the grand opening of the Marriott Marquis Clock Lounge in Times Square and went on to work there for seven years, cultivating her skills and captivating diverse audiences with her unique musical style. In addition to her five-star experiences in New York City hotel bars and her no-star gigs in small regional lounges, Goldsby's musical adventures have taken her to exclusive island resorts, Third World countries, and the castles in Europe where she currently performs. She has recorded two solo piano CDs: *Somewhere in Time* and *Twilight*. You can visit her web page at www.goldsby.de.